THE
DYNAMICS
OF REAL ESTATE
CAPITAL MARKETS
A PRACTITIONER'S PERSPECTIVE

BOWEN H. "BUZZ" McCOY

ii

ULI–the Urban Land Institute
1025 Thomas Jefferson Street, N.W.
Washington, D.C. 20007-5201

Library of Congress Cataloging-in-Publication Data

McCoy, Bowen H.
    The dynamics of real estate capital markets : a practitioner's perspective / Bowen H. "Buzz" McCoy.
        p. cm.
    ISBN-13: 978-0-87420-972-3
    1. Real estate investment—United States.
    2. Commercial real estate—United States.
    3. Business ethics. I. Title.
        HD255.M372 2006
        333.33'22–dc22

                                    2006026239

10 9 8 7 6 5 4 3 2 1
Printed in the United States of America.
Second Printing 2007

ULI–THE URBAN LAND INSTITUTE is a nonprofit education and research institute that is supported by its members. Its mission is to provide responsible leadership in the use of land in order to enhance the total environment.

ULI sponsors education programs and forums to encourage an open international exchange of ideas and sharing of experiences; initiates research that anticipates emerging land use trends and issues and proposes creative solutions based on that research; provides advisory services; and publishes a wide variety of materials to disseminate information on land use and development. Established in 1936, the Institute today has more than 32,500 members in over 80 countries, representing the entire spectrum of the land use and development disciplines. The Institute is recognized throughout the world as one of America's most respected and widely quoted sources of objective information on urban planning, growth, and development.

PROJECT STAFF

Rachelle L. Levitt
Executive Vice President,
    Information Group
Publisher

Dean Schwanke
Senior Vice President,
    Publications and Awards

George Kelly
Scholar in Residence
Project Director

Nancy H. Stewart
Director, Book Program

Lori Hatcher
Director, Publications Marketing

Libby Howland
Manuscript Editor

Betsy VanBuskirk
Art Director
Book and Cover Design

Susan S. Teachey, ON-Q Design, Inc.
Desktop Publishing

Craig Chapman
Director, Publishing Operations

This book is dedicated to all the women and men, investment bankers and support staff, who worked with me with such intelligence, energy, and integrity to build the real estate platform at Morgan Stanley.

To Helen
Enjoy the cycles!
Buzz McCoy

Bowen H. McCoy

Bowen H. "Buzz" McCoy was employed by Morgan Stanley & Co. from 1962 to 1990, where he served as general partner, managing director, and president of Morgan Stanley Realty. He is a life trustee of the Urban Land Institute and a past president of the Counselors of Real Estate. *National Real Estate Investor* magazine named him one of the "real estate icons" of the 20th century. McCoy currently operates Buzz McCoy Associates in Los Angeles, where he conducts a consulting business along with his philanthropic, teaching, and writing activities.

McCoy's book on values-based leadership, *Living into Leadership: A Journey in Ethics*, will be published by Stanford University Press in spring 2007.

Acknowledgments

I would like to thank ULI's Cheryl Cummins, Rachelle Levitt, and Dean Schwanke for their prompt and enthusiastic support of this project. Tony Downs, who has been a wonderful friend for over 25 years, generously responded with alacrity when invited to write a foreword. Kristina Kessler, editor in chief of *Urban Land*, shepherded many of these articles into print. She has been pleasant and easy to work with over the years. The same applies to Gloria Bowman, editor for many years of *Real Estate Issues*, the publication of the Real Estate Counselors in which many of these articles first appeared. This book would not have come together without the yeoman work of George Kelly, scholar in residence at ULI, whom I had the privilege to teach while he was a student at the Lusk Center for Real Estate at the University of Southern California. I also appreciate Libby Howland's intelligent and thoughtful editing on the book manuscript.

I have been a member of ULI since 1975. It has meant a great deal to me, both personally and professionally. The friendships run broad and deep, starting in the early years with Roy Drachman, Ernie Hahn, Jerry Hines, Charlie Shaw, and Marion Smith and building up over the years to good friends far too numerous to name. To all of you who have touched my life, including the ULI staff, many thanks.

Contents

Changing Tools and Processes

PART 4: REAL ESTATE CAPITAL MARKETS IN THE 2000S

Investment As Affected by 9/11

A Maturing Asset Class

PART 5: VALUES-BASED LEADERSHIP

Character and Personal Responsibility

Globalization of Business Ethics

Ethics and Real Estate

Foreword

BY ANTHONY DOWNS

Bowen H. "Buzz" McCoy is both a pioneer and a legend in commercial real estate circles. He was one of the first people to bring Wall Street's mind-set into real estate markets. For more than 40 years, he has labored to educate real estate professionals about what the infusion of Wall Street money and thinking would do to real estate. At the same time, he has been trying to figure out what this "marriage" of two businesses would become as it endured through several real estate and financial cycles. The essays in this book set forth his observations and speculations on how that relationship has progressed. Since his essays cover a period of immense changes in both Wall Street and real estate, they provide a running commentary on how both institutions have fared.

In person, Buzz is a tall, lean gentleman who thinks fast, talks fast, and always challenges people. He has made many friends at all stages of his multifaceted career. He was the first businessman I met who chose running as a hobby before it became popular—and he might be encountered jogging along big-city streets or hiking mountain paths in Nepal.

In his quest to establish clearer thinking about real estate finance, Buzz headed a real estate credit task force for Alan Greenspan in the early 1990s, and subsequently convened and endowed an annual finance symposium—both of which were run by the Urban Land Institute, of which Buzz is a life trustee as well as former president of the

Urban Land Foundation. As an attendee of the McCoy Finance Symposium for many years, I believe it is the most informative single annual event available for understanding real estate markets.

Beyond real estate capital markets, Buzz also has focused on the role of ethics in real estate and business in general. He began this pursuit well before the current outbreak of corporate scandals, bringing his rigorous analytical skills to a crucial business issue.

Most of the essays in this collection grapple with a fundamental tension in real estate markets: Each real estate project serves an essentially local market, but the financial conditions vital to its success are set by global factors. Thus, successful real estate development or investment requires understanding both local markets and global capital market flows. Moreover, the relationship between these two aspects of real estate has undergone radical changes since the 1960s when Buzz began trying to meld Wall Street and main street in Morgan Stanley's real estate deals. When he was putting together those early deals, real estate finance was essentially separated from larger global financial conditions by institutional arrangements that isolated sources of property finance from stock and bond capital markets. Banks and insurance companies were the main sources of capital for commercial real estate.

The 1970s saw a real estate boom early in the decade that crashed in 1974 and 1975. Then rapid inflation set in, and another real estate boom occurred in the late 1970s when investors treated real estate as a hedge against inflation. Then the Federal Reserve under Paul Volcker set out to quash general inflation by pushing interest rates to record levels, peaking in 1982. Real estate, which is highly sensitive to interest rates, was drastically affected by these general credit conditions. Over the following two decades, interest rates gradually declined. Because lower interest rates basically favor real estate investment, massive amounts of capital—including a lot from overseas—flowed into real estate in the 1980s, stimulating one of the greatest commercial property building booms in history. The flow of capital into real estate was furthered by the deregulation of savings and loan institutions, which flooded commercial property markets with capital derived from their federally insured deposits.

The resulting overbuilding of all types of commercial property reached a climax in 1990. The savings and loan industry essentially went bankrupt, federal regulators ordered banks and insurance companies to quit financing real estate, and property markets collapsed. The nearly complete withdrawal of private financial capital from real estate forced most developers into default. But it also caused many developers and owners to shift to public financial markets through the formation of real estate investment trusts (REITs) and the floating of public shares on Wall Street. To make up for the absence of bank and insurance company money, the development of commercial mortgage–backed securities (CMBSs) created a channel for debt funds to flow into real estate. These institutional changes set the stage for the most complete merger of Wall Street finance and the real estate industry in history—a merger with consequences that are still working themselves out in today's markets.

Buzz's essays describe this dynamic period of fundamental change in real estate capital markets from the viewpoint of one of the field commanders on the ground, as he was busy helping to make specific real estate deals throughout this period. The articles included in this collection repeatedly mention three fundamental issues: 1) the absence of a standardized method for measuring the returns to real estate projects and hence the difficulty of establishing their value; 2) the lack of transparency in real estate markets compared with the stock market; and 3) the resulting tendency of individual developers to overbuild based on their inaccurate knowledge of what was actually happening on the ground, as well as an arrogant belief in their own ability to succeed regardless of what others were doing.

As the 1990s progressed, interest rates declined further and real estate slowly recovered from the collapse of prices and credit availability brought on by catastrophic overbuilding in the 1980s. With the proliferation of REITs and CMBSs, credit flowed into real estate from nontraditional sources—mainly pension funds and financial institutions that had previously focused almost entirely on stocks and bonds. But the sensational performance of the stock market in the 1990s caused most financial capital to flow into corporate equities—and almost ignore real estate. That happened even though property market conditions were outstanding in the late 1990s, with low vacancies and high rents and profits. Then, with the bursting of the "Internet bubble" in 2000 and the shock of 9/11 in 2001, world stock markets collapsed just as spectacularly as real estate had in 1990. The NASDAQ composite lost over 60 percent of its value, and the Dow Jones Industrial Average and the S&P 500 also fell sharply.

This bear market in stocks soon demonstrated how deeply real estate finance sources and Wall Street finance sources had become integrated as a result of the structural changes described above. With REITs and CMBSs as vehicles along with newly expanded private equity funds, capital fled out of stocks and bonds into real estate markets. The "Niagara" of capital that flooded into real estate amounted to the greatest inflow of funds in history. At the same time, central banks all over the world were cutting interest rates and pumping up monetary liquidity in order to prevent the stock market collapse from causing a general recession. And the United States was running record trade deficits financed by the purchase of U.S. Treasury securities, largely by foreign central banks. Therefore, U.S. property markets were suddenly awash with more capital than ever before—right at the time when vacancies shot upward and rents fell sharply because of the drop in general business caused by 9/11 and the 2000 stock market debacle.

This unique combination of deteriorating space markets and sensationally soaring capital inflows produced several unusual impacts on real estate. One was a boom in housing prices throughout the developed world (except in Germany) as households shifted capital out of stocks and into their homes. Rising prices led to a boom in housing construction and homeownership, enabling many homeowners to cash in on rising equities and use some of those funds to sustain high levels of consumption, which kept the U.S. economy expanding. A second unusual impact was that, while vacancies in commercial property markets rose and rents fell, the competition among investors to put their capital funds to work in real estate pushed commercial property values ever higher. This drove capitalization rates to their lowest levels ever, in spite of deteriorating incomes from the properties involved.

As the prices of most stocks continued to fall through 2001 and 2002, REIT shares began rising steadily and attracted large amounts of investment capital. Record amounts of money flowed into CMBSs to finance ever costlier purchases of real properties by investors trying to put their money to work somewhere. Never had the newly strengthened dynamic connections between Wall Street and real estate finance been so clearly demonstrated.

Fortunately, this immense flow of financial capital into real estate has not yet (at least as of June 2006) generated a building boom in new commercial property similar to that of the 1980s. However, conditions in space markets began improving in 2005, when increasing prosperity and strong government spending caused vacancies to fall and rents to stabilize and begin rising, which provided some greater justification for higher property values.

Still, most of the increase in prices through 2005 was caused by a decline in cap rates as investors bid prices upward without corresponding increases in property profitability. The Federal Reserve had driven the federal funds rate down to only 1 percent in 2003, giving borrowers a great spread between the cost of capital and what they could earn with it. This stimulated the formation of many private equity funds for buying up real estate properties with higher leverage than REITs could muster. But the Federal Reserve began raising the federal funds rate in 2004, in hopes of raising mortgage rates to slow the real estate boom. By May 2006, the funds rate had reached 4.8 percent, which finally pushed mortgage rates up enough to began slowing housing markets.

As long-term interest rates began rising in 2006, the frenzy in investment property markets slowed somewhat. But because of many uncertainties in the world, stock markets were unable to sustain a significant rally. That fact, plus the threat of rising interest rates in bond markets, kept money in real estate because it had shown the highest overall yield among asset classes for several years.

In fact, for investors a paradigm shift of sorts had occurred. Pension funds and other financial institutions had finally decided that real estate is indeed a separate asset class, with prices that move differently from those of stocks and bonds. As of today, these financial institutions have decided to keep a larger share of their total assets in real estate than in the past. But if stock markets took off, some of the funds that have recently moved into real properties would surely move back into other stocks. Even with these allocation changes, most pension funds and other institutions still fall short of having 10 percent of their assets in real properties—a share that Buzz has been advocating for decades. They should listen to him!

As of mid-2006, tons of capital are still available for investment in real estate. Much of it is in private equity funds raised by property advisory firms that have moved into the asset placement business. But rising interest rates, high construction costs, and continuing high vacancy rates have slowed what would normally have been the response to such capital availability and general prosperity—that is, a new building boom in commercial properties.

After the 2005 McCoy Finance Symposium, Buzz himself concluded that now is the time to prepare for some type of coming downturn in property markets. So cyclical forces still operate on real estate markets—and on capital markets generally. But as described above and in the articles collected in this book, the immense institutional changes that have merged real estate capital markets and general financial capital markets have forever changed how these capital markets will interact and behave in the future.

The essays included in the values-based leadership section of this collection express Buzz's thinking about the role of ethics in business. He has been teaching ethics courses to business school and real estate classes for several years. Just reading the daily newspapers shows how significant are the ethical principles and practices he espouses, and the high costs to society of people's disregarding them.

Altogether, this book presents the front-line thinking of a leader in real estate finance who has applied Wall Street concepts to real estate over the years. He has used those concepts well as he fought through the many ups and downs of property markets from 1960 through 2006. If you want to discover how a truly successful real estate finance expert felt about that turbulent period, no one will be able to tell you better than my longtime friend Buzz McCoy.

Anthony Downs
The Brookings Institution
Washington, D.C.
July 14, 2006

PART 1

The Dynamics of Real Estate Capital Markets: An Overview and Thoughts on the Future

An Overview and Thoughts on the Future

This book of 36 readings comprises a selection of articles (plus one symposium summary) that I have written over the past quarter century. These readings provide insights into the evolution of real estate capital markets over the past 35 years. Although for the most part the selected articles focus on conditions at a particular time, in their entirety they provide a unique perspective on how real estate, an asset class that is interest rate–sensitive, responds to the various supply/demand and capital market cycles.

Real estate is notably a cyclical business and the chronological arrangement of the articles in this book intentionally emphasizes the importance of cycles. The part 2 articles are concerned with the integration of real estate into the capital markets system in the 1970s and 1980s. The part 3 articles focus on the 1990s, a period of globalization in real estate markets and a period of turmoil and restructuring in U.S. real estate capital markets. The part 4 articles cover the 2000s (through 2005) and are concerned mainly with investment uncertainty, the importance of transparency to capital markets, and unprecedented liquidity.

Following the decade-by-decade story of real estate capital markets, the final part 5 articles focus on values-based business leadership, reflecting on the fact that real estate is essentially a people business. A successful real estate practitioner must sustain a reputation over a career lasting decades, which requires the ability to build long-term, trust-based relationships as well as a set of personal values to help make the tough ethical calls that will have to be made.

A Practitioner's Perspective

I have practiced real estate investment banking for a third of a century and have been involved in overall capital market activity for almost 50 years. Like most practitioners, I have always lived in the moment. But I have made it a point to try to discern long-term trends, because I think that the key to attaining wisdom over time is an understanding of such trends. Along the way, I have participated in a wide variety of corporate and asset-based financings.

I joined the investment banking firm of Morgan Stanley in 1962, right out of Harvard Business School. At that time it was a small firm of 140 individuals, and $7 million in capital. Despite its boutique size, it was at the time the dominant firm on Wall Street. I was a corporate finance specialist. Each finance professional was expected, over time, to become proficient in all the firm's product lines—public capital markets, mergers and acquisitions, private placements, project finance, and the like. On any given day, I might be found in Dayton, Ohio, working on a public utility; in Melbourne, Australia, working on financing an iron ore project; or in Paris working for the largest aluminum company in France. Eight years after joining Morgan Stanley, I was invited to become a general partner.

About the time of my partnership, Morgan Stanley invested in a joint venture with Brooks Harvey, a highly respected real estate finance firm in New York City. While I was not well versed in real estate finance, I had gained experience in project finance entailing the structuring of layers of finance around predictable cash flows from projects, and in private placements involving the direct negotiation of financial terms with large insurance companies. As a corporate finance specialist, I had worked on the acquisition of a shopping center development company and I was just beginning what became seven years of work for the James Irvine Foundation, owner of the Irvine Ranch in southern California.

I was asked by a senior partner to serve on the board of Brooks Harvey and to become involved in the business. Another partner, Ed Matthews, five years my senior, was asked to run the Brooks Harvey business and to integrate it into Morgan Stanley. The Brooks Harvey investment gave Morgan Stanley the largest real estate presence of any major investment bank at the time. Lazard Frères had made an investment in Corporate Property Investors, which was run by Disque Deane. Deane had worked earlier at Hurd & Co. with Ben Lambert, who went on to form Eastdil Realty. Merrill Lynch soon bought Hubbard Westerfeld, another old-line real estate firm. At the time, none of these operations reached the scale of the Morgan Stanley/Brooks Harvey joint venture.

Morgan Stanley pushed Brooks Harvey aggressively, and the joint venture opened up branch offices in Los Angeles, San Francisco, Chicago, Houston, Atlanta, Washington, D.C., and Boston. Morgan Stanley itself had no branch offices at that time. Brooks Harvey also formed a private equity real estate investment trust (REIT), a real estate development company, and a joint venture with Mitsubishi Estate, the largest real estate company in Japan.

Then in March 1973, to my dismay, my good friend and partner Ed Matthews resigned his partnership at Morgan Stanley to become chief financial officer of AIG, a post he held for the next 25 years. Morgan Stanley did not have a deep bench at that time, so I was asked to head up the entire real estate operation—a position for which I felt woefully unprepared. The senior partners had asked me to go into real estate "for a couple of years." I'm still at it 30 years later. The rest, as they say, is history.

It turned out that 1973 was the year of the collapse of the commercial-paper market, continuing financial distress of major companies such as Penn Central and Chrysler, and the worst-performing commercial real estate markets since the 1930s. Through Brooks Harvey's development company and my participation on the investment committee of the Brooks Harvey REIT, I was in a position to see the distress in the real estate markets before it was broadly reported. Because I lacked experience and perspective, I became convinced that the deterioration in our investments was all my fault. I canceled a second-round financing for the REIT, closed several of the branch offices, and downsized the Brooks Harvey New York City staff.

As conditions began to improve in the mid 1970s, we built Brooks Harvey back up and completed its integration into Morgan Stanley. During the last half of the decade, we performed many important financings for new clients such as Trammell Crow, Jerry Hines, and John Portman. We also accomplished several landmark sale transactions—including Monumental Properties, the Irvine Ranch, Tishman Realty, and Ernie Hahn's shopping center business.

Morgan Stanley validated these successes by buying the rest of Brooks Harvey and incorporating it into a new firm, Morgan Stanley Realty. We had little competition of consequence on Wall Street at this time. The real competition among Wall Street firms in real estate capital markets began in the 1980s, when Claude Ballard moved from Prudential Insurance to Goldman, Sachs and firms such as Solomon Brothers, First Boston, and Drexel began to trade real estate mortgages.

When I started my involvement in the real estate capital markets around 1970, I was one of the few senior investment bankers on Wall Street participating in these markets. At that time, real estate financing rates were administered by institutions such as insurance companies and savings banks, and they were essentially delinked from capital market activity. Morgan Stanley's activity in the real estate debt and equity markets at that time, in fact, did much to bring real estate finance into the capital market system.

In 1975, with the sponsorship of Jerry Hines and Marion Smith, I became a member of the Urban Land Institute. That was one of the best decisions I ever made. Over the years, ULI has been for me a powerful learning experience, a marvelous source of new business, a broad platform from which to serve others, and the springboard for several long-lasting relationships built upon deep trust and affection. Roy Drachman and Charlie Shaw, both past presidents of ULI, served as trustees of the Brooks Harvey REIT.

In my early years at ULI, I became involved with the Program Committee, and I suddenly found myself in front of a thousand or so people introducing the likes of Peter Jennings, Tom Brokaw, or Condi Rice. ULI afforded me numerous opportunities to appear on panels and to make speeches, allowing me to deepen my presentation skills. Over the years, I have chaired the Urban Development/Mixed-Use and International Councils; served on the Denver Convention Center advisory panel, the Awards for Excellence jury, and the Nominating Committee; and chaired the Investment Committee, the ULI Credit Task Force, and the 1992 Los Angeles fall membership meeting. For five years I was president of the Urban Land Foundation. I also have served as vice president and as treasurer of ULI. My involvement with ULI was good for business. At one time, Morgan Stanley was doing business with all but a single member of the ULI Executive Committee.

Another organization from which I have benefited greatly is the Counselors of Real Estate. The Brooks Harvey staff included five people with CRE designations, and they were among the most talented and wise real estate practitioners with whom I have dealt. I learned an immense amount from them, and I always included them on my project teams. In 1980, I was asked to address the organization's annual convention. I reworked the speech I gave there as an article for *Real Estate Issues*—"Adventures in Marketing Large Real Estate Portfolios." This speech/article, which is the first article in this collection, apparently caused the Counselors of Real Estate to invite me to become a member. Many years later I was honored to serve as the organization's president.

Throughout my career, one of my constant roles has been to interpret and explain the real estate business and capital market behavior to clients as well as colleagues. If I had kept all my client presentation books over the years, I would probably have needed to sublet a warehouse for them. In the early 1970s, I spoke at one of the first *Institutional Investor* magazine conferences on real estate investments—at which time I proudly proclaimed that within a few years pension funds would be investing 10 percent of their assets in real estate. More than 30 years later that boast remains unfulfilled.

As I continued to speak on real estate finance at various investor and trade association conferences, I began turning my speeches into articles, more than 50 of which have been published in *Urban Land*, the Urban Land Institute magazine, and *Real Estate Issues*, the Counselors of Real Estate magazine. Covering some 30 years of real estate finance activity, these articles individually reflect the capital market events of the particular time at which they were written. As time went on, I broadened my journalistic focus to include values-based leadership, a subject to which I have given much thought and about which I have taught at the university level. Besides *Urban Land* and *Real Estate Issues*, my articles on real estate capital markets and values-based leadership have appeared in a number of other publications—including *Harvard Business Review*, *Wharton Real Estate Review*, *Stanford Business*, and the UCLA School of Management's journal.

Like a good pack rat, I kept copies of all my articles that have been published. I was very pleased when the Urban Land Institute determined that a collection of some of these articles might provide useful insights into real estate capital markets.

Real Estate Capital Markets in the 1970s and 1980s: Articles 1 to 4

The initial group of articles, "Real Estate Capital Markets in the 1970s and 1980s," comprises four articles published between 1981 and 1988. They explore two themes—1) the gradual emergence during this time period of real estate as an investment asset class, and 2) the securitization of real estate finance.

The 1970s commenced with the worst commercial real estate downturn since the 1930s. REITs had only recently come on the scene, primarily as mortgage investors, and most failed to survive the downturn, giving these investment vehicles a bad name for several years. Pension funds began cautiously to put their feet in the real estate waters.

In the mid-1970s, the federal government initiated some significant financial deregulation policies, and the loosening of restraints on financial institutions led to a slackening of investment discipline, which carried forward into the 1980s. Capital flows into real estate were augmented by foreign investors from the Middle East, Japan, and Canada.

By the early 1980s, inflation was rampant and interest rates went sky high. By the late 1980s, these conditions had stabilized, and an excess of investment funds became available to commercial real estate, which fostered an overbuilding binge that took many years to work off.

Real Estate Emerges as an Asset Class

Article 1. An early use of investment banking techniques for commercial real estate transactions is described in the first article in this collection, **"Adventures in Marketing Large Real Estate Portfolios" (1981)**, which tells the story of Morgan Stanley's marketing of four major transactions involving the Irvine Ranch, Tishman Realty and Construction, Monumental Properties Trust, and the Ernest Hahn Company, that were, in effect, orchestrated auctions. In executing them, Morgan Stanley brought high standards of execution and sophisticated procedures from its investment banking business to the commercial real estate business. Many of our innovations, such as rigid bidding procedures, confidentiality agreements, and written protection from third-party brokers, later became standard procedure on Wall Street—not only in the real estate business but in the mergers and acquisitions business as well.

There are many claimants to the "invention" of real estate investment banking. Ben Lambert, the creator of Eastdil Reality, a pioneering firm in real estate finance, has a fair claim to it. Salomon Brothers used to claim that it invented real estate finance, but in actuality Salomon began trading commercial mortgages about a decade after Morgan Stanley had acquired Brooks Harvey. In its 2000 centennial issue, *National Real Estate Investor* magazine recognized that Morgan Stanley played a pioneer role in creating this business. If so, it was these four transactions that put us on the map.

Of particular note in these four transactions was the difference in the pricing of publicly held commercial real estate assets compared with privately held assets. At times in the market cycle, privately held assets are valued much higher than assets held in public companies; and at other times the reverse is the case. During the period covered by the article, public markets were demoralized and private owners would pay much higher values for real estate assets. Tishman, for example, was prevented from paying dividends and its stock price was around $8 a share, yet we were able to sell the individual assets out of the company for an equivalent of $27 a share, almost 3.5 times as high as the company's shares. Monumental was selling at $18 a share, including the insurance company assets, yet we sold the real estate alone for the equivalent of $70 a share while the insurance company continued to trade around $20. Ernie Hahn was almost bankrupt from overspending on new projects, but when we took his centers out from under the public structure they sold for three times the value they had been trading for.

The private market premiums were immense, and we caught Wall Street napping. Of course, we had to maintain absolute secrecy during the one to three years it took to execute these transactions. We saw what was happening, and we hoped to keep it a secret as long as we could.

[Note: see articles 5 and 16 for more on pricing anomalies in real estate markets.]

Article 2. By the mid-1980s, financial deregulation had fundamentally changed the capital availability picture for real estate, which is described in **"Financing Real Estate in the 1980s" (1983)**, a summary of market conditions in the early 1980s and a discussion of the "changing game" of financing real estate in terms of the different players. The article was my initial attempt at prognostication, and I did pretty well for a rookie—especially with my brave pronouncement that the Dow Jones might reach 2000 in the 1980s!

In the early 1980s, interest rates were high and real estate was "overpriced" relative to other assets. The article does not say it, but this overpricing was going to get a lot worse by the end of the decade. Because of volatility in the capital markets and better computational tools, internal rate of return (IRR) calculations were replacing the capitalization rate approach to valuation. Financial deregulation had led financial institutions to bid for deposits and to put more emphasis on "spread" banking. By the middle of the decade, many commercial banks and savings and loans had become overly aggressive in making open-ended construction loans and funding real estate joint ventures in order to book a return over their cost of funds.

In the early to mid-1980s, tax-shelter syndications were luring individuals into overpaying for real estate. (The tax shelters were legislated out of existence later in the decade.) During this time, I was a member along with Charlie Shaw of a delegation from ULI that was invited by Bob Dole, chair of the Senate Finance Committee, to breakfast in the Senate Caucus Room—and the tax code was a topic of discussion. We explained to the senator how a rapidly changing tax code makes it difficult to plan a project that may take five to seven years or longer to entitle.

My prediction in this article that pension funds would prefer to invest in a liquid, appreciating stock market rather than in real estate assets proved valid, as did my prediction that insurance companies would be selling shorter-term products and thus investing for shorter-term returns.

The fact that there is a five-year gap in my writing on real estate capital markets between article 2 and article 3 may signify the real estate industry's self-satisfaction in the mid-1980s. We had resolved the issues of the early 1970s, and the high interest rates of the early 1980s were abating. The stock market was soaring. Most institutions preferred financial assets over real estate assets. Office buildings were going up everywhere. The mortgage officers at commercial banks and S&Ls were competing with one another to get money out. We were upset that Congress had done away with tax syndications, but otherwise things were good. In fact, they were great. What a swell party! The few doomsayers who stood up at ULI meetings and complained about overbuilding and excesses in the system were not invited back.

Article 3. Foreign investors added to the real estate frenzy of the late 1980s, which was characterized by undisciplined overbuilding on a scale not seen before and which led to the terrible real estate crisis of the early 1990s. In **"Japanese Investment in U.S. Real Estate" (1988)**, I argued that the Japanese would be players in the U.S. real estate capital markets for some time to come.

It was only natural that Morgan Stanley would bring its international business relationships to bear in the real estate business. A third of the investors in the firm's private equity REIT, which was formed in the early 1970s, were international. They included Mitsubishi Estate, Kuwait Investment Company, several private Swiss banks, the private investment firm of the Agnelli family in Milan, and others. Also in the early 1970s, Morgan Stanley established a joint venture with Mitsubishi Estate, the largest real estate firm in Japan, to develop real estate in the United States. We also facilitated a joint venture between Equitable Life Assurance and Nippon Life, the largest insurance company in Japan, to invest in a Manhattan office tower—which was the first office building purchased by a Japanese institution. The endorsement of such activity by Nippon Life led to a wave of further purchases by Japanese investors. Morgan Stanley also facilitated a joint venture between John Portman and Mitsubishi Estate to construct the Bonaventure Hotel in downtown Los Angeles.

Starting in 1973, I traveled to Japan on real estate business at least once a year for many years and I spent considerable time educating Japanese investors on the benefits of owning U.S. property. As the opening paragraph of this article says, one learns how to deal with a counterparty in a different culture only when things go wrong. I had plenty of experience in this regard, reworking the Portman/Bonaventure joint venture as well as a Morgan Stanley Realty office building project in Portland Oregon that had gone awry. In the article, I attempt to support the Japanese investor's point of view (why not, they were terrific clients!) and to explain their investment rationale.

My prediction here that the U.S. trade deficit would persist for several years appears to have held up pretty well, as has my prediction of the depreciation of the dollar against the yen, which has gone from 135:1 at the time this article was written to below 100:1 subsequently. I am pleased that I suggested that Japanese owners spend more time on tenant service, property management, and leasing—even though that admonition went unheeded. In the early 1990s, the owners of ARCO Towers in downtown Los Angeles turned off the escalators and air conditioning at 6:00 p.m. to "save money," much to the chagrin of their few remaining tenants.

What happened in the late 1980s of course, is that the Japanese went crazy. Individual entrepreneurs and flight capital joined the ranks of disciplined, institutional investors and bid up the price of all types of real estate. In the late 1980s, Morgan Stanley was given an assignment to sell some unentitled land on the Kona Coast of the

Big Island of Hawaii. We thought it was worth $30 million, but Japanese buyers eventually paid $136 million for it. In the early 2000s, astute U.S. investors bought the land back for $24 million. So goes the cycle.

The Commercial Real Estate Securities Market Matures

Article 4. New mechanisms and forces were bringing real estate financing increasingly into the money and capital markets. These are explained in **"The New Financial Markets and Securitized Commercial Real Estate Financing" (1988)**. The article also puts securitization into historical perspective, arguing that securitized commercial real estate financing was not a new phenomenon in the late 1980s. In a way, this was my response to Salomon Brothers' claim that it had invented securitized real estate finance. The article refers to the layered, structured finance of receivables going back to the late 1950s as well as layers of debt based on "take or pay" contracts in project financings. And it points out that many sophisticated techniques—such as caps, swaps, futures, multicurrency trades, and the like—had recently evolved to deal with market volatility.

Despite all their sophisticated techniques, the commercial real estate securitized markets remained largely untested at that time—and they still do. Valuations were derived by trial and error. Complex sets of cash flows were computerized and traded, with neither buyer nor seller really understanding the true worth of the underlying asset. Pricing anomalies produced windfalls and losses, as the markets adjusted to the new techniques. Principal/agency problems developed as certain institutions that benefited from government-insured deposits bulked up their balance sheets with riskier and riskier investments. In certain cases, "zombie" thrifts "corrected" their balance sheets with billion-dollar, 24-hour repos in order to remain qualified as government-insured deposit institutions. The excesses were building.

Real Estate Capital Markets in the 1990s:
Articles 5 to 19

The second group of readings, "Real Estate Capital Markets in the 1990s," comprises 15 articles published between 1990 and 1999. They explore four general themes—1) the evolution of valuation methods, 2) the globalization of real estate capital, 3) turmoil and the restructuring of capital markets, and 4) changing tools and processes.

The early 1990s saw the worst real estate depression since the 1930s. The fundamental cause was the market's overreaction to financial deregulation in the mid-1970s. Before deregulation, safe and conservative government-insured deposits were invested in safe investments. After deregulation, financial institutions were allowed to access capital and make investments relatively unconstrained by regulations. The growing practice of spread banking increased the cost of funds and pushed institutions to make riskier and riskier investments, including investments in real estate.

Institutions without sophisticated real estate experience began offering open-ended construction loans, loans with high loan-to-value ratios, and joint venture equity investments in real estate. Financial pro formas showed high rates of escalation in rents continuing unabated for the next ten years, along with much lower inflation rates for expenses. Market studies for new urban high-rise office buildings were based on assertions by their developers that the building's superior location and design, or even the personality of its owner, would make it outperform the already constructed empty building next door.

It came to pass that many major financial institutions saddled with poor real estate loans and investments would have been bankrupted if they had marked their real estate to market. Federal regulators stepped in, and the flow of capital to the commercial real estate markets essentially dried up for several years. ULI established a real estate credit task force that, along with other ULI initiatives, played a role in restoring confidence to the commercial real estate capital markets. (The real estate depression affected ULI itself, leading it to downsize the organization and to cancel a long-scheduled membership meeting in London.)

By mid-decade, new risk-based capital rules, a new tax-enhanced version of real estate investment trusts, the mobilization of opportunity funds, and the proliferation of commercial mortgage–backed securities had helped restore the demoralized capital markets.

Valuation Methods Evolve in Response to Volatility in Capital Markets

Article 5. By the mid-1980s, advances in computers and software were providing buyers and sellers with the computational ability to value properties and portfolios using various and changing assumptions in each year of the projection period. Differing assumptions about rental rates, lease terms, expenses, and the like created a market in which buyers and sellers were quoting wildly different cap rates for the sale of the same property. **"Capitalization Rate in a Dynamic Environment" (1990)**, an article on changing techniques for valuing real estate—changes caused by increasing volatility in the capital markets—grew out of a paper I presented at the 15th Pan-Pacific Congress of Real Estate Appraisers in Seoul, Korea, in 1990 at the invitation of the Real Estate Counselors. In it I review a variety of valuation techniques, including a computer-driven method of building up a componentized rate of return, called dynamic rate of return analysis.

For 20 years following World War II, capital markets had remained fairly stable. Over this period, long-term interest rates rose from roughly 2 percent—the rate at which the Federal Reserve Bank "pegged" interest rates during the war—to a fairly stable 4.5 percent. In the summer of 1966, it was a real shock when Standard Oil Company of Indiana, a company with AAA-rated corporate debt, paid 6 percent for long-term debt. Rates kept going up, and by the early 1980s short-term money had climbed to about 20 percent.

A couple of years ago, I was asked to teach a real estate valuation class at USC's Marshall School of Business. When I resurrected and updated this article, I determined that I would not write it much differently today.

Article 6. Using John M. Keynes' characterization of the unintended bad consequences of an otherwise positive act as a "moral hazard," **"Real Estate and Moral Hazard" (1993)** takes a look at the moral hazard entailed in the misuse of government-insured deposits, potential mark-to-market accounting adjustments (rules), and the degeneration of appraisal terminology and methodology.

Mark-to-market real estate accounting requirements, for example, would wipe out the equity of many institutions—the result of about $400 billion of short-funded real estate assets in the commercial banking and insurance company systems with no obvious means of repayment, causing real estate finance to remain severely constrained.

The misuse of government-insured deposits by institutional real estate investors to fund increasingly risky undertakings could be seen as a moral hazard of the government banking-insurance system. Deposit insurance financed, in large part, the rampant overbuilding of the 1980s. Valuation issues loomed large in the real estate capital markets at this time. There was little good information, and the spreads between possible future values and current distressed values were huge

One moral hazard not discussed in this article concerns loan workouts. At the time, I had been retained by a couple of developer friends to help work out their bank loan problems. In some cases, a 25-year relationship with never a disagreement was not enough to dissuade the banks from pulling their loans—resulting in abnormal losses for the banks as well as the developers. Opportunity funds mobilized to purchase distressed assets at rock-bottom prices and made a fortune on them. I discovered that developers who told the truth and made a full disclosure tended to be run over, while the most difficult and obstinate developers who lied about their cash reserves and hid assets usually came out pretty well. I was observing a perverse variation of Gresham's Law: "Bad currency drives out good currency."

Article 7. Written in response to the ongoing crisis in the real estate capital markets, **"Price Differentials in Public and Private Markets" (1995)** takes a historical perspective on persistent pricing anomalies in real estate markets—markets that are generally "more imperfect than perfect." In particular, it includes a discussion of the wide pricing anomalies of the 1970s represented by the four major transactions that are the subject of article 1.

"Administered" pricing in the debt markets is discussed. In the 1970s, large institutions—primarily insurance companies—performed their overall investment asset allocations as part of their annual budgeting cycle. Real estate mortgages and real estate equities were assigned a budget to invest at the beginning of the year. Capital markets were so stable that quite often these allocations remained unchanged. As the year wore on, senior investment officers would price their mortgages not based on market conditions, but on how close they were to meeting their quota. Performance reviews rewarded officers who invested their budgeted amounts for the year.

As a result, private debt markets became delinked from public markets. At one time in the 1970s, Morgan Stanley discovered it could do a sale-leaseback of a corporate headquarters building for a Baa-rated regional bank or public utility for as much as 250 to 300 basis points below where the company's corporate debt would be trading. Most mortgage investment officers at insurance companies were delighted with the credit quality we could offer them compared with a typical real estate deal, and they thus ignored the public markets.

In the late 1970s, certain innovations—the "spread" trading of debt instruments off of Treasuries and the increasing transparency of the real estate capital markets—caused such pricing anomalies to disappear. But it was great fun while it lasted, and Morgan Stanley had little competition at the time.

Real Estate Operates in a Global Marketplace

Article 8. When **"Why Foreign Capital Flows into U.S. Real Estate Are Drying Up" (1991)** was published, Japanese and European investors were pulling back from the U.S. real estate market. The article concludes: "The market for foreign investment in U.S. property will be far from buoyant in the 1990s. None of the conditions—a valuation methodology compatible with financial markets, investment liquidity, or healthy local property markets—is met. The time has come to hunker down, size down, and manage assets."

The pessimism that characterizes the early 1990s is beginning to show up. Given the time lag between the writing and the publication of a magazine article, by the time this article appeared (July 1991) overbuilding had become obvious and real estate had become delinked from the capital markets. Valuation techniques were viewed as flawed and arcane. Appraisals were not keeping up with current market conditions. The best advice to investors would have been: "Tighten your belts and hold on to your tenants!"

Article 9. Despite the confusion in the U.S. real estate marketplace, real estate practitioners were on the lookout for opportunities in newly developing markets. Billed as a introduction for real estate practitioners interested in becoming China watchers, **"Does China Meet the Preconditions for Long-Term Investment in Real Estate?" (1995)** summarizes long-term investment prospects for China. Many of the observations come from a two-week study tour sponsored by ULI, in which I participated.

The article sets forth a list of preconditions for long-term investment in emerging economies in general and evaluates conditions in China against these criteria. It concludes that although China fails to meet the preconditions, it is experiencing tremendous investment flows. A partial explanation is that investment paybacks are fast, making the investments essentially short term in nature.

ULI's study trip to China was popular. It was my fifth trip to China. My first three trips, beginning a decade earlier, were with my friend Trammel Crow. I had also ridden Chairman Mao's East German–built private train from Beijing to the border of the former Soviet Union. While on the 1995 ULI study trip, I celebrated with my daughter's in-laws—who are native-born Chinese and who helped ULI organize the study tour—the birth of our first mutual grandchild.

Article 10. At the start of **"Real Estate: Global or Local?" (1999)**, I ask the rhetorical question: "Why should whatever happens to the Thai baht affect the ability to finance local real estate?" My conclusion on the question of "global or local" is that although real estate is a local and private business, its financing costs are to some extent driven by world events. Thus real estate is a local business operating in a global marketplace.

The link between the pricing of domestic real estate capital and international capital markets is complex and not fully understood. Capital markets do not like surprises. At times of uncertainty there is flight to quality in the capital markets. When a series of surprises came one after another in 1998, capital was withdrawn from emerging-markets debt, lower-grade corporate debt, and real estate debt, causing spreads to Treasuries to double overnight.

Why, I ask, is commercial real estate debt lumped with emerging third-world countries and junk bonds? The answer is basically the lack of transparency in real estate finance. Commercial mortgage–backed securities (CMBS) portfolios have not been seasoned through a down market. We do not have a good process for distressed CMBS workouts.

Turmoil Leads to Restructuring

Article 11. In 1992, roughly two years into the real estate credit crisis, capital markets were healthy, the stock market was flourishing, there was plenty of liquidity in the system, and many of the financial institution issues had been "resolved," but there was no money for real estate. Writing from my experience as chair of the second ULI Real Estate Credit Task Force, but expressing my own—not necessarily the task force's—interpretation of the credit situation, I explain, in **"The Withdrawal of Credit from Real Estate" (1992)**, why credit, which is in plentiful supply in the capital market, is not available for commercial real estate. And I suggest that the prospects for short-term remedies are dim and predict another three years of difficulty, through mid-decade.

Among the reasons for the withdrawal of credit: as an asset class, real estate lacked transparency; appraisals were unrealistic; accurate data, including rent data, were unobtainable; risk-based capital rules limited the exposure of banks to real estate; and REITs and commercial mortgage–backed securities had not yet been a factor in the recovery.

It is far easier to understand what is occurring in the capital markets if you are a player rather than a passive observer. I know exactly when the credit crunch of the early 1990s began—after mid-December 1989, when Bank of America funded the purchase of the SeaFirst headquarters building in Seattle, and before mid-January 1990, when Security Pacific Bank pulled in a bank line of credit from Don Koll, which he had planned to use to purchase the real estate assets of Union Pacific Railroad. Morgan Stanley was involved in both transactions, which together mark the harsh and abrupt change in attitude of the commercial banking system toward funding real estate commitments.

The banks had come under the scrutiny of the Comptroller of the Currency, and any funded or unfunded real estate liability was a big problem. For many banks, adding capital reserves was a survival issue. Real estate was suddenly "toxic." Loan portfolios had to be sold immediately, and there were no buyers. The price of the common stock of many major banks began to fall, affecting the personal net worth of senior officers.

My experience with Security Pacific and Don Koll made me aware of the abrupt change in the real estate credit situation, and I asked to lead a breakout panel at the spring 1990 ULI meeting to discuss the credit crisis. However, most developers had not received the message or remained in a state of disbelief, and the panel was sparsely attended. Six months later, the word was definitely out—there was standing room only at a plenary session on the credit crisis at the fall 1990 ULI meeting, a session cochaired by Stan Ross and Carl Reichardt, CEO of Wells Fargo Bank.

ULI's members responded quickly and responsibly to the 1990 crisis, contrasted with their relative indifference to the overbuilding of the 1980s. Following the fall meeting, ULI formed a Real Estate Credit Task Force, with Don Riehl as chair, to stay on top of what was happening in the capital markets. Early on, the task force met with Alan Greenspan, chair of the Federal Reserve Bank, who charged it and ULI to provide him with early warning of major changes in real estate capital markets. The successor to the task force, the McCoy Finance Symposium (which I endowed and which succeeded an interim ULI Credit Symposium), continues to meet to this day and a senior staff member of the Federal Reserve Bank attends its meetings.

Article 12. By 1994, the destruction of the old way of doing things was continuing, and some signs of the new creative real estate financing techniques were beginning to surface. **"The Creative Destruction of Real Estate Capital Markets" (1994)** is, in effect, another report from the ULI Real Estate Credit Task Force, which I was still chairing. We were still in a deep real estate recession. Hopeful signs for the future lay in the rebirth of real estate investment trusts (REITs), commercial mortgage–backed securities (CMBSs), opportunity funds, and the emergence of far greater transparency and flows of information in the real estate capital markets. I suggest here that if industry practitioners can solve some ongoing problems, the new capital market forms that are arising out of the destruction of the last four years may reduce the costs of real estate capital.

By this point of time in the credit crunch crisis, the ULI task force had succeeded in getting a number of leading financial institutions—such as Prudential Insurance, Teachers' Insurance and Annuity, Citicorp, Lehman Brothers, and others—to agree to pool their real estate databases and consider funding the development of a national market-rent index in order to provide greater transparency to the marketplace. Such cooperation was unprecedented. Of course, as conditions improved the offers to participate were withdrawn.

Article 13. It's 1997. Whew! The crisis is over. **"Commercial Real Estate Financial Trends" (1997),** a report from the ULI Credit Symposium, looks at the likely direction of the real estate capital markets over the next five years. Stability is predicted. The credit crisis had restored discipline to the markets. New or improved financial instruments, such as REITs and CMBSs, had proved very useful in taking out the banks. But, are they providing only an illusion of liquidity? The public markets are providing needed transparency to the industry. Pension funds are struggling to intellectualize the proper returns from real estate as an asset class, thinking in terms of spreads over the presumed risk-free Treasury rates, thus further linking real estate into the capital markets. The prediction: "If the self-discipline the industry was forced to acquire in the early 1990s can be maintained, together with improvements in the flow of real estate data, the millennium could prove to be a golden age for commercial real estate investment."

Article 14. If industry people had been as diligent in recognizing indications of over-building in commercial real estate markets in the late 1980s as they were in the early 1990s, perhaps things might have been different. **"Irrational Exuberance" (1998)** is a "point of view" article that looks at ways by which we can protect real estate markets from their unlimited propensity to "irrational exuberance," the term used recently by Alan Greenspan to describe stock market bubbles. It lists a number of common-sense indicators of overbuilding, all of which were plainly present in the late 1980s, and a list of new indicators related to trends in securitization, technology, and consolidation—all of which affect our ability to predict commercial real estate cycles.

Article 15. Commercial real estate in 1998 was in market equilibrium for the first time in many years, the result of ongoing trends in securitization, technology, and con-solidation. "Have these new trends," I ask in **"Tragedy of the Commons: Will It Be Different This Time?" (1998)**, "served to dampen the volatility of the real estate cycle, or is the real estate development game just the same old game being played out in a new wrapper?" The article examines the excesses of the 1980s as a phenomenon known as "the tragedy of the commons," from an 1833 parable that describes the conflict for resources between individual interests and the common good. In the parable, the vil-lage commons is overgrazed to the point where there is no fodder left; each individual animal owner had felt entitled to their own share of the common good, and there had been no sense of the collective responsibility to conserve or renew the food supply. No one individual is responsible for the devastation of the common good, but it is devas-tated and trust is lost.

Applied to commercial real estate, the "tragedy" can play out as follows: If individual entrepreneurs attempt to get an edge on the market by not sharing insider information, the result will be a lack of transparency—which, in turn, leads major institutions, such as pension funds, to think of real estate as an insiders "rigged" game; they therefore pull their capital out, thus raising the cost of capital for all real estate development.

I conclude that the kinds of systems that might produce the transparency need-ed to prevent overbuilding—a national rent index and new federal reporting require-ments for banks and real estate finance companies, for example—are "probably too draconian to withstand the political and regulatory process." And I suggest, somewhat cynically, that the presence of imperfections in the real estate markets, with all the concomitant windfalls and losses, is why we find real estate such an entertaining and stimulating place to make a living.

Article 16. In the late 1990s, wide disparities in pricing between public and private markets were once again, as in the 1970s, a possibility. Public markets had pretty much taken commercial banks out of the real estate lending business. But, the wake-up call of 1998 was that public securities markets can dry up quickly for reasons that have absolutely nothing to do with the quality of the underlying real estate assets. After the debt crisis, private market players came roaring back into the market. **"When Markets Clash" (1999)** looks at recent events in the real estate capital markets as part of the evolving clash between public and private markets (as covered also in articles 1 and 7), and ponders on the issue of transparency versus entrepreneurship. It concludes: "The industry wants the world to be predictable, while it remains unpredictable. In a thoroughly predictable, transparent world, profits are limited. . . .Without the clashing

---

McCoy Symposium Reports

A number of the articles throughout the book are reports that came out of the annual McCoy Finance Symposium or its predecessors, the ULI Real Estate Credit Task Force and the ULI Credit Symposium, which Tony Downs in the foreword to this book, calls "the most informative single annual event available for understanding real estate markets." A chronological list of the symposium-based articles included in the book follows:

- "The Creative Destruction of Real Estate Capital Markets" (1994)—article 12
- "Commercial Real Estate Finance Trends" (1997)—article 13
- "When Markets Clash" (1999)—article 16
- "Real Estate: Global or Local?" (1999)—article 10
- "Toward Greater Transparency" (2000)—article 24
- "Capital Constraints" (2001)—article 25
- "Will It Ever Be the Same Again?" (2002)—article 21
- "Disconnected Markets" (2003)—article 22
- "Capital Markets Equilibrium?" (2004)—article 26
- "Managing for the Crisis" (2005)—article 27
- "Is the End Near for Unrestrained Capital Flows?" (2006)—article 28

of the public and private markets, the industry would lose much of its unique character, as well as many of its opportunities."

The article is one in what was to become a series of informal reports on the annual meetings of the McCoy Finance Symposium (formerly known as the ULI Real Estate Credit Task Force and then the ULI Credit Symposium). The symposium met in December 1998, at which time the shockers were the Russian/Asian debt crisis of the previous summer followed by the Long-Term Capital Management crisis, which shook everyone's confidence in the newly liquid REIT and CMBS markets for public real estate debt and equity. The value of REIT stocks plummeted and CMBS spreads over Treasury rates widened dramatically.

There will always be cycles and tradeoffs between public and private markets. The potential for capital markets to be delinked from underlying real estate assets should motivate all major users of real estate capital to have access to multiple sources in both the public and private markets.

Changing Tools and Processes Play a More Prominent Role

Article 17. Successful investment in real estate by a large pension fund requires a competent, motivated staff and benchmarking of performance; advisers must be rewarded—or not—on the basis of such benchmarking. Based largely on the lessons learned from an advisory assignment to study a large public pension fund's processes for investing in real estate, **"Pension Funds' Investment in Real Estate: A New Model" (1996)** discusses the role of real estate in pension fund portfolios and the pension fund advisory business.

I had been intrigued with the potential for real estate investment by pension funds from my earliest days at Brooks Harvey. In the late 1970s, I was invited to address a conference of the major United Kingdom pension fund managers on the topic of property investment in the United States. In the mid-1990s, I obtained an assignment to re-engineer the real estate investment process of one of the largest pension funds in the country. I undertook to evaluate the fund's procedures, looking for both good and bad practices. I met with many of the most successful pension fund advisers to validate what I had determined to be good practices. This article is a précis of my final report to the pension fund. I also presented these findings to a conference of the Pension Real Estate Association (PREA), the professional group for pension real estate advisers.

Pension funds need to implement good practices and the real estate markets need to provide better information (transparency) for pension funds to meet that target 10 percent asset allocation that I predicted 30 years ago.

Article 18. **"Public Process Counseling" (1996)** proposes a framework for public process counseling, based on my participation in assignments like a citizens committee to comment on a city of Los Angeles ordinance on the allocation of sewer permits, a ULI panel to choose the location of a new convention center in Denver, and a task force to examine the economic condition and financial structure of the city of Los Angeles. "Process counseling," it concludes, "is far more complex than transactional counseling."

In my career, I have spent considerable time in public service and teaching activities. Some of these activities have involved pro bono real estate counseling. After I had completed a number of such counseling projects, it occurred to me that many real estate practitioners are involved in community improvement activities on a pro bono basis. It was to leverage this involvement that I wrote this article describing some of my activities and drawing some conclusions on how to be effective at such work.

Article 19. Written when not so many real estate professionals had gotten on board the computer train, with the view that they would soon have to if they wanted to continue to perform at a competitive level, **"My Computer and Me" (1997)** is a personal story about the trials and tribulations I endured in entering the computer age.

In addition to so many other things, I owe my computer prowess to ULI. More than ten years ago, my wife and I attended a ULI midwinter leadership conference in Tucson at which one of the speakers, Jennifer James, a dynamic and attractive college professor, challenged all of us to become computer literate. I left thinking: "Who needs it?" but my wife, two months later, gave me a birthday present of a computer and nine hours of instruction (from a very attractive instructor). The article describes my computer-learning adventures and mishaps from then on. Of course, ten years later, I cannot live without it.

Real Estate Capital Markets in the 2000s: Articles 20 to 28

"Real Estate Capital Markets in the 2000s" comprises nine articles published between 2000 and early 2006. They explore two general themes—1) the effects of 9/11 on investment in real estate, and 2) the maturing of real estate investment as an asset class.

Just when we began to think that the real estate market had returned to normal (what is "normal" in these cyclical markets?), 9/11 threatened new turmoil. Two market conditions helped the industry avert another nosedive: the capital constraints that operated in the 1990s and relatively low interest rates. The constraints on capital flows in the 1990s precluded overbuilding and gave commercial real estate markets plenty of time to work off the excesses of the 1980s. In some markets, including the downtown Los Angeles office market, it took almost 15 years to reach equilibrium. The interest rates that prevailed over a sustained period of time in the early years of the new century seemed to many people to be abnormally low. In fact, they were about the same as they were when I started at Morgan Stanley in 1962; but it had taken us 40 years to get back there.

By mid-decade I was predicting the end of such low interest rates and cautioning against overborrowing at cheap rates; as rates rose and loan-to-value ratios went down accordingly, there was the danger of getting caught in a liquidity squeeze. Capitalization rates of as little as 5.5 percent seemed ridiculously low, but justified in the eyes of some investors on the basis of the lower relative return to cash, bonds, or stocks. Obviously, a rising stock market would wipe out real estate's relative advantage. Lower capitalization rates for completed projects reflected rising replacement costs and lengthening land entitlement processes.

I also reminded investors that commercial mortgage–backed securities had never been tested in a stressful market and that real estate investment trusts could become stressed at the later stages in their life cycles. By mid-decade, opportunity funds were providing excess liquidity to the markets. Furthermore, I worried about the inexperience factor—too many "developers" in the marketplace who have never experienced a down market like that of the early 1990s. To be truly seasoned, real estate practitioners must have seen both ends of the cycle.

9/11 Shocks the Market

Article 20. Written shortly after 9/11, **"Clouds of Uncertainty" (2001)** provides a brief overview of the likely near-term direction for real estate and various segments of the capital markets. It advises borrowers where possible to lengthen maturities and move from floating-rate to fixed-rate debt. It predicts wider debt spreads, increases in the cost of equity capital, and more tenant power. It predicts that what is considered "normal" will change.

September 11, 2001, was the next big shock to the market after the credit crunch. After much debate, ULI decided it would not cancel its planned semiannual meeting in Boston in October. The meeting was well attended, with many of the sessions, as well as the trustees meeting, devoted to our reaction to the terrorist attack.

Article 21. In the immediate aftermath of 9/11, the transaction market was frozen, with a wide spread between perceptions of value by buyers and sellers. Property operating expenses, especially for insurance, were increasing. Tenants were avoiding high-rise office buildings. Equity values were decreasing, although the decline was still not reflected in appraised values. "Yes and no," said the participants at the December 2001 McCoy Finance Seminar to the title question: **"Will It Ever Be the Same Again?"** **(2002).** They agreed that the economic slowdown would last until at least mid-2002, but then disagreed on the recovery, with half saying lack of consumer confidence would make it sluggish and half saying that the economy would adjust to uncertainty.

The sense of the symposium was that insurance, security, concentration of personnel, communications, and travel will feel the effects of 9/11 for some time to come—but also that we must try "to separate out the long-term impacts of terrorism from the negative impact of the recession," which will pass much sooner than the terrorist impact. The recommendation of the symposium was that developers should stay as liquid as possible, cut overhead, and hold on to tenants. The economy will grow again, but to develop real estate in it will require more equity and self-discipline.

Article 22. A little more than a year after 9/11, the capital markets were awash in liquidity and seeking investments, while commercial property markets, on the other hand, were experiencing weak rental conditions and high vacancies. Based on the deliberations of the ninth annual McCoy Finance Symposium that met in December 2002, **"Disconnected Markets" (2003)** tells real estate developers to "use the current attractive financing markets prudently, retaining an ample supply of equity in their projects." The disconnections between the capital and property markets, said symposium participants, require us to distinguish between the investor perspective and the developer perspective. At this point in time, real estate fundamentals were weak and expected to deteriorate further.

But reliable numbers were still elusive. Despite all the work of the finance symposium and its predecessors, in 2003 it was still difficult to determine net effective rent levels and true estimates of unoccupied space, especially where rent was still being paid.

Debt was cheap, and developers and owners tended to overborrow. The article recommends basing pro forma calculations on interest levels 200 basis points higher than current market rates and reducing the loan-to-value ratio in order to mitigate refinancing risk. It advises practitioners to avoid speculative risk and wait for an improved economy, which is expected by mid-decade.

Article 23. In a deflationary environment, debt becomes an intoxicating siren, and borrowers should be wary of overborrowing at cheap rates, which could be stepping into a "liquidity trap." **"New Conditions? Suggestions for Dealing with the Possibility of a Deflationary Environment" (2005)** notes that even if the overall economy manages to avoid deflation, which is likely, the commercial real estate industry and specific geographic areas may experience deflationary conditions; and it provides some specific suggestions—managing inventories, cutting costs, developing an action plan, and so forth—for dealing with the possibility of a deflationary environment, many of which could prove beneficial even if a deflationary cycle never materializes. In sum, "the best advice always is to tightly manage and plan businesses—and run a little bit scared."

Real Estate Matures As an Asset Class

Article 24. Whether real estate would continue to be viewed as a separate asset class or become more fully integrated into the global capital market system was the major issue engaging the attention of the participants at the December 1999 McCoy Finance Seminar, reported in **"Toward Greater Transparency" (2000)**. When real estate is viewed as a separate asset class and thus delinked from the capital markets system, it may be mispriced, and such mispricing can create opportunities. The role of the Internet in commercial real estate transactions was also a topic of much discussion.

As the article's title indicates, the participants in this symposium generally supported the idea of more transparency in real estate investments. They noted that real estate loans and investments have been moving into the public markets, but that real estate has relatively less transparency than the capital markets have come to expect—resulting in a restricted volume of investment funds in the real estate capital markets and in a risk premium in mispricing real estate capital.

Article 25. The greater transparency that was called for in the 1999 McCoy Finance Symposium (article 24) "still has not materialized," report the 2000 symposium participants in **"Capital Constraints" (2001)**—and the disconnect between public and private markets continues to be maintained. Other selected observations from the symposium: 1) After a long absence, pension funds are beginning to move back into core real estate and single-asset transactions; and trophy real estate is making a comeback. 2) Real estate credit remains attractively priced, but it is more difficult to access because lending capacity has sharply diminished from a decade earlier. Borrowers can expect higher due-diligence standards and widened spreads. 3) The liquidity squeeze in both debt and equity markets is providing excellent market discipline.

Article 26. Real estate capital markets are approaching equilibrium, according to the December 2003 McCoy Finance Symposium as reported in **"Capital Markets Equilibrium?" (2004)**—a condition predicted for mid-decade by participants in previous symposiums. Low-cost debt has lasted far longer than we had anticipated, and it has led to lower capitalization rates as well. When interest rates rise again, however, those who overborrowed may find themselves in a liquidity trap. The present equilibrium is recent and may be short-lived. We may overshoot once again, basing prices on aggressive income assumptions and leveraging. The flow of investment funds into the market makes this a very real risk. The symposium participants are concerned about the new generation of retail stock brokerage real estate syndicators, who have raised significant funds but are likely to obtain only mediocre returns, "giving real estate investment a bad name in the marketplace once again."

Article 27. The December 2004 McCoy Finance Symposium report, **"Managing for the Crisis" (2005)**, finds commercial real estate remaining in a benign state. Rental rates, capitalization rates, and interest rates are competing in a race of sorts, with excess investment funds driving down capitalization rates while rising expenses and declining rents drive down net operating returns from property. For real estate owners, the real race will be between property returns and interest rates—if rental rates rise sooner and faster than interest rates, all will be fine, but if the reverse occurs owners can be caught in a liquidity trap as they try to refinance deals.

The current lower-than-normal returns on real estate do not much worry symposium participants, who see in them "evidence of a declining risk premium for real estate caused by greater transparency and price disclosure in the public markets, the benefits of securitization, and banking consolidation, among other factors." Still, the odds are 30 percent, according to symposium participants, that a major shock that could cause a crisis like those experienced in 1998 and 2001 will occur in the not-too-distant future. To prepare for such an eventuality, real estate practitioners who have lived through the crises of the past will operate prudently and keep some liquidity for the buying opportunities ahead.

Article 28. **"Is the End Near for Unrestrained Capital Flows?" (2006)**—a report on the December 2005 McCoy Finance Symposium—begins: "It appears we are in for another cycle—it is time to manage debt structures prudently." The participants agree that the presence of higher interest rates and more risk in the system spells the near end of the "perfect calm." Mainly because most markets are in equilibrium and overbuilding has not occurred, a crisis has so far been avoided. However, the fact that capitalization rates are as low as 5.5 percent is a worrisome indication that the market may have overreached once again. Debt underwriting standards have deteriorated. In structured debt deals, loan-to-value percentages have moved up into the 90s. It would be ironic if the financial instruments that alleviated the credit crisis of the early 1990s became contributors to a real estate credit squeeze in the next few years. The market may be forgetting the financial discipline learned so hard in the 1990s. Proceed with caution!

Values-Based Leadership: Articles 29 to 36

The last group of readings, "Values-Based Leadership" comprises eight articles published between 1983 and 2002. They explore three general themes—1) character and personal responsibility, 2) the globalization of business ethics, and 3) ethics and real estate.

I was in my mid-30s when I was asked to take over the real estate unit at Morgan Stanley. In the course of that assignment I terminated several individuals and made key decisions regarding compensation and promotions. Several of the individuals I was "leading" were ten, 20, or even 25 years older than I. I became aware of the responsibility I had for others, and I tried to take it very seriously. The education I received at Harvard Business School proved extraordinarily applicable, and the rest I learned by trial and error—making plenty of mistakes.

After 20 years of service, I took a six-month sabbatical from Morgan Stanley (initiating the firm's sabbatical program). I trekked in the Himalayas, taught at Stanford Business School, and studied moral philosophy one day a week with a theologian at a seminary in Berkeley. My thinking was that I knew enough about organizational theory and had gone through plenty of on-the-job training, but that I lacked grounding in the philosophical and theological underpinnings of ethics and values-based leadership. A focus of my sabbatical was, in effect, an Oxford-like tutorial in which I read two books a week, met with my adviser one morning a week, and did practical fieldwork in the afternoons. One important lasting result of my sabbatical was a long friendship with the theologian, which helped me feel more comfortable in teaching, speaking, and writing about business ethics.

Seeking Ethical and Emotional Maturity

Article 29. "**The Parable of the Sadhu**" (**1983**), an article that has been widely reprinted and referenced, tells the story of encountering a dying pilgrim (a sadhu) on a climbing trip in the Himalayas. The experience had a powerful impact on my thinking about corporate ethics. Although some might argue that the experience has no relevance to business, it was a situation in which a basic ethical dilemma suddenly intruded into the lives of a group of individuals. How the group responded I think holds a lesson for all organizations no matter how defined.

After almost 20 years at Morgan Stanley, 12 as a general partner, I decided I needed a time out to do some things I otherwise might not accomplish. Accordingly, I took a six-month sabbatical. In the first three months, I trekked with a companion for 600 miles in the Himalayas. In the second six months, I taught two sections of a full-term course on the management of financial institutions at Stanford Business School and spent one day a week at the Pacific School of Religion, a seminary in Berkeley, boning up on moral philosophy.

The Himalayan adventure was purely for me. The teaching was to see if I could do it—in preparation for life after Morgan Stanley. The seminary was to fill in some missing pieces. I had been running the real estate unit for almost a decade, giving me plenty of hands-on operating experience, and I felt well prepared in organizational theory from Harvard Business School. In my experience, leadership was values based, and I wanted to see what a better understanding of moral philosophy could add to my leadership skills.

While at the seminary, I read an advertisement in the *Harvard Business Review* offering a $4,000 prize for the best ethics "case" submitted by a practicing business person. I wrote this article, and it won the prize. "The Parable of the Sadhu" has been in the Harvard Business School curriculum for 25 years, and is used as well by many other business schools, corporations, and not-for-profits. A Google search turns up several hundred references to it. It has, in short, become a "classic" in business ethics. In fact, a few years ago *Harvard Business Review* reprinted it as a classic. The "case" was even filmed, in a joint venture between PBS and Harvard Business School, with Arthur Miller of Harvard Law School leading a discussion of the situation.

The continuing ambiguity about what was the "right" thing to do, as well as the exotic nature of the situation, have helped give this article a long shelf life. Rules-based ethicists would take a utilitarian approach—the greatest good for the greatest number. Values-based ethicists would state that the rules no longer apply. Read the parable to see where you come out.

Article 30. Prepared for a 1995 conference of the Counselors of Real Estate on the shared ethical responsibility of individuals and their institutions, **"On Business Ethics" (1994)** attempts "to frame a definitional language" by briefly explaining major types of ethics: normative ethics, Kantian ethics, utilitarian ethics, social justice ethics, religious ethics, and communitarian ethics. Then it suggests an overlapping model of practical ethics based at the intersection of moral philosophy/theology, social ethics, and corporate ethics. Finally, it proposes a five-step process of ethical decision making. I conclude with this observation: Ethics "is a lifelong process of growth and maturation that, by its very nature, can never be perfect or complete.

Morgan Stanley's real estate unit provided me with a real-time laboratory for testing myself as a leader. As time went on, I became more and more interested in developing leadership skills and in evaluating my impact on the organization. Even before retiring from Morgan Stanley, I began teaching graduate-level leadership courses in business schools. In particular, I have taught a six-hour leadership module, usually twice a year, since 1989 at the Lusk Center for Real Estate at the University of Southern California.

Article 31. I devoted one of my "The President Speaks" columns in *The Counselor* (Counselors of Real Estate) to a review of the book *Emotional Intelligence* by Daniel Goleman—a book that argues that people who are emotionally adept, who know and manage their own feelings well and who read and deal effectively with other people's feelings, are at an advantage in any domain of life. I believe that this piece, **"Emotional Intelligence Provides Key to Life Success" (1997)** is one of the most important things I have written. Leadership is about keeping one's emotions in check and being, in the midst of a crisis, a point of comfort to others. Countless highly intelligent, driven individuals failed at Morgan Stanley because they lacked emotional maturity. Peter Drucker emphasizes emotional maturity in his book on the leader of the future. How, you may ask, does one attain such maturity? Fundamentally, by leading an integrated life and finding peace within oneself. Religion can play a powerful role, as can a deep-seated humanism.

Moving Toward a Global Ethic

Article 32. Published shortly after 9/11 exposed America to transnational terror, **"Toward a Global Ethic?" (2001)** argues that the need to think globally is even more pressing than before. "A move toward a global ethic," it says, "requires discovery of those aspects of universal humanity that transcend barriers."

Globally integrated capital markets and worldwide communications networks have made isolation from the rest of the world difficult. An understanding of cultural differences is important. It is possible to distinguish aspects of different cultures that promote—or discourage—economic growth. Many cultures have to change in order to participate in the global business model that is rooted in capitalism, a system that these cultures may traditionally consider to be inhumane.

In the West, we rely on institutions, such as universities and large corporations, to take care of us. Many of us learn to trust these institutions. In third-world countries, family ties remain far more powerful. We often mistake deeply imbedded family-based cultural norms for cronyism. If we want to really "think globally, act locally," we must understand cultural and social differences. There will always be differences, and the differences must be celebrated.

Article 33. Whether or not Enron officers broke the law (and they did), they broke trust with the public. **"Breaking Public Trust" (2002)** is my initial reaction to the Enron scandals, and it suggests that "the best outcome of Enron's collapse would be confirmation of ethics as crucial to business decision making." This scandal raises issues of the trustworthiness of public accounting firms, law firms, management consulting firms, boards of directors, financial reporting, business leadership, and even the stock market. If the U.S. capital market is the model for the world, Enron also broke trust with institutions throughout the world.

Trust is not easily created, but it is easily destroyed. The proper response to scandalous corporate lapses that can destroy public trust is not to pile on more rules and regulations, like those in Sarbanes-Oxley, but to focus more on honoring leadership and values in the business community. Ethics must become a crucial component in making business decisions.

Applying Ethics to Real Estate

Article 34. I wrote **"Real Estate Ethics"** (**2000**), which concerns the importance of teaching ethics in business school, for the *Wharton Real Estate Review* at the behest of my good friend Peter Linneman. It is an update of article 30, with the addition of a great deal of my continuing thinking on the subject of real estate ethics. The article includes a list of typical ethical dilemmas that my USC students have experienced in their working lives—for example: When does networking become spying? When does puffery become lying? When does playing hardball become deception?

Article 35. **"A Question of Ethics"** (**2000**) excerpts a discussion panel on the social responsibility of business, which I organized as part of the Stanford Business School's celebration of its 75th anniversary. In addition to myself, the panelists were Milton Friedman, who many years ago had framed the debate over the social responsibility of business, and two professors at Stanford Business School, one liberal and one conservative. The spirited debate was filmed and shown on some PBS stations.

Article 36. The final article in this book, **"Free-Market Environmentalism"** (**2001**) — written at the start of the George W. Bush administration when two free-market environmentalists had just joined the Cabinet, one as administrator of the Environmental Protection Agency and the other as secretary of the Interior Department—focuses on the philosophy of free-market environmentalism.

I love the outdoors, and I have a stake in how we as a society might best protect important natural resources. I have hiked some 10,000 miles of wilderness areas, including 1,000 miles in the Himalayas. I admire ULI's standards of smart growth as an attempt to balance various interests.

I have been exposed to the issues of environmental protection from various perspectives. One weekend in the 1970s, after I had spent the week drafting a public debt prospectus for Consolidated Edison Company of New York concerning the funding of a pumped-storage electric power plant at Storm King Mountain on the Hudson

River—a plant that I thought was environmentally sound and made great sense—I led a hike over Storm King for the Appalachian Mountain Club. I had to listen all day to rabid environmentalists describing the plant as a criminal activity.

The concept of free-market environmentalism makes great sense to me, and I am a supporter of the Property and Environment Research Center in Bozeman, Montana. I was pleased when the Real Estate Counselors asked me to write something about free-market environmentalism.

It is a philosophy that is grounded in property rights, voluntary exchange, common law liability protection, and the rule of law—all of which seek to integrate environmental resources into the market system. Basically, it applies rational economics and utilitarian models to evaluate the cost and benefits of environmental protection. When a regulation costs many times more than the calculated benefits to society, it is wrong—at least from an economic point of view.

Clearly some issues are moral, and go beyond rational calculations. Pure air and water and gorgeous sunsets have aesthetic values. They cannot be evaluated solely in dollars and cents. Given human nature, rewards and punishments should remain available. However, free-market environmentalism offers a creative and positive way out of the morass of overregulation and endless litigation. It offers more balanced and effective solutions.

Current Thoughts on the Future of Capital Markets and the World of Real Estate

Toward a Global Marketplace

This book's reprinted articles trace the changes in real estate capital markets from the 1970s through the mid-2000s. Now I turn to what trends I see in store for real estate going forward. Cycles will, of course, continue to play out. A myriad of predictable but basically unknowable factors—say renewed inflation, rapidly rising oil prices, hurricanes, or terrorist activities—will cause the cycle to speed up or slow down, to deepen or flatten. Real estate professionals should always be ready for the unanticipated. They should always keep some financing flexibility, both for downside protection as well as for unexpected buying opportunities. Those who went through the early 1990s know what it is like to have the banks drive your business plan; no one wants to repeat that experience.

For the near term:

- I worry that the commercial mortgage–backed securities (CMBS) market still has not been through a distressed cycle. When it does hit bad times, how will property owners handle the decisions to delay and defer payments or fund tenant improvements? Who will pay for the workout process? Who will perform the workouts? Under stress, what will happen to the lower-rated B tranches? How will new issues of CMBSs be structured?

- I think that there are still too many REITs. Sarbanes-Oxley requirements provide one more reason why private is better. The consolidation of REITs will continue, and the number of REITs moving from public to private will grow.
- As the supply/demand situation continues to improve, large-scale urban development and urban infill will enjoy a renaissance.
- Opportunity funds will feel increased pressure to meet their stated terms for termination and liquidity. They will respond by selling assets, going public, and the like.
- Pension funds will grow in size to 1.5 to two times their current dollar amount, providing large sums for real estate investment at current allocation levels. They probably will not grow their real estate asset allocation to 10 percent. (Then again, now that I have rescinded my forecast made 35 years ago that they would get to 10 percent, they probably will!)

Over the longer term, markets will continue to fluctuate. Although we seem to have developed a much higher level of sophistication in applying monetary policy, we will still have swings of recession, deflation, rapid growth, inflation, and excessive speculation. In the real estate sector, with its reliance on interest rates and its entrepreneurial excesses, the swings will be wider than for the economy as a whole. The best practitioners will know where we are in the cycle and how to retain financial flexibility without overborrowing or getting caught up in excess euphoria.

Looking at Real Estate through the Prism of Economic Cycles

My formal university training was as an economist, and I remain connected to that profession in several ways. For three years I served as chair of the Center for Economic Policy Research at Stanford University, and I have continued to maintain friendships with Ken Arrow, Mike Boskin, John Shoven, John Taylor, and other people there. Also, I have served on the executive committee of the Hoover Institution for many years, where I became acquainted with Milton Friedman and several other notable economists. Steve Roach, chief economist at Morgan Stanley, and Ben Friedman, economics professor at Harvard, are among my longtime friends, along with economists Tony Downs, Peter Linneman, and Ken Rosen. Economics is the prism through which I see the real estate world. I might even be termed a "real estate economist" myself, though I do not claim the title.

I see the real estate world as a series of discontinuous cycles—the public market pricing cycle, the private market pricing cycle, the interest rate cycle, and the localized real estate supply and demand cycle. General economic cycles—of which I have lived through five or six in my professional life—overlay the specifically real estate cycles.

A way to "understand" real estate—and to make a fair amount of money from it—is to keep an eye on all these cycles as they play out in relationship to one another, creating pricing and value anomalies and opportunities for profit. Of all the people I have run into over the past 45 years, Sam Zell probably does this the best.

Another important truth to remember about real estate: There is no such thing as passive real estate. We are forever falsely trying to convince ourselves and others that real estate is passive. Put a mortgage on it; put it in a REIT; put it in an adviser's hands; put it in a CMBS portfolio (where a bunch of bad assets suddenly, in aggregation, become one very good asset)—but always remember, there is no such thing as passive real estate. I am thankful for my hands-on experience in running a REIT and a development company for Morgan Stanley. Even in a debt position, you have to know the property—how it makes money, what it is competing against, whether it is on the way up or the way down, what attracts tenants to the building, what tenants need, the schedule for normal and extraordinary maintenance and repairs, and so on and so forth. Otherwise, sooner or later, you will be in for a big, unhappy surprise.

Fundamental Values

A long-term career in real estate is sustained by people and trust, not by money and power. If you can compete in a rough-and-tumble business and sustain long-term trust relationships with people, you will make plenty of money. On the other hand, if you are continually trying to hit the ball out of the park and looking for the next deal, and if you view your clients as people you can take advantage of, you will burn out—and you are likely to be a bit lonely. I am proud to say that as a sole proprietor, without the great engine of Morgan Stanley behind me, I am still doing business with people with whom I have maintained relationships for 15, 20, 25, and even 30 years.

My strongest advice, looking back over almost 50 years of professional life, is to know who you are—what your values are. Take a long-term point of view. Learn from your mistakes. Know what is it you are willing to lose for. Regard your profession not as an unending series of deals, but as a series of long-term trust relationships that you carefully nurture.

Real estate is a valid profession. To this day, I can travel to almost any major city in the United States and see projects that Morgan Stanley helped to finance. It gives me great satisfaction to know that, in our way, we helped shape the built environment of so many cities, provided jobs, and promoted community. All of us in the business world, if we live constructive lives, contribute to the well-being of society. If we wish, we can see our own businesses as a canvas on which we live out our personal values. I hope that you who are reading this book will see the potential in the real estate business for adventure, success, and a noble calling.

PART 2

Real Estate Capital Markets in the 1970s and 1980s

An Emerging Asset Class

Growing Securitization Issues

Note to readers: In part 1 of this book, the author summarizes the key issues and points covered in the individual articles, and offers additional commentary to provide context and a longer-term perspective. Commentaries on articles 1 to 4 may be found on pages 8 to 11.

1 Adventures in Marketing Large Real Estate Portfolios

This article is based on a speech presented by Bowen H. ("Buzz") McCoy on January 30, 1981, at the midwinter meeting of the American Society of Real Estate Counselors in Las Vegas, Nevada.

The four transactions presented cover some 20 major urban areas throughout America and involve all types of commercial property. They also involve politics, corporate raiders, lawsuits, fraud, deceit, and allegations of murder. These adventures belong to my work with Morgan Stanley & Co., one of the leading U.S. investment banks. Its real estate financing and counseling activities are carried on by Brooks Harvey, a 65-year-old firm that in the past two years has sold or financed $3 billion worth of commercial real estate.

From these experiences I will attempt to draw some conclusions about what we have learned by executing the assignments, which not only underline the interesting content of the counselor's work, but also offer insights into factors contributing to success in large transactions.

Irvine versus Joan

Starting in 1971, I worked as a counselor for the James Irvine Foundation for seven years. The Irvine Foundation held as its principal asset 54 percent of the common stock of the Irvine Company, which in turn owned 80,000 acres comprising 22 percent of Orange County, the southernmost contiguous county to Los Angeles County.

Called the Irvine Ranch, the area is an old Spanish land grant with an interesting history. At the inception of our assignment, I read a monograph published by the Huntington Library and filled with tales of cowboys, Indians, rustlers, robbers, and young James Irvine riding his bicycle from San Francisco to inspect his property.

The property included a regional shopping mall, an office park, a hotel, a number of single-family homes and apartments, golf courses, marinas, perhaps the best industrial park in the nation, 3.5 miles of pristine Pacific coastline beachfront, agricultural land on the ranch and in the San Joaquin Valley, and the Flying "D" Ranch on the Gallatin River.

There were other shareholders in the Irvine Company, including a 22 percent block controlled by Joan Irvine Smith and her mother, Athalie.

The immediate problem was to value the foundation's holding of Irvine common stock in order to comply with the Tax Reform Act of 1969 as it applied to holdings of private foundations. At the time, the Irvine Foundation carried its total holdings in the ranch at one dollar. Our valuation would become the basis for the charitable payout requirement to be levied on the foundation by the Internal Revenue Service. The assignment in its own terms was challenging, as it included such problems as judging developmental time horizons, discount rates for raw land, capitalization rates for various types of income property, and valuations of single-family ground leases. Added to this was the as yet undefinable impact of the newly formulated requirements for environmental impact studies, the California Coastal Initiative restriction on 3.5 miles of oceanfront, and the newly generated "last in" exclusionism of the residents of the town of Irvine.

The foundation trustees cautioned us that Joan Irvine might be less than conservative in her approach to value, and that any value arrived at was likely to be challenged ultimately in the courts. Ms. Irvine had brought 15 separate lawsuits against the foundation to break its control over the property. She felt the property should have been left to her mother and herself, as James Irvine's granddaughter. After we were employed, it was discovered that Joan Irvine had implicated the foundation in the death of her grandfather, James Irvine, who drowned while fishing in the Gallatin River on the Flying "D" Ranch, as well as in the death of her father, Myford Irvine, who eventually was deemed a suicide by the California Supreme Court. It was later learned that Joan Irvine had supported a rider to the 1969 tax bill that lasted all the way to the Senate Finance–House Ways and Means Conference Committee. The rider would have made it unlawful for any charitable foundation to own 20 percent or more of any county in the United States.

This is not meant to disparage Joan Irvine, but serves to point out the elements of high drama and complexity that her role brought to this assignment. While we were not influenced by her strong feelings against our client, it was soon clear that the relationship between the two principal shareholders was contentious, adverse, and frozen in past emotions.

This was a serious deficiency having an adverse impact on value. Anyone who ultimately might wish to purchase the foundation's 54 percent interest would step into its shoes, and would have to deal with Ms. Irvine to gain control of the ranch.

There was thus a "control" premium in the valuation of this delicate piece of property. The foundation's 54 percent holding did not represent control while Ms. Joan Irvine and her mother held a blocking position. The blocking position impaired value to the foundation and put Ms. Irvine in the catbird seat with respect to the Internal Revenue Service (which was interested in a high value for charitable payout purposes), the state of California attorney general (who was required by law to approve major sales of foundation assets), and any prospective purchaser of the foundation's shares.

Another problem was the fact that the foundation owned shares of common stock, not real estate; and because of Joan Irvine it was not in full control of the asset, its disposition, or its development plan. Recognizing this lack of control, were we to value the shares or the underlying asset?

We valued the shares and treated the land as burdened by fragmented control, old Proposition 13 (the coastal initiative), a slowdown in development because of environmental impact studies and the like, a 30-year development cycle, and a discount rate on raw land of 15 percent. A discounted cash flow model for the development of the entire Irvine Ranch with absorption projections for each segment of possible land use was constructed. Those lands with more than a 30-degree slope were eliminated and longer-term development of the coast frontage was assumed.

Based on these studies, the prices of common stock of some 30 publicly traded land or development companies, a prime rate of 14 percent, and an annualized housing start rate of 800,000, we opined that an offer to purchase 100 percent of the shares of the Irvine Company by Mobil Oil Corporation for $200 million was within a range of fairness. Ms. Irvine, heavily influenced by the relatively small portion of the ranch that was fully developed, thought all the shares were worth $1 billion. She felt that the Mobil deal was "too close" an arrangement between the trustees and Mobil, and that we were unprincipled agents of the foundation. She made her point of view known to the Internal Revenue Service, the California attorney general, and several others who had a more than purely academic interest in the proceedings.

Ms. Irvine should have realized that her interests and those of our client were compatible. We wished to cover the market and achieve the highest offer for the foundation's shares, letting the market tell us what it was worth. What Ms. Irvine apparently did not realize was that her contentiousness alarmed potential purchasers and depressed potential value.

Back at the ranch we found ourselves locked in a deal with Mobil. The foundation required a court adjudication of fairness of a firm offer in order to sell, as only such a process could secure the California attorney general's approval. Without a firm offer there could be no such court proceeding. Mobil bargained hard, saying its offer would hold only so long as the trustees would not shop it. Because we and the trustees felt the Mobil offer was fair, we decided not to market the shares but to proceed through the courts for confirmation of fairness. We could only react to unsolicited inquiries from other prospective purchasers.

This posture lasted for 18 months. During this period no other bona fide offer was received. Joan Irvine intervened effectively in the court adjudication. Also during this time the economy began to recover from the oil crisis of 1974–1975, interest rates came down, and housing starts increased.

At one point we felt Ms. Irvine and the other family interests were agreeable to a share-for-share stock swap with Mobil. Mobil stock was then at $30; today it is at $80 after a stock split. Thus, its offer would have become a $1 billion tax-free transaction. But that offer fell apart.

After 12 months, Mobil was advised that unless we could produce a record for the judge that the shares had been aggressively offered to the market, Ms. Irvine probably could continue to delay final approval. This was one time when Joan Irvine's strategy helped us. Mobil's attitude was that its price of $200 million had been in the public domain for 18 months; since no other offers were forthcoming, it released the trustees from the "no shopping" constraint.

We made 113 offerings throughout the world and barely got Cadillac Fairview into the picture before the judge could rule. Later the Taubman-Irvine (Joan)-Ford-Bren-Petrie-Fisher-Allen group came in and the judge said: "This is just a court-monitored auction!"

In the spring of 1977, I was on the witness stand in Superior Court, Orange County in Santa Ana for three weeks, testifying as to value and the body of our work over seven years. The IRS, the attorney general, and Joan Irvine were on the other side. During those three weeks almost every query I could think of, and some I hadn't, were served up.

A couple of months later, Taubman overbid Mobil by ten cents a share or $800,000 in what became the last round, and, as a friend of mine says, "he stole the ranch!" for $336 million. Joan Irvine had a 10 percent interest in his consortium.

The Tishman Liquidation

While Irvine was moving to its 18-month flashpoint, we were employed as adviser and agent to liquidate Tishman Realty and Construction, a 50-year-old publicly traded real estate company with 17 major office building properties located in Los Angeles, San Francisco, Chicago, Cleveland, Rochester, and New York City. It also held development properties, raw land, a prominent construction and construction management organization, a leasing and management company, and a research organization. Common stock was $8 a share, and Bob Tishman felt the intrinsic value of the real estate was far greater.

An added problem was that losses on 1166 Avenue of the Americas, resulting from the almost complete demoralization of the New York City major corporate office rental market, had put Tishman into a corporate retained earnings deficit, which, under New York corporate law, prevented the corporation from paying common stock dividends. Since real estate cash flows could not be reported for corporate accounting reasons, the dividends had been the major support for the stock price. At that time, the only major real estate company to have gone private in an asset liquidation was Oliver Tyrone.

An added fillip was that a significant minority position in the common stock was held by Sy Scheuer, a prominent corporate asset liquidator.

Bob Tishman needed someone who could analyze, appraise, package, and sell the 17 urban office towers and the construction company, deal with the New York Stock Exchange and the Securities and Exchange Commission, aid in gaining shareholder approval for the sales, deal with the corporate raiders—especially during the liquidation—and deal with the financial press and the arbitrage community, which were just beginning to see real estate values in publicly traded real estate stock.

Tishman chose our firm. We studied each individual property including leases, expense escalations, stops, conformity to local fire codes, possible additional expenses to an institutional purchaser, and local market supply/demand factors. Projections of lease rollovers, re-rents, and increases in occupancy expense were prepared as well as offering procedures and confidentiality agreements. This was the first of the major institutional portfolio sales. A third of the property was located in Manhattan and it was during the most critical part of the marketing period that the New York *Daily News* ran the headline, "Ford Says New York Drop Dead!"

Looking back at what astute buys Olympia and York made for Uris and Equitable for Tishman, we tend to forget what courage it took at the time—two classic examples of "fishing in troubled waters." We sold John Tishman's construction business to Rockefeller Center Inc.; he has since repurchased it, but the Tishman shareholders got their money for it.

The shareholders ultimately received $27 a share, or a 340 percent premium in value compared to the stock price when we began. The confidentiality agreements worked, and the arbitrageurs were caught napping. The deal stayed ahead of the stock price all the way.

Marketing Monumental

The Meyerhoff family in Baltimore had developed a significant regional shopping mall and multifamily residential real estate portfolio as owner/developers in the 1960s. Like Sea Pines, Ernie Hahn, Cousins, and many others, the Meyerhoffs desired a stock market listing that gave added value over the intrinsic real estate asset values and also provided liquidity for family members. Accordingly, they purchased Monumental Life Insurance Company of Baltimore and merged their real estate into Monumental, keeping the public shareholder group. The Meyerhoff family, including their son-in-law Jack Pearlstone, controlled approximately one-third of Monumental Life.

In the 1970s, the stock market was in the doldrums and real estate suffered the greatest loss in value since the depression. Monumental sold for $18 a share and in the minds of its board of directors, the market accorded zero value to either the real estate assets or the life insurance assets. Utilizing local counsel, the directors evolved a plan of action. The assets of Monumental were divided into two classes. All the real estate was placed, tax-free, into a liquidating trust known as Monumental Properties Trust. The life insurance assets remained in Monumental Corporation. Each shareholder received a number of shares of Monumental Property Trust equal to their holdings in Monumental Corporation.

The Internal Revenue Service ruled that no corporate tax was payable and taxed each shareholder only at capital gains rates, a ruling that will not be given in the future. To meet the standards of the ruling, all the assets had to be sold within one year. The burden of proving to the IRS that this could not be done was on the trustees. If the deadline were not met, a double tax would be imposed.

The plan was approved by a shareholder vote, and Harvey M. "Bud" Meyerhoff, managing trustee of Monumental Properties Trust, went out looking for an adviser, talked to all the household names, and picked us.

Along with the competitors and the logical buyers, we believe that the way to sell income property is from projections and analysis of internal rates of return, even though this requires a heavy amount of front-end work. Bud Meyerhoff wanted to be in the market with all 75 income properties within 60 days. Insisting on 120 days of quiet, intensive analysis, I told him that more work in the beginning would save time in evaluation, commitment, and closing.

A team of 18 assembled to study and evaluate the 75 properties located in Boston, Buffalo, Baltimore, Atlanta, Miami, New Orleans, Houston, Dallas, and Oklahoma City. There were 18 major regional shopping malls, 17,000 apartment units in 41 separate projects, four office parks, four strip shopping centers, an urban parking garage, and raw land.

Each property had to be analyzed. Projections were prepared for 1,500 mall tenants, including buyouts, space cut-ups, overage rents, re-rents, common area maintenance charges, taxes, roof repairs, promotion budgets, and pads for added anchors. We also had the 17,000 apartments and the other properties to contend with, as well as the competition and conducting the area market studies.

After that came pricing, the packaging, and the sourcing. Questions included: What process will induce the best offer? Should it be sold as one package? Should we skim the cream? What is the largest dollar price that will still provide broad market access? How many prospective buyers can physically be processed, negotiated with, and closed with? How do we provide a "scarcity value" for the property? How do we persuade anyone to spend the $250,000 required to analyze all the properties properly, if they don't know they will be a buyer?

Efforts produced 2,000 written or telephone inquiries to which we responded, plus continual press inquiry and unrelenting inquiry from the arbitrageurs who followed the transaction closely. During Thanksgiving week my key stalwart fainted from exhaustion at Northlake Mall in Atlanta. Three people worked all day New Year's Day in Baltimore, and the Monumental people worked side by side with them.

By Monday after New Year's 1979, four months from kickoff, we were in the market. The 18 regional malls were offered in three packages at $120 million each over existing mortgages. The marketplace told us we were ingenious in creating indifference, or shall I say equality, among the three. The apartments were in seven packages; the miscellaneous properties were individually offered. A complete set of our full-disclosure, internal rate of return cash flow projections was about three feet high.

We were able to obtain commitments on the 75 properties in a ten-week effort. Substantially all the sales were closed within one year of our employment. Gross value exceeded $900 million. Shareholders whose combined shares sold for $18 received $70 for Monumental Property Trust and retained a share of Monumental Corporation, which sold in the $20s.

We are proud of the end result of closure on the terms of commitment. Throughout the closing process we stayed involved, and became experts at such matters as overage rent apportionment, tax apportionment, leaky roofs, number of stripes in the parking lots, and dike maintenance such as in New Orleans. It is interesting to note that one apartment complex nine miles from Three Mile Island was closed; and another one originally had been syndicated to a soon-to-be-assassinated Iranian.

The major properties—the 18 regional malls—generated six offers. The three highest were from domestic institutions; the three lowest, offshore institutions. Jack Pearlstone particularly had predicted these properties would end up in foreign ownership. I think the reason is the way we offered them: We played to the sophisticated buyer who could understand the projections, discounted cash flow, and internal rate of return. They also understand matters such as the logic of buying out the leases of underperforming tenants, cutting up space, and moving theaters to a freestanding location to increase mall space.

Analyzing Ernest Hahn

At the same time as the Monumental transaction, we were analyzing the real estate and various corporate alternatives for realizing the intrinsic asset value of the Ernest Hahn Company for its shareholders. Hahn owned 54 regional shopping centers of which 28 were operational and the balance were under construction or development. Although Hahn controlled 18 percent of the regional mall space in the state of California, it was also active in 14 other states from the Sunbelt to the East Coast. In addition, Hahn had a very active construction company, a development organization, a management and leasing business, and a strip center development subsidiary.

Our teams were in the field analyzing properties, the competition, and the market; projecting rents; and developing valuation techniques to analyze the risks inherent in projects under construction or development.

Taxes became a major constraint. The Monumental ruling was not available. Hahn Corporation was a "dealer" and Ernie was a greater-than-5 percent stockholder. The consequence was double tax at ordinary rates to Ernie as well as to the other large shareholders. The difference to Ernie alone between a single tax at capital gains rates and a double tax at ordinary rates was substantial.

The only logical way to escape the tax problem was to sell the common stock instead of the real estate assets. Yet this appeared to be an immediate impediment to sale. The stock was publicly traded at $18, far less than the asset values. A stock sale implied all or none. Wouldn't it be more logical to sell the operating centers to an institution and the construction and development centers to an entrepreneur? Only real estate people could recognize the future values, but real estate people don't buy common stock, especially with all those contingent liabilities. Furthermore, we knew that an opinion in writing in the proxy statement to each public shareholder stating the transaction was fair to him had to be provided. Could we do a tax deal for Ernest Hahn that would still provide fair value for the public shareholder?

Again, a three-foot pile of setups was prepared that included a separate package for each of the individual centers and our confidentiality agreements. For this one we also had a 20-minute, three-screen sound-and-light show with background music depicting 56 properties and including some shots of Ernie.

As background material to support a classic "bait and switch" marketing effort, we prepared a lengthy annotated balance sheet detailing each individual actual or contingent asset and liability of the Hahn Company and tying back into each individual property being offered. It was invaluable in converting prospective purchasers from the assets to the common stock without any meaningful erosion of value.

After lengthy negotiations with the outside directors and several thousand dollars of analysis, we hit the market in January 1980—just in time for the 20 percent prime rate, severe disintermediation in the life insurance industry, and the return of the Deutsche Bank and its friends to the bunkers.

Although we had a safety net to fall into, we gave Olympia & York six weeks to verify our data including the tax position. This resulted in an offer from Trizec to buy, at $55 a share, 300 percent of the stock price when we obtained the assignment and 200 times earnings per share.

The frenzy of Wall Street caught up with the transaction. Ahead of the deal most of the time, the arbitrageurs inhibited the marketing. Prospective buyers were justified in feeling the stock was overpriced. As insiders, we could not discuss this.

The closing process was a horror. Two of my best people were in California for three weeks, seven days a week, 14 hours a day. Nevertheless, Hahn closed on schedule like clockwork, and the shareholders were all paid by mid-December.

Achieving Successful Transactions

The counselor's role is to bring order and structure out of chaos and indecision, to bring patience and quiet understanding out of high emotion and confusion. How does one succeed at bringing about complex transactions on a major scale and in all types of market conditions, which may never have been accomplished before?

Hard Work. The president of Morgan Stanley has in his office a cushion upon which is stitched: "The harder I work, the luckier I get!"

Front-End Analysis. Provide enough analysis to make the investment decision as easy as possible for the most sophisticated investor.

Credibility. Back up and double check every number and every assumption in your presentation.

Competition. Every major investor will say: "Deal with me exclusively and I'll give you my best offer because I know I'll get the product." Not true. We all respond to competition.

Narrow Market. Limit the market enough to maintain scarcity value. Be confident in your judgment to know what is fair value without injuring the market with your offering.

Clear Offering Procedures. Lay out the offering procedures up-front and stick to them.

Know Your Customer. Limit your efforts to those with a proven record of closing similar deals on time. Check out new market entrants thoroughly, and do it yourself.

Disclosure. Be sure you have made full disclosure of every possible defect in the deal before commitment, so you don't lose credibility and waste months of effort by the deal unraveling during closing.

People. Have bright, highly-motivated, well-paid people work for you. Make them look good and share the credit. Allow them to make mistakes, to risk, and to grow. Remember, you can't look at 125 regional malls all by yourself.

Confidence. Avoid ego and hyperbole and exude quiet confidence, even when you are not certain how you're going to get the deal done. Most clients in major deals already have a lot on their minds.

Flexibility. Be flexible and listen. Don't tell the market where the market is. Learn something about the deal from every potential investor.

Decisiveness. Be decisive. Seek market opportunities and have confidence in your judgment when markets open up. Don't wait for another offer to confirm value.

Market Leadership. Be personally committed to the project in order to educate the market to do something perhaps risky and innovative. Make your market judgment a self-fulfilling prophecy.

Source: *Real Estate Issues*, spring/summer 1981.

2

Financing Real Estate in the 1980s

The real estate industry in the United States has been challenged in recent times by economic uncertainty. There are several possible future directions for the economy, ranging from continued inflation with ever higher interest rates, to deflation with recession, to disinflation with slow growth and relative stability. The current trend seems to be toward the latter, with perhaps a three-to-one probability that there will be slow growth and disinflation in the near term. This means that a real annual growth rate of around 3 to 5 percent might be realized as the U.S. economic recovery takes hold. The prime interest rate may drop to as low as 8 or 9 percent by the end of 1983.

A Tough Transition

While general economic conditions may be stabilizing, the real estate industry still has some major adjustments to accomplish. The transition from inflation to disinflation will be rough. Relative to financial assets, real estate has become overpriced, and the hyperinflation that has prevailed in the industry will have to be eliminated over time.

In the early 1970s, the real estate industry enjoyed a stable environment in which traditional capitalization rates were applied to fairly constant income flows. This was followed by a period in which there was serious overfinancing by commercial banks and REITs, and by 1975 the U.S. real estate financing industry closed down for a while.

In the late 1970s, after the industry worked off its earlier excesses, there were major opportunities in most urban markets, particularly in the office area. New building costs reflected the inflation that had begun in 1973. As buildings were constructed to meet pent-up demand, they provided a rental umbrella for owners of older property that enabled them to double or triple rents and still undercut rents in the new buildings. Since income flows were escalating rapidly, many investors and developers moved away from capitalization rates and went to the internal rate of return concept. Property was sold under the assumption that inflation would continue at 12 percent, with prices doubling every six or seven years. Now, as disinflation has begun, that rapidly escalating real estate market has been curtailed. Office rental markets will now be driven by space availability in relatively older structures with lower capital costs. As supply runs ahead of demand, the cost of new structures will no longer set market rates.

Real estate finance and investment will adjust to disinflation over the next year or two. The more fundamental issue is the effect of the diversification and competition now taking place within and among financial institutions as a consequence of deregulation and further integration of worldwide financial markets. Questions have been raised about who will be financing real estate in the years ahead. The game will change, but how much?

Individual Investors

In 1982, there was more real estate sold to individual investors through syndicators than ever before. The individual investor seems to be drawn into the real estate market every seven or eight years. In the early 1970s, individuals came into the market and purchased a large proportion of the REIT securities. They left the market as those securities depreciated in value. Now they are back again. It remains to be seen how important a role these investors are going to perform in a bull stock market. In a bear stock market, which prevailed for 12 years, the retail stockbroker had a hard time making a living, particularly when commission rate structures were lowered sharply, and brokers looked for products with high commissions to promote. Oil and gas and real estate are products that have high commissions.

Because of the high commissions and expenses involved, property sellers view dealing with individuals in real estate as a hindrance unless the individual is willing to pay a higher price than the institutions. Individuals are willing to tolerate these charges when they are convinced that real assets are better than financial assets. This is usually the case in an inflationary environment. At this time, bonds and stocks are performing better than real assets. In the mid-1980s, individuals are likely to forsake real estate in favor of equities and bonds.

A possible future trend is the "securitization" of real estate in which tax benefits as well as the more recent institutional concepts of debt-equity joint ventures or convertible debt instruments are offered to individuals through public offerings. It should be noted again, however, that the increased costs and fees of public distribution will result in individuals paying higher prices than institutions for property.

Banking Institutions

In this new era of competition among financial institutions, the thrift institutions must compete for savings on an equal footing with other financial institutions. They have to diversify away from their familiar role in housing finance. Those institutions that will survive, namely those that are entrepreneurial, are those that are taking advantage of their greatest asset—their retailing capability. The aggressive ones are trying to shift from the housing finance business in order to compete toe-to-toe with institutions like Sears and Citibank in offering financial service centers for individuals with checking, portfolio management, counseling, brokerage, insurance, automobile financing, and the like. The only way thrift institutions can continue to play their role as a prime source of capital for housing will be through the provision of new equity or tax incentives that can compete for savings.

Commercial banks will not play the major role in real estate finance in the 1980s. As was the case in the mid-1970s, commercial banks tend to be fully committed at the moment with a large proportion of open-ended construction loans to developers who were avoiding the institutional debt/equity structures. When such loans were made, both borrowers and lenders felt that rates would come down soon. With declining interest rates at present, commercial banks are seeing increased competition from insurance companies and pension funds, which are offering seven- to ten-year "bullet" loans. Commercial banks are likely to remain conservative investors in real estate through the mid-1980s, although selected individual banks will remain aggressive.

Pension Funds

Despite much of the talk of the last ten years, pension funds are also unlikely to become the major factor in real estate investment. Their investment departments are staffed by common stock and bond buyers, who are rewarded for their market timing and portfolio balance. This places a premium on liquidity and current return. Aggressive management of fixed-income investments has become very important. It is too much to expect these people to be equally expert in real estate investment; the fields are too different.

Real estate requires intimate knowledge of local markets. If one wishes to buy an auto stock, there are four or five to choose from. If one wants to buy an office building, there are at least 30 major markets. One would have to understand nearly 100 submarkets if he were to master the national office building market alone, and then there are also shopping centers, hotels, industrial property, and the like. The insurance industry has the capacity to monitor and know those markets. The pension funds, generally speaking, do not have such direct knowledge.

A major service has been provided in recent years by the pension fund intermediaries such as the life insurance companies with separate accounts and various closed-end or open-ended funds. Many of these funds now have several years of actual results over the business cycle, which should make it easier for the pension fund managers to choose among them.

If the Dow Jones average reaches 2000 in the 1980s, as some think it might, it will be far easier for the pension funds to go in their accustomed direction of concentrating on stocks and bonds. A pension fund manager in real estate at a time when financial assets are favored over real assets would be pursuing a view contrary to most managers.

Insurance Companies

Real estate, along with government bonds, has been the bedrock investment of life insurance companies for the past 180 years. These institutions invested in farm and home mortgages long before they invested in corporate bonds and far longer than they have invested in common stocks. Indeed, most of the largest insurance companies did not invest in common stocks until the early 1960s.

The largest portion of trained people in long-term real estate investment have been employed in the insurance industry. The presence of such expertise within the insurance industry is likely to lead to a continuing interest in real estate as an investment using either their own funds or intermediated funds from other sources. Insurance companies have been very active intermediaries for pension fund assets, and they have already begun to act as intermediaries for international investment in U.S. real estate.

The insurance industry has suffered as a result of high interest rates and inflation. Policyholders cancelled, cashed-in, or borrowed on their policies. With disinflation and slow growth, however, the traditional insurance products are likely to come back, albeit in a different or modified form. The insurance companies will be creating future liabilities for which they will have the opportunity to match assets, and there is no reason why real estate will not continue to be part of the asset base. If the life insurance product of the future has more of an equity component and is of a shorter term, those characteristics will be matched up in how the companies will invest and participate in real estate development.

Foreign Investors

Foreign investors will increasingly find U.S. real estate an appropriate vehicle for investment, though the total investment in the aggregate is unlikely to approach even that of U.S.-based pension funds. Whether or not there is a stable economy for the rest of the decade, more and more overseas investors view the United States as the broadest, deepest, and safest capital market in the world in which to invest. For some, investment in U.S. real estate is an opportunity not to be missed.

Japan provides a good example. There are only six or seven life insurance companies in Japan, and the largest has close to half the market. Much like the Canadian banking industry, the Japanese insurance industry is very concentrated. These Japanese insurance companies are real estate investors. Real estate investment may account for 10 percent of their assets, but their major domestic market for investment is Tokyo, with the next largest market being Osaka. They have been encouraged to diversify their investments outside Japan.

Large pools of foreign capital tend to be invested the same way the U.S. insurance companies have invested over the long term. Initially, they invest in their local economy. Then, as they outgrow that economy, they begin conservative investments elsewhere. In the last ten years this has been true in the Middle East as well as in Japan. Foreign institutions buy U.S. government bonds first, then cautiously begin to buy high-grade corporate credits. Gradually they work their way up the risk spectrum to single A–rated corporate debt instruments and begin to work into common stock investment. Real estate is most often at the end of the cycle. It is relatively easy to understand what U.S. government paper is worth or what an AAA corporate bond is worth. Real estate is much more specialized.

The recent Canadian experience reflects the highly localized character of U.S. real estate markets. Fueled by a concentrated national banking system and feeling that opportunity for major investment was constrained within Canada, investors from that country aggressively entered U.S. markets in order to maintain the growth rates they had sustained over the previous ten years. Canadian investors began to fill a vacuum created by U.S. investors after 1973–1974. They jumped in quickly without always having intimate knowledge of the local markets. Given the decline in interest rates, it remains to be seen whether they are now going to be able to work their way out in each case. Some of them appear to be overextended in terms of what they paid for property as against what they are going to be able to obtain in rents in a down market. Some of the land holdings probably will not be developed for several years. Canadians will continue to be a factor in our markets in the 1980s, but not to the extent of recent years.

Advising foreign investors requires particular knowledge of taxes, foreign exchange, required government approvals, and the like. Each international market is unique, with its own investment parameters, varying from conservative long-term investors to highly entrepreneurial investors seeking a quick return.

Localized Markets and the Entrepreneurial Developer

As the Canadians and many institutional investors have learned, it is very difficult to institutionalize the real estate process in the United States. In a country with the scale and diversity of the United States, the strong local developer who is attuned to growth and expansion possibilities in the market and who has a thorough understanding of the development process, the zoning process, the value of property, and the inherent growth dynamics of the local market—and who is not counting on corporate move-ins from outside—is invaluable. It also helps to have a couple of certain tenants with which to start off each project. An outside developer cannot just buy blocks of land assuming that the local market will automatically respond. Some of the demand has to come with the project itself.

In addition, every real estate deal needs a catalyst—someone who can get a half dozen to 50 people committed to a project. This is why, in the future financing of real estate, the joint venture approach will remain important. The local entrepreneur's creativity and risk taking will continue to be needed, but it will have to be teamed up with the capital that large institutions can provide. Investors want to be equity partners, but they cannot invest without the entrepreneurial developer.

Developers of the 1980s and 1990s?

Where are we going to find the entrepreneurial developers of the 1980s and 1990s to replace the sole proprietor entrepreneurs of the 1950s, 1960s, and 1970s? Will it be possible to provide the same kinds of rewards to the developers of the next two decades as were provided over the past three? In retrospect, real estate was one of the best businesses to be in during the post–World War II decades. It was supported by the demand left over from the depression and World War II, compounded by the postwar baby boom. The tax incentives and lending practices that evolved enabled developers who were successful to become extremely wealthy. The odds are that this same combination of incentives, as well as opportunities, will be more limited in the future.

What kind of people are going to be motivated to take all the risks that are necessary in development—risks that are far greater today? It can take six or seven years to build a regional shopping center. The time value of money is far greater than the old 3.5 to 4 percent interest. The risks are greater and the rewards are less.

Space users are more sophisticated today in realizing the value of their land positions and occupancy leases. The typical build-to-suit corporate headquarters building where the developer ends up with a major equity position and the corporate occupant is content with a conventional lease is changing.

Still, even after measuring the risks and rewards, and in comparison with other opportunities, real estate provides abundant opportunities for careful, risk-managed entrepreneurs. The entrepreneurial developer will need more capital behind him to get started. That seems to be the way the industry is now going, with the debt-equity joint venture financing that has evolved in recent years. Such arrangements are here to stay. This is so, in part, because it is the only way to capitalize a new generation of developers as they start out.

Renewed Opportunities

While we are in for a rough transition in the near term, there are still opportunities, especially in residential. Any time there is a supply/demand imbalance of the kind we face in single and multifamily housing, there is opportunity. If the purchasing power and financing are available, as a bonus of disinflation, the demand for housing should persist well into the 1990s.

Older properties are going to be valuable over the next few years. At a time of oversupply in office space, the older buildings will put pressure on the rental rates that can be charged for new space in a down market. Entrepreneurs are going to take advantage of the lower costs in certain cities as the boom in some of the other markets creates a competitive cost disadvantage.

The opportunities will be there, but they cannot be defined in the abstract. The developer has to be out there seeing the market, dealing in particular property. Real estate development has never been, and is unlikely to be, a business that can be run by remote control. That is why we will continue to see many of the same kinds of players in the business in the later 1980s and 1990s as we know today.

Source: *Urban Land*, January 1983.

3

Japanese
Investment
in U.S. Real Estate

Barring a major disruption in oil prices or world trade, the Japanese will be investing in U.S. real estate for some time to come.

The history of dealing with Japanese investment in U.S. real estate can be characterized by two axioms: 1) one only learns how to deal with another when things go wrong; and 2) renegotiating a transaction and restructuring a financing are the real tests of a long-term relationship.

One project that had to be renegotiated with the Japanese involved the Westin Bonaventure Hotel in downtown Los Angeles. The project was financed with equity from Mitsubishi International Corporation and a long-term fixed-rate mortgage from Equitable Life Assurance. Although the hotel was completed on time and at projected cost, room rates and occupancy levels did not meet pro forma projections; the hotel consequently had operating deficits equal to about 20 percent of initial project cost.

To protect its initial investment and prevent others from reaping the benefits of stabilized returns, the Japanese equity investor had to be convinced to provide additional funds to cover the hotel's operating deficits. At the same time, the advisory firm arranged a refinancing program that diluted the developer partner, brought in a tax-shelter equity investment group, extended loans from banks, and established a first-mortgage accrual program.

Almost ten years later, a project involving the Pac West office building had to be renegotiated. The building was completed on time and within budget, but the leasing period became extended, and a leasing deficit of 20 percent of the project's cost had to be funded. The renegotiations with Mitsubishi Estate Corporation and Meiji Mutual Life Insurance Company took 15 months to accomplish and required four trips to Tokyo to obtain the additional funds and to reallocate partnership losses.

Perception versus Reality

There are a number of misconceptions commonly associated with Japanese investment in U.S. property.

Overpayment. In almost all cases when Japanese institutions paid the highest price for a property in this country, a prospective U.S. purchaser was right behind. Recently, evidence indicates that the initial return requirement for Japanese purchases is increasing.

Huge Investment Totals. Japanese investment, while large in recent years, accounts for only 8 percent of the total foreign investment in U.S. property.

Limited Investment Preference. Japanese investment never has been limited to existing high-rise urban office buildings. Beginning in the early 1970s, Japanese capital has been invested in residential land deals, development, hotels, office buildings, and shopping centers and industrial property.

Low-Cost Tokyo Takeout. Interest rates in Japan have been significantly lower than they have been in the United States. For a time, Japanese banks were willing to lend on the unrealized appreciation on property owned in Japan. Such loans obviously entailed exchange risk if they were utilized to purchase U.S. property. More recently, this type of speculative lending has been discouraged. Although U.S. affiliates of Japanese banks have lent dollars to Japanese borrowers, they have done so only at prevailing U.S. interest rates.

Why Do They Do It?

Institutional equity investment by the Japanese in U.S. property totaled $5 billion during 1984–1986, with $3.3 billion in 1986. Investment increased to $7 billion in 1987, and an increase to $10 billion is predicted for 1988, prompted by several factors.

Lower Returns on Real Estate in Japan. Returns on real estate in Japan typically are 1 percent to 2 percent, making the 7 percent to 8 percent return on U.S. real estate appear uncommonly attractive.

High Land Cost in Japan. Land cost for an urban office tower is about 20 percent of the total project cost in the United States but 90 percent of the project cost in Japan. Land may cost as much as $3,000 or even $5,000 per square foot in

Tokyo. At a floor/area ratio of 10:1, the land cost per rentable foot is $300 or higher, requiring a rent of as much as $45 per foot annually to achieve a true equity return by U.S. standards. This makes almost any office building purchase in the United States appear attractive at $300 per foot, including the fee interest.

Yen/Dollar Exchange Rates. During the period when returns on U.S. real estate were falling, the Japanese still made more than acceptable returns on U.S. investments because of favorable exchange rates.

Liquidity of U.S. Real Estate. An active trading market in U.S. real estate among principals as well as an active market in real estate mediated by brokers provide Japanese investors with a perceived way out of U.S. investments, which has not existed within their own marketplace.

Cheap Financing. Japanese real estate has appreciated significantly in recent years, and a large portion of the unrealized gain is being utilized as collateral to support borrowings from the Japanese banking system to acquire U.S. property. The Japanese banking system has been highly liquid and is aggressively establishing a position in the U.S. real estate market.

Tax Incentives. U.S. depreciation schedules, tax rates, provisions for interest deductibility, etc., are much more liberal than Japanese tax breaks on real estate.

Where Do They Go from Here?

A close look at the Japanese and the U.S. economies provides the basis for predicting future investment in U.S. real estate by the Japanese. Strong appreciation since 1985 pushed the yen to historic heights. Despite some retreat (10 percent) from the highs against the dollar this year, the yen remains one of the strongest currencies in the world. Thus, the yen will remain an attractive currency with which to purchase U.S. assets. Yen appreciation has, however, reduced Japan's export volume and encouraged imports. The drop in export volume is beginning to have a positive impact on the U.S. trade deficit; the deficit is narrowing faster in the physical volume of goods than in dollars because of the yen's appreciation.

The Japanese domestic economy has experienced a dramatic shift from export-driven growth to internal, consumer-driven growth. Domestic consumption has grown so extensively, it has made up for the drop in exports. The Japanese economy also has experienced growth in housing and in major construction. Behind the strength in domestic demand are strong gains in real disposable income. Inflation is less than 1 percent per annum and is driven down by cheap imports. A high personal savings rate of over 15 percent (compared to a U.S. savings rate of less than 4 percent) suggests that domestic consumer spending will continue to expand.

Japanese exports to the United States are continuing at high levels, even though the Japanese are absorbing large foreign exchange losses because they are being paid in weak dollars. Japanese export profits have been cut severely as they have held onto market share. Meanwhile, at current exchange rates, Japanese labor costs have risen over the past four years from 50 percent of U.S. labor costs to close to parity. Because of foreign exchange losses and rising labor costs, it has been estimated that, before long, the Japanese will produce more than 1.5 million automobiles a year in the United States.

Large U.S. trade deficits will continue for several years and require capital inflows. In recent years, the foreign private sector has not been willing to make the required investment, and foreign central banks have had to take up the slack. When the dollar was weakening, foreign investors were discouraged from buying U.S. financial assets (U.S. Treasury securities, corporate bonds, and corporate equities), because of repeated currency losses. But now that the dollar is close to its low ebb, long-term direct foreign investment in manufacturing and real estate assets is extremely attractive. Multinational corporations worldwide have 15 percent of their plant and equipment located offshore; the Japanese have only 3 percent of their manufacturing capacity offshore.

U.S. economists say the dollar will fall another 10 percent to 15 percent against the yen at a current exchange rate of 135:1 before trade patterns reverse and reflect the changes in consumer spending patterns that have occurred in the United States. Such a decline in the dollar carries with it higher interest rates and a heightened risk of recession. Even if the dollar falls, however, it will take at least four years to nullify the trade deficit. Thus, for the next three to five years we may expect to see continuing reinvestment of excess liquidity by the Japanese in the U.S. marketplace. The Japanese will shift their portfolios among the debt markets, the stock market, direct manufacturing investments, and real estate as their perception of markets changes.

Conclusion

The Japanese have established a highly visible position in U.S. real estate, and they no doubt will add to this position. In certain markets, such as downtown Los Angeles, they actually may be able to exercise a degree of market control within the next few years.

However, the Japanese come from a landlord's marketplace in which annual rents can equal $120 per square foot and landlords require a three-year rental deposit up-front. It is difficult to shift mentally from such a landlord's market to a tenant market. The Japanese, therefore, must become educated to provide tenant service, and they must develop first-rate property management and leasing capabilities.

Source: *Real Estate Issues,* fall/winter 1988.

4

The New Financial Markets and Securitized Commercial Real Estate Financing

Real estate securitization relates real estate more closely to money and capital markets.

Real estate securitization relates real estate finance closer to the money and capital markets. This has become increasingly more intense since the mid-1970s as linkages among all types of financial and nonfinancial assets have been established.

The concept of securitization of assets has been around for a long time. Back in 1962, when J.I. Case Company went bankrupt, money was raised to pay off the company's senior creditors by setting up a sales finance captive subsidiary and securitizing Case's accounts receivable. In the course of the exercise, many of the same functions were conducted then that are performed today on the assets underlying a collateralized mortgage obligation (CMO). We utilized statistical analysis of the average remaining life, the default patterns, the delinquent payment frequency, and the average transaction size for each receivable.

In the mid- to late-1960s, bauxite and iron ore facilities in Australia were financed by pledging 25-year commercial contracts, primarily with Japanese companies, in support of private placements and public offerings of debt in both the domestic U.S. and the eurodollar markets. Additional security was provided through a first-mortgage lien on the facilities.

In the early 1970s four Orbach's retail stores were financed. The stores were owned privately by a Dutch family that wished to avail itself of cheap financing by guarantying payment of principal and interest, but the family did not wish to give up its privacy. Accordingly, enough net worth was shown to a commercial bank to obtain the bank's own guaranty in support of the financing. This was a form of securitized finance.

Real estate investment trusts of the 1970s were a means of introducing real estate assets into the securities markets, just as CMOs and master limited partnerships are today.

The following discussion focuses on the characteristics of the new financial markets that have led to the recent growth of securitized real estate finance.

Characteristics of the New Financial Markets

Linkages

In recent years, increasing linkages have been observed among all financial markets and financial and nonfinancial assets. In the mid-1970s as interest rates climbed and corporations such as Penn Central and Chrysler faced financing problems, a number of corporations had difficulty raising capital, including regional banks and public utilities. At the same time, the mortgage departments of several insurance companies were having difficulty finding good-quality real estate in which to invest their allocated funds.

A series of sale-leaseback transactions of lower-grade credits were executed on corporate headquarter facilities at interest rates as much as 250 to 300 basis points lower than the issuer's corporate cost of borrowing. This was accomplished because the mortgage side of the insurance companies had more available funds than good investments, and the securities side was less liquid.

When one major life insurance company wished to avoid this anomaly, its chief economist sent a memo to all the field officers saying: "Do not make a mortgage loan on any corporate real estate at a rate less than the Aa utility rate posted in your daily newspaper." The memo described a very crude but effective method of creating a proxy rate for real estate. Thus, in this and many other instances, capital market linkages to real estate were born. Most recently, these linkages have been seen in Standard & Poor's rating of office buildings and Moody's rating of particular cities from a real estate point of view.

Volatility

The stock market can move 30 to 50 points in a day or, at the extreme, as many as 300 to 500 points. The prime rate itself moved from 12 percent to 20 percent during the period of 1979–1980.

Even as interest rates have come down, the real rate of interest has stayed higher than is customary. How does one develop a project with three-, five-, or seven-year development cycles in the face of such interest rate volatility? A variety of interest rate risk management techniques have evolved—options, swaps, caps, futures, options on futures—but the techniques themselves have, at times, increased volatility and thus the underlying risk in the market.

Institutionalization

Investment decision making has become more and more institutionally controlled. Single-point decisions have supplanted the plurality of decisions made by thousands of individual investors as they have become increasingly insulated by independent retirement accounts, pension funds, money market funds, and mutual funds.

On the New York Stock Exchange, trades of 1,000 shares or more increased from 70 percent of total volume to 90 percent of total volume in just eight years (1978–1986). This is a sea change in stock ownership, with individual ownership reduced from 30 percent to 10 percent of total volume. During the same period, large trades of 10,000 shares or more increased from 23 percent to 52 percent of total volume as institutions dominated the market.

During the period 1979–1987, institutional holders of corporate debt increased from 76 percent to 93 percent. The departure of the thousands of individual trades, which used to dampen volatility, has added further to the swings in the markets.

Internationalization

Global markets have arrived, along with 24-hour trading. Consequently, all assets are linked through currency swaps, and fixed- and floating-rate obligations are made fungible by interest rate swaps. Pockets of opportunity arise as various currencies or maturities fall out of line or investor preferences change. A real estate transaction may be financed on a floating-rate basis with the rate reset every 30 days and then swapped into a 12-year fixed-rate obligation. A U.S. dollar real estate transaction may be financed in New Zealand dollars or Japanese yen or German deutschemarks and swapped back into U.S. dollars for funding. Each maturity for a securitized real estate financing trades at a negotiated spread over the comparable maturity U.S. government obligation, thus linking all market rates together.

Securitization

Securitization simply takes an asset or an obligation to pay (a commercial contract or a lease) and converts it into a financial obligation that has readily identified characteristics and can be accordingly rated to risk in the international capital markets. Securitization can be accomplished by having a project rated in one of the major investment-grade categories by a respected rating service such as Moody's or Standard & Poor's. It also may be accomplished by having a high-credit party add its credit (credit enhancement) to the transaction through a guaranty, letter of credit, or similar arrangement. Japanese banks have been particularly active in this area because they retain high credit ratings as a class, have lower funding costs than U.S. banks, and are more competitive on fees as they build their global business.

Deregulation

Now a worldwide phenomenon, deregulation commenced in the United States during the mid-1970s with the removal of regulations covering funding costs for financial institutions. This initial step led to spread banking, which allowed financial institutions to focus closer on funding sources and costs and to seek out assets and transactions that provided a spread not only over the average cost of funds but also over their marginal costs. Spread banking created a closer link between the asset and liability side of balance sheets and caused pricing and thus money markets to become more volatile.

Deregulation of financial institutions and spread banking placed a premium on higher-yielding assets (foreign loans, real estate, junk bonds, etc.) and increased the risk profile of many financial institutions. It also placed great pressure on operating costs, created a desire for fee income (which does not require funding), increased the need for permanent capital (to increase credit quality and access to cheaper funding), spurred new product innovation, and caused a shift to other businesses away from service businesses.

Certain thrifts moved into brokered loan funding and junk bond investments. Certain commercial banks changed into fee-driven investment banking transactions. Investment banks took over a large chunk of traditional commercial bank funding of corporate America through commercial paper, floating-rate notes, and market auction preferred stock and moved into principal and merchant banking activities.

To be successful in this environment, financial institutions needed to have a full array of products, global reach, a large capital base, a willingness and talent for managing risk, an ability to seek out market anomalies, and the discipline to avoid and cut back commodity or low-margin businesses.

Sophistication

In 25 years, the computer changed financial institutions from slow-paced Dickensian establishments, where MBAs looked up stock prices in yellowing *Wall Street Journals*, to highly sophisticated, electronically driven enterprises engaging in futures, options, program trading, and multicurrency transactions. Many bankers have computer screens on their desks that can be programmed to retrieve and display whatever worldwide data may be relevant to their own transactions.

With computers, portfolio managers and investors think and act more like traders. Dealers amass an array of software resources and capital to stay ahead of investors. A new product idea, innovation, or knowledge of a mismatch somewhere in the money or capital markets has a half-life measured in nanoseconds as worldwide computer and communications networks buzz 24 hours a day.

Restructuring

The competitive pressure to achieve return on capital and reduce operating expenses has focused attention on underperforming assets and lines of business. Business units that may be redundant or irrelevant to one enterprise may become much more productive as a part of another enterprise. The constant review of business units and capital allocations has created even greater motivation for managers to aggressively run their businesses.

The Mechanics of Securitization

To understand securitization, three discrete aspects of a transaction are highlighted: 1) credit support, 2) funding, and 3) interest rate risk management techniques.

Arranging Credit Support

This phase of the securitization process begins with traditional real estate financing and involves identifying and negotiating with an institution that is prepared to accept credit risk for a particular project. Considerations include location, construction, completion, rent roll, and sponsorship. Such discussions may be held with conventional sources (U.S. banks, insurance companies, pension funds) or with unconventional sources (a new entity established to provide financial guaranties, rating agencies, foreign banks, Japanese trading companies or other foreign industrial corporations with excess tax credits). At the conclusion of this phase, funding may be obtained directly or it may be supported by a bond type rating, a letter of credit, or a guaranty of some nature.

Identifying the Funding Source/Structuring the Financing

This phase involves the cheapest source of financing that will accept the credit support—locating wherever in the world it exists, in whatever currency, and at whatever maturity. The least expensive source of financing may be commercial paper, fixed- or floating-rate eurodollar notes, a floating-rate private placement in yen, a domestic public offering, or a foreign currency.

The funding is chosen from a hodgepodge of floating and fixed, dollar and non-dollar alternatives. Lowest financing cost is optimized and the result usually is short-term, floating-rate nondollars—completely unsatisfactory to fund a long-term U.S. dollar asset. Hence, phase three.

Interest Rate Risk Management Techniques

An array of techniques has evolved (and is evolving) to convert wholesale funds into retail funds, to match the funding source to the project's needs, to meet construction draw schedules, to create a simple medium-term fixed-rate loan, and to hedge against possible future interest rate movements. It is beyond the scope of this article to detail these techniques; but usually they involve the intermediation of risk preferences of financial institutions and capital users throughout the world. Floating-rate obligations are swapped for fixed-rated obligations, various maturities on the yield curve are traded, and currencies are swapped. Each party to the transaction has a preference or opinion of the trend in interest rates, the slope of the yield curve, or the relative strength of certain currencies. Swaps may be entered into merely to cover a previously exposed position. They may be arranged by a financial intermediary on an agency basis (where both counterparties are located) or on a principal basis (where the position is taken uncovered by the intermediary itself).

As the market has broadened, several hedging techniques have developed, including forward swaps, accreting swaps, caps, and accreting caps, that fundamentally add an option to a swap transaction in order to accomplish certain timing/hedging objectives.

All these techniques carry fees, and the fees widen and narrow as investor preferences change and as outlooks for the future direction of interest rates and currency fluctuate. Basically, the more the perceived risk at any time, the higher the fees. In each case, the cost of the hedged transaction must be compared to the current borrowing rate and the premium paid must be compared to the unhedged interest rate risk.

Case Study: Trammell Crow International Partners

New ground was broken in 1986, when $180 million was raised for Trammell Crow International Partners (TCIP). A diversified fund of 16 industrial, retail, and office properties owned by this company was placed in a limited partnership structure, against which $90 million of equity was raised from a syndicate of Japanese institutional investors and $90 million of securitized debt was obtained.

The perceived finite capacity for equity in Japan led to a capital structure that included debt. Credit enhancement was required to obtain a broad market for the debt. The cash flows from the portfolio were finite; returns had to be provided to the equity; therefore, the cost of debt became critical. The strategy was to obtain credit support for the debt, sell the debt only after equity placement was reasonably assured, and get the best price for the debt.

Credit support was arranged by purchasing a guarantee from Financial Security Assurance (FSA), which was founded in the fall of 1985 as the first monoline insurance company to provide financial guaranties for corporate debt issues. FSA was rated AAA by Standard & Poor's. FSA had $205 million in equity capital and had been involved in $2 billion of transactions at the time of the negotiations.

FSA became actively involved in the structuring of the debt instrument as guarantor, and it performed extensive real estate due diligence on the properties. After negotiations among the Trammell Crow organization, FSA, and ourselves, the portfolio consisted of 16 projects in six diversified markets. FSA obtained a cross-collateralized first-lien position on the properties. The appraised value of the portfolio, as submitted by Joseph J. Blake & Associates, exceeded the purchase price for the portfolio. The initial-year loan to value on the debt was 52 percent, and the cash flow coverage of debt service was approximately 1.9 times.

With a guaranty from FSA, a AAA-rating debt was secured. The debt was funded on a ten-year bullet loan basis in the international capital markets. In order to mitigate principal repayment risk, a defeasance reserve was established to commit the partnership to reserve funds to repay principal 18 months prior to maturity and to defease the entire amount within six months of maturity.

Additional support was negotiated by FSA. The appraised value of partnership assets must be at least 125 percent of the partnership's secured debt; semiannual net operating income (before debt service) of the partnership must be at least 125 percent of debt service; and other tests must be met before additional indebtedness may be incurred.

By the time the partnership equity was committed, interest rates had become quite volatile. During the period of June through August 1986, the ten-year U.S. Treasury bonds ranged in yield from 6.93 percent to 8.01 percent. Spreads off Treasury bonds widened as yields decreased, and swap spreads also widened. Japanese institutions, the initial target for the debt, were not prepared to pay for the funding structure that was being offered. The lack of liquidity inherent in a real estate asset–based transaction further narrowed the investor market.

By mid-August, the international capital markets had been canvassed but investors could not be found who were willing to focus purely on the credit enhancement and not the underlying real estate.

In order to facilitate the transaction and close on the equity, Morgan Stanley, in late August, purchased all the debt as principal, locking in a rate to TCIP that was priced from an interest rate that was within two basis points of the lowest ten-year U.S. Treasury yield in over eight years.

This example illustrates the complexity of securitized real estate debt and the need for financial intermediaries to assume risk and act with a principal-oriented mentality to make markets perform.

Interest rate risk management techniques were less important here because the issue was denominated by U.S. dollars and was set at a fixed rate with a relatively low interest rate level.

Case Study: Parklabrea Finance Corporation

Parklabrea, one of the largest residential real estate complexes in the United States, is located in the mid-Wilshire Boulevard district in Los Angeles. On October 31, 1986, May Department Stores sold a portion of the Parklabrea complex (approximately 2,800 of the total 4,000 apartment units) to a subsidiary of Forest City Enterprises. May retained the remainder of the complex in a joint venture agreement with Forest City. As part of the consideration for the sale, May received from Forest City a $165 million promissory note and first-trust deed for a term of 12 years.

May had several objectives in this transaction: liquefy the $165 million note by either selling or financing against it at a low cost of borrowing; obtain financing to match the 12-year maturity on the underlying note; remove the asset from its balance sheet and minimize any continuing contingent liability; and book the gain on the 1986 sale of the real estate to take advantage of the lower capital gains rate. This meant May also was aiming for a year-end closing on the liquification of the note.

Most of the conventional real estate lenders showed little interest in the transaction due to its 12-year maturity, large size, and age and because it was a residential property. Also, conventional lenders were wary of asbestos, methane gas, and earthquake risk associated with the project.

The structure finally chosen took into account the current market conditions and realized all May's objectives. To achieve the objective of removing the asset from its books, May sold the $165 million promissory note to a newly created third-party subsidiary, Parklabrea Finance Corporation, which issued the bonds.

The issue totaled $165 million and the bonds had 12-year maturity (five years noncall). By keeping the 12-year term, the issue was so specialized it would appeal only to particular segments of investor demand, namely portfolio investors who were looking for long-term investments. The eurodollar floating-rate market was chosen because this market offered the lowest cost of borrowing.

One of the most important aspects of this transaction was its multiple levels of guaranties. The first and most important was a full guaranty of the issue's principal and interest once again by FSA. The second level was provided by May (rated AA3/AA-)

through a partial guaranty of the principal and a shortfall guaranty of the interest payments. The final layer of security was the property itself.

Why were so many layers of guaranties needed? The aim in paying FSA a fee for its guaranty was to make a complicated real estate deal simple and marketable to investors who were not sophisticated in real estate analysis. Consistent with its no-loss underwriting policy, FSA, in turn, required May to provide the partial guaranties in addition to the first mortgage on the property.

The Parklabrea bond issue was launched on Monday, December 1, and it was priced at the London Interbank Offered Rate (LIBOR) plus 25 basis points. Once the floating-rate funding was completed, an interest rate swap had to be executed with a 12-year term to satisfy May's objectives. A 12-year term is too long to optimize the market, and so once again, to effect the transaction, Morgan Stanley took the swap as principal and provided a 12-year, fixed-rate funding to May at a cost, including all fees, of 9.35 percent.

Conclusion

Securitized real estate finance attempts to make real estate fungible so it may be traded like a bond. But is real estate fungible? Can an array of financial techniques make a real asset a financial asset? Perhaps so in good times. What happens in bad times?

Sam Zell addressed this issue in his article "Modern Sardine Management" in *Real Estate Issues* (v. 2, no. 1, 1986): "The current attempt to develop securitized commercial real estate only extends the separation of the investor from the risk he is taking. Securitization converts mortgages into a commodity that blurs the risk to the investors."

Putting it another way: Does marketability guarantee liquidity? Probably not, at least not throughout the full market cycle. Just as in the days when erstwhile merchant bankers were swapping beads around the campfire: Caveat emptor!

Source: *Real Estate Issues*, spring/summer 1988.

PART 3

Real Estate Capital Markets in the 1990s

Evolving Valuation Methods and Pricing Issues

Globalization

CONTINUED

Note to readers: In part 1 of this book, the author summarizes the key issues and points covered in the individual articles, and offers additional commentary to provide context and a longer-term perspective. Commentaries on articles 5 to 19 may be found on pages 11 to 21.

5 Capitalization Rate in a Dynamic Environment

In the dynamic world within which we live, the capitalization rate is no longer a valid real estate calculation by itself, and it does not add much to investment analysis even when used in conjunction with other techniques.

This paper was given at the 15th Pan Pacific Congress of Real Estate Appraisers, Valuers and Counselors, Seoul, Korea, September 1990.

The thesis of this paper is that, in the case of property sales, the capitalization rate is the notational result of an often prolonged and arduous negotiating process, a calculation that is derived after the fact. The capitalization rate in and of itself is meaningless unless it is placed in context. What cash flows are being capitalized? Are buyer and seller utilizing similar assumptions? With what rates of return is the capitalization rate being compared? What can the buyer do with the property?

As will be shown, deficiencies with the capitalization rate become pronounced in the dynamic economic environment in which we currently live and the environment we are likely to experience in the future.

The volatility of the property sale market makes it more difficult for the real estate practitioner to rely on the capitalization rate as a basis for valuation of a property for other purposes. The practitioner must know a great deal more than is generally known about the transaction to utilize the derived capitalization rate for any other purpose. For example, how useful is it to know that the Stanford Court Hotel in San Francisco or the Bel Air Hotel in Los Angeles traded on a 1 percent nominal capitalization rate?

This paper will review the dynamic economic environment in which we live, discuss the difficulty of determining which cash flows to capitalize, describe alternative valuation techniques and modern portfolio theory and the buildup of a componentized rate of return, and review the reasons why aberrations occur in the capitalization rate.

The Dynamic Economic Environment

The capitalization rate was an extremely useful tool when the world was stable. We enjoyed a low interest rate and a low inflation rate environment for 20 years following World War II. During that time, there was little capital market volatility as we know it today. A rental stream and an expense stream could be capitalized for 10, 20, or even 30 years without burdening the calculation with too many assumptions. We now live in an age of volatility, with a greatly enhanced computational capability, which makes the simplistic techniques of the past less relevant. Let us examine some of the factors that have led to this new age.

Globalization. We talk today of globalized capital markets, but globalization is a highly imprecise term meaning entirely different things to different practitioners. At a minimum, this concept encompasses such factors as 24-hour trading in money and capital markets and assets that are linked through currency and interest rate swaps. A real estate transaction may be financed on a 30-day revolving floating-rate basis, which is later swapped for a financing on a medium-term fixed-rate basis in a different currency.

A variety of new global financing techniques has evolved, including options, swaps, caps, futures, or options on futures. These new techniques have enhanced the ability of real estate investors to access capital market activity, but they have also increased the volatility of the marketplace. Now, a real estate developer in Omaha must be concerned about efforts of the Bundesbank or the Japanese Ministry of Finance to control their country's domestic monetary base. In fact, as capital market linkages progress, it will become more and more difficult for any central bank to establish unilateral domestic monetary policy.

With all these capital market linkages, what real rate of return should the practitioner be attempting to protect? How does one build up a capitalization rate for a long-term project that will protect against swings among a half-dozen major economies that are out of synchroneity?

Securitization. The securitization of real estate assets has come about as large capital market players, initially U.S. insurance companies and pension funds, sought to develop the means of integrating traditional real estate investment analysis into modern portfolio theory to make overall portfolio asset allocation decisions. This integration of real estate into modern portfolio theory means that real estate can no longer be considered a "special" asset with characteristics that justify its insulation from worldwide economic events.

Institutionalization. The thousands of individual trades that served the purpose of dampening volatility in the past have been converted through the institutionalization of savings by pension funds, insurance companies, money market funds, mutual funds, and the like into single-point decisions made by powerful forces. This concentration of decision making has made capital markets much more volatile and risky and has increased the real rate of return required for long-term investments.

Deregulation. Deregulation of financial institutions, begun in the United States, has spread to other major capital markets. In the years ahead, there will be increasing pressure for deregulation, especially in Japan. The removal of regulations covering funding costs for financial institutions led to the bidding up of the cost of funds, which in turn led to the booking of more risky assets. As a result, the risk profile of many financial institutions has increased considerably, and the overall credit quality of these institutions has decreased. In certain capital market segments, such as U.S. thrift institutions and commercial banks, this has led to a sharp curtailment of the amount of capital available to real estate.

Sophistication. Only 25 years ago, calculations were made laboriously on electromagnetic calculators, and the results were noted on yellow accountancy workpapers. But now, with the proliferation of personal computers and computer networks, a sole real estate practitioner has unparalleled computational ability. This greatly enhanced capability allows the practitioner to manipulate data at will, building in different inflation assumptions for each variable for each year, if desired. Because such capacity is available, use of a single capitalization factor for a project makes a practitioner appear to be lazy as well as unsophisticated.

Hand in hand with computational ability goes database information retrieval. Not many years ago, the real estate practitioner's database was a stack of yellowing *Wall Street Journal*s. Within a few years, we will all be linked by fiber optics, and we will each have in our offices a single device for computation, communication, data retrieval, video conferencing, and the like. Most of the information revolution is still ahead of us, and it will have a significant effect on the industry. Real estate liquidity at present suffers from a lack of specific, local information. The information revolution should make real estate more liquid and even more closely connected to the worldwide capital market system.

In summary, real estate exists in an economic environment that is linked to an increasingly sophisticated, integrated, and worldwide capital market system. Real estate therefore cannot insulate itself by claiming the uniqueness of specific locality. The paradox is simply this: To be a participant in the global financial system, real estate must become fungible.

Cash Flow Analysis

Before moving along to a discussion of real estate valuation techniques, let us for a moment refresh ourselves on cash flow analysis and in particular on how cash flow analysis relates to the current dynamic economic environment.

The volatility in capital markets combined with the volatility in real estate markets creates the need for the practitioner to be much more analytical in determining which cash flows to value. The availability of increasingly powerful analytical equipment makes sophisticated analysis much more practical than it was in the past.

In the case of an office building, for example, differences occur among cities and among investors regarding the appropriate means of measuring the leasable area upon which rents are calculated. This item alone can produce a material distinction between what a buyer and what a seller think is the actual capitalization rate. What is a normal frictional vacancy rate under prevailing real estate conditions—3 percent, 5 percent, or 10 percent? When initial rents are discounted through rental concessions or excessive tenant installation allowances, what number is utilized as base rent for calculating new rent on tenant rollovers? Should a real estate recession be programmed into a ten- or 15-year cash flow model? Should rents be inflated every year? Should rents in some years remain flat or be reduced? How do we account for deferred maintenance? How about fire and safety code violations or asbestos removal? How do we deal with more exacting standards in the future?

In an apartment complex, how do we account for the replacement of carpeting and refrigerators over a ten-year cycle? What is normal maintenance?

In a shopping mall, what do we allow for the cost of cutting up a large, 20,000-square-foot space into smaller units? How do we adjust for the expense of decking the parking area in order to create more freestanding tenant space? What premium do we exact from the one potential buyer for whom our regional mall provides tenant control within a market segment? How do we account for the cost of removing toxics from the subsoil under a parking lot built over a sanitary landfill?

In the case of a hotel, how much do we expend as a replacement reserve? Can we actually reduce expenditures on food and beverage service through operating efficiencies? Should we view telephone operations as a service or as a profit center? Should we rehabilitate three floors into an all-suite, concierge operation? What value enhancement does the property receive from a particular acquirer's reservation system and convention booking expertise?

The complexities of actually operating a property and integrating it into a prospective purchaser's overall business is far more complex than capitalizing a net rental stream. It is here that value is created and capitalization rate discrepancies occur.

Alternative Valuation Techniques

Let us examine briefly the range of alternative techniques of valuation to place the capitalization rate in proper perspective.

Internal Rate of Return. Internal rate of return gained great acceptance in the United States during the period of high inflation that ended in the early 1980s. This methodology allows one to pro forma re-rent at much higher rates in the future, inflate expenses, and capture in present dollars the resale of property in a future year. Computer-driven software has been developed over the last ten years specifically for internal rate of return analysis by particular property types. As will be discussed, the internal rate of return calculation for a project is perhaps the best linkage into modern portfolio theory, making real estate a fungible capital market investment under asset allocation modeling.

Particular problems with this methodology on a stand-alone basis include: 1) the built-in assumption that the investor's opportunity rate for reinvestment remains constant and can be realized over the term of the investment; 2) the fact that cash flows may swing widely from negative to positive over the investment period and yet appear "smooth" in the final analysis; and 3) the exactness and predictability of the analysis, which make the inherent property management and leasing functions appear disarmingly mechanistic.

Net Present Value. Net present value or discounted cash flow analysis is based upon the same theory of compounding of the rate of investment return as the internal rate of return calculation, but it computes a dollar amount rather than an overall investment yield. It is useful when annual returns vary widely, and it is particularly useful for analyzing investment in a particular project. It is not useful, however, in comparing returns to other projects or other forms of investment.

Market Sales. Market sales have always been useful as indicators of value, so long as they have met the basic appraisal definition of a free market transaction. The more homogeneous the product type and the broader the list of transactions, the more useful this technique becomes. A problem in today's market is that bellwether transactions resulting from a prolonged worldwide auction of a trophy property are too often claimed to be proxies for market value in general.

Replacement Cost. Replacement cost is always a good test of value. Other than superb locational dominance or zoning constraints, one wonders why anyone would ever pay more than the replacement cost for a property. Replacement cost also may provide a secondary indication of value in a temporarily overbuilt market when obtainable rents cannot support asking prices.

Residual Sale Value. Residual sale value is really a subset of the internal rate of return calculation. It is worth highlighting, however, because in many cases it drives pricing. Investors justify purchases at seemingly high prices by assuming that they can "turn property around" (i.e., they can rehabilitate the property or reposition it in the market) and support a windfall sale price at a future date. Another phenomenon in recent years has been "capitalization rate arbitrage," which simply involves selling a property at a lower capitalization rate than the one used to purchase the property. One example of capitalization rate arbitrage is Marvin Davis's resale of the Beverly Hills Hotel in 18 months to the Sultan of Brunei. Another example of capitalization rate arbitrage is the differential in pricing of regional shopping malls over the past 15 years. In the mid-1970s, contract base rental income traded on an 8 percent basis, with overage rental income trading on a 12 percent basis. In the late 1980s, all income was undifferentiated and traded on a 5 percent basis.

In raw, undiscounted funds, the residual sale in some cases can amount to 50 percent of the funds returned to the investor. When discounted, depending on the timing of the assumed sale, the residual sale can provide 100 to 200 basis points toward the internal rate of return.

Gross Income Multiplier. Gross income multiplier is derided by the computer whiz kids as archaic and overly simplistic; yet real estate veterans still find it a useful calibration for analyzing apartments quickly when they are out of the office, and it has become a useful rule of thumb for evaluating community shopping centers as well.

Years to Investment Payback. Years to investment payback suffers the same criticism as the gross income multiplier; yet it is very useful to individuals who have a full career's experience with thinking in these terms.

Dynamic Rate of Return. Dynamic rate of return analysis is ultrasophisticated and extremely useful in allowing analysis to focus on possible weaknesses with laser intensity by "unbundling" various components of return. This analysis is a further refinement of internal rate of return analysis, and it is computer driven:

■ Unburdened cash flow analysis allows one to analyze the separate components of a mixed-use project, the individual leases of an office building, or the impact of a variety of financing or refinancing plans and to model redevelopment of an aspect of a project and the like.

- Sensitivity analysis allows one to measure the impact of an internal rate of return in a hotel project, for example, on changes in room rate; occupancy; food and beverage income; furniture, fixtures, and equipment allowances; and the like.
- Probability-risk adjusted rate of return analysis allows one to measure by statistical sampling. For example, one may compute for a hotel the internal rate of return assuming a 25 percent probability of a 65 percent occupancy, a 50 percent probability of a 70 percent occupancy, as well as a 25 percent probability of a 75 percent occupancy.

Cash-on-Cash Yield. Cash-on-cash yield returns are really a subset of the capitalization rate approach. In order to overcome the disutility of the capitalization rate approach in a dynamic environment, many investors now calculate the cash-on-cash return in each individual year of their investment horizon. Others focus on cash-on-cash yields in the initial, third, fifth and tenth year. Still others calculate an undiscounted arithmetic ten-year average cash-on-cash yield on a project. Such methods correct many of the deficiencies of the simplistic capitalization rate approach and can be very useful analytic tools. They do not, however, create a real estate rate of return that is useful in modern portfolio theory.

Modern Portfolio Theory

Computer-driven analytics have had great impact on the entire capital market investment process. The capital asset pricing model and modern portfolio theory have attempted to quantify investment risk and to develop coefficients of performance for various classes of assets, including real estate. As the investment process has become more sophisticated, computer-driven baskets of securities have been developed, including a model based on the entire Standard & Poor's index of 500 common stocks; a futures index based on the Standard & Poor's index; a "South Africa–free" common stock index; an index based upon the Shearson-Lehman bond index; indices of Japanese, German, Hong Kong, or Thai common stocks; program trading; and the like.

Historical rates of return and exposure to risk and volatility have been calculated for various classes of assets, including real estate. The proxy investment yield for real estate that most closely parallels the Standard & Poor's stock index or the Shearson-Lehman bond index in the capital asset pricing model is the internal rate of return calculation. Thus, real estate is being driven more and more to conform with this particular methodology in order to gain access to large multi-asset class capital pools, such as pension funds and insurance companies. An obvious problem in making real estate conform to this model is that there is no method for measuring real estate prices on a daily basis. Appraisals are not valid because they are determined after the fact, and price volatility is eliminated.

The entire movement toward the securitization of real estate is driven by the same motivation. Managers of large capital pools want to think of real estate debt and equity investments as just another fungible asset class. They therefore attempt to secure Moody's or Standard & Poor's bond type ratings for real estate, either through high-credit tenants or the purchase of someone else's credit (credit enhancement) for a fee, so real estate debt will appear to resemble a high-grade bond in the capital markets.

The continuing worldwide institutionalization of savings creates even larger capital pools with single-point decision making. In order for real estate to access these capital pools, it must assume the trappings of modern portfolio theory and appear to be fungible, giving up the uniqueness of location, design, marketing, and specific performance.

The paradox is obvious. Appraisers with a lifetime of experience and judgment are replaced by 28-year-olds with a computer terminal. Huge errors in judgment are committed. Billions of dollars are lost. Real estate is removed from reality. But the world goes on.

One ray of hope is that the computer revolution has just begun. The computer today is where the electric dynamo was 100 years ago when it provided light to manufacturing processes driven by steam-driven crank shafts and overhead pulley systems. Once the computer is fully integrated into our work and our lives, say in about the year 2015, the individual should become liberated once again from these huge, multinational organizations, and a plurality of localized decisions may once again drive international financial transactions.

Componentized Rate of Return

It may be useful to withdraw for a few moments from market-driven transactions and contemplate an ideal rate of return, whether capitalized, internal, discounted, or otherwise.

Real rate of return is the basic component of any rate of return calculation. It is meant to measure that riskless rate of return, free of inflation that a long-term investor ought to expect. As a result of considerable regression analysis over a period of many years, the real rate of return expected in the United States at present is around 3 percent.

Inflation assumption is the next component of a return calculation. What is the normalized inflation expectation over the term of the investment (say ten years), which, if earned, will protect the real rate of return? The expectation in the United States today is about 5 percent, which creates an inflation-protected nominal rate of return of 8 percent.

Risk and volatility have in recent years added a premium to this inflation-adjusted real rate of return. The added risk premium did not exist prior to the period of high inflation experienced in the late 1970s. Adding on a risk premium of 100 to 200 basis points provides us with a risk- and inflation-protected rate of return of around 9 percent to 10 percent. This is within the trading range of U.S. government long-term bonds and is just about what the return has been on U.S. common stocks over a long-term period.

Real estate premiums can be built up over and beyond this standard rate of return to account for additional illiquidity, additional risk (for example, a hotel), the burden of management, cyclicality, complexity, overleverage, overbuilding, and the like.

It would not be difficult to establish that the nominal rate of return for real estate should be in the area of 13 percent to 15 percent in the United States at present. Why the market returns are 300 to 400 basis points lower than this in generally overbuilt markets shall remain the subject for a different inquiry.

Reasons for Aberrations in the Capitalization Rate

As one can infer from the remarks to this point, there are many reasons for aberrations in the capitalization rate. It is very difficult to encapsulate in a single simplistic notation the multitude of analytics and emotions produced by a drawn-out negotiation. A few of the reasons for capitalization rate aberration are summarized here.

- "Collectibles" is one way to phrase the interest in so-called trophy real estate. One man's Van Gogh is another man's Beverly Hills Hotel. Yield is immaterial. Pride of ownership and possession is paramount.
- Capitalization rate arbitrage has been referenced previously. Below certain levels, it may become the adult version of "musical chairs." Where does the elephant sit? Wherever it wishes to.
- Strategic buyers are seeking an asset that empowers and enhances other assets they already own. This was true of Nestle in the purchase of the Stanford Court Hotel in San Francisco to anchor its U.S. system. It was true of the Corporate Property Investors' purchase of the Monumental shopping center portfolio to improve its dominance in markets like Atlanta and Boston. It was true of Trammell Crow Company's purchase of Jack Benaroya's 40 percent of the industrial property in Seattle.
- Long-term investment horizons cause certain investor types, notably Japanese insurance companies, to accept lower initial returns.
- Different perceptions on how an asset may be marketed or even physically configured cause value discrepancies, particularly between investment type buyers and operating type buyers.

Conclusion

In the sophisticated and dynamic world in which we live, the simple capitalization rate approach to value is no longer valid in isolation and does not add much to investment analysis even when used in conjunction with other techniques.

As for me, I use a matrix of valuation techniques, shifting my focus from property to property. Internal rate of return is a benchmark, but I am always suspicious of what it glosses over. I favor various forms of dynamic rate of return analysis, as well as cash-on-cash yields in each year and replacement value.

I never fail to see the property in its urban or suburban context. I walk the neighborhood and the roof, check the boiler room, and talk with the tenants. I get a feel for the property, the market, the appeal, the politics, and the management. I suppose you could label my approach "the Gestalt theory of investment valuation." It is what it is.

We each concoct a valuation stew of our own making. Whatever yours is, *bon appetit!*

Source: *Real Estate Issues,* fall/winter 1990.

6

Real Estate and Moral Hazard

A look at real estate today and the truth about financial markets.

There is plenty of credit available and at attractive rates. It is just not available to real estate. This is true for several reasons, primarily because of the one- to 12-year oversupply of commercial real estate, depending on product type and location. The overborrowing binge of the 1980s has created a huge backup of short-term financed real estate assets held primarily by commercial banks and insurance companies. This classic mismatch of long-term assets financed on a five-year, nonamortizing basis was created in the expectation that supply and demand of product would remain in balance and that credit would be available to refinance the debt as it came due. Neither assumption was accurate. As a result, loans are being called, and the value of much commercial property, because of wholesale liquidation, has plummeted to as low as $.40 on the dollar.

Despite the agony of the past three years, there remains close to $400 billion of short-funded real estate assets in the commercial banking and insurance systems. Much of this debt will come due in the next three years. Thus, it becomes simple to predict a credit crunch in commercial property lasting well beyond the midpoint of this decade.

Repercussions of poor lending practices have struck at the core of these financial institutions. Rating agencies such as Moody's and Standard & Poor's have lowered the credit ratings of financial institutions having "excessive" real estate assets in their portfolios, creating serious funding problems for certain entities. Likewise, financial institutions wishing to issue equity securities to bolster their capital ratios have run afoul of security analysts who also take a dim view of "excessive" real estate holdings.

At a time of relatively low, short-term borrowing rates and relatively high, long-term Treasury rates, banks are enjoying historically wide earning margins by short funding and investing in "riskless" government securities. At the same time, banks are avoiding the high costs of originating, underwriting, monitoring, and defending to regulators and others any new real estate loans. The impact of this real estate credit allocation will resonate well beyond the current decade, much as debt aversion extended well beyond the 1929–1933 depression.

On the margin, one may expect to obtain real estate finance from REITs and other public vehicles, securitization, wealthy individuals, foreign investors, and certain pension funds. Nevertheless, without significant participation from commercial banks and insurance companies, real estate finance will remain severely constrained.

Risk-Based Capital Rules

The late John M. Keynes coined the phrase "moral hazard" to describe unintended bad consequences of an otherwise positive act. One may trace the current overborrowing and overbuilding of commercial real estate to the moral hazard from the misuse of funds raised by government-insured deposits. Relatively inexpensive "riskless" capital was utilized to fund increasingly risky investments. The fact that the federal government guaranteed the deposits changed the demeanor of certain bankers from that of stewardship to that of imprudence. Compounding this was the federal government's lack of zealous regulation, the politicization of the regulatory process by certain members of Congress, and overall government policies that resulted in interest rates rising precipitously in the early 1980s, causing thrifts to choose increasingly risky projects.

The cure for the misuse of government-insured deposits has been the implementation of risk-based capital rules for both banks and insurance companies. Putting it simply, banks are not required to have equity capital to invest in U.S. government securities and must hold about 8 percent as a capital reserve against commercial, industrial, and real estate loans. These rules, whether applied by regulators or by the private sector arbitrators of capital access (rating agencies, security analysts, accountants, etc.) compound the trend of highly liquid banks loading up on government securities and going out of the commercial loan business. The moral hazard to risk-based capital rules is that once again banks are short funding long-term assets. Just a whiff of inflation from the new Democratic government could flatten out the yield curve and create a banking crisis on a scale seldom before imagined.

Risk-based capital rules will stifle the current economic recovery, hinder the growth of small business, and change the traditional temporal intermediation function of banks to being risk-averse investment companies with deteriorating talent to underwrite loans and evaluate risk.

Mark-to-Market Accounting

The accounting profession, the Securities and Exchange Commission, bank regulators, pension fund administrators, and the credit-rating agencies are united in proposing that financial institutions mark their assets (loans and investments) to market. At present, investment banks mark to market, while commercial banks and insurance companies do so only for publicly traded securities. Pension funds in particular are anxious to develop a basis for periodic market valuations of real estate assets in order to incorporate real estate into the capital asset pricing model and make real estate truly fungible with other financial assets. As laudable as the notion may be, it ignores the specificity and idiosyncratic nature of individual large commercial real estate projects. Moreover, any attempt to write all real estate assets to current liquidation value in a market severely lacking in both willing purchasers and willing sellers would threaten the stability of our financial system.

Public policy efforts should be focused on continuing to allow banks to hold real estate assets for future recovery while keeping short-term interest rates low, thus allowing the banks wider than customary margins to build reserves for future real estate write-offs. A multiyear solution to the real estate problem, while prolonging the agony, will preserve the stability of our banking system.

It is ironic that, under the prevailing low, short-term interest rate structure, banks are now realizing larger profits on restructured, classified real estate loans than they did before when the loans were paying their contracted rate of interest.

Valuation Terminology

Another form of moral hazard in the current environment is the degeneration of appraisal terminology and methodology and of appraisers themselves. A typical scenario has a developer explaining his property to a bank in terms of a ten-year hold to recovery and a "discounted investment value," while the bank is examining the same property in terms of a three- to five-year hold and a "current market value," and simultaneously the bank examiner is scrutinizing the same property in terms of immediate disposition and a "liquidation value." All three parties argue with one another while utilizing terminology that the others do not comprehend. The property may, or may not, have an "intrinsic value," but whatever that value is, it is impacted by the capital structure and holding power of its current owner.

This current cacophony of terminology is creating increasing dissatisfaction and confusion with the appraisal process. More and more individuals add to the confusion by attempting to clarify the issues. Kenneth Leventhal & Company suggests classifying real estate assets as follows:[1]

- Quality assets with acceptable cash flows (given the weak economy) and some long-term potential. Such assets could be held or sold.
- Assets that could be rehabilitated and converted to new uses and then either held or sold.
- Problem assets that must be restructured, held until the economy and market improve, and then sold.
- "Trapped" assets that cannot be sold because they are in litigation or bankruptcy.

James R. Cooper of Georgia State University suggests these categories:[2]

- *Investment value*—an optimistic view of the value of a property if held in a financially stable, long-term portfolio and sold in the future in a stabilized market.
- *Market value*—the most probable price for cash that a property will bring if sold in a competitive and open market under all conditions requisite to a fair sale, both buyer and seller acting prudently, with available financing and no undue stimulus.
- *Current value*—the most probable selling price under whatever conditions exist at the date of appraisal.
- *Liquidation value*—the price an owner is compelled to accept when the property sale is mandatory with less than reasonable market exposure; the lowest price that a democratic capitalistic system produces under conditions of market failure; a buyer-dominated market.

The degeneration of appraisal terminology has been abetted by underqualified government regulators requiring documentation that, at times, has been unnecessary and irrelevant. The confusing state of the market has been acknowledged by the Appraisal Institute. In June 1992, its special task force issued a report on value definitions. Yet a past president of the Counselors of Real Estate, James Gibbons, has stated: "We do not need more definitions. We have enough; and they are well understood; the recent difficulties arose from inappropriate data inputs. Our major difficulty seems to be inadequate or faulty communication."[3]

Valuation Methodology

FIRREA [the Financial Institutions Reform, Recovery, and Enforcement Act of 1989] and government regulations have forced wholesale appraisals of real estate loans and investments held by financial institutions. Real estate professionals are complaining more than ever about the inadequacy and irrelevancy of the appraisals they receive.

Tens of millions of dollars are being spent on appraisals that have no use in business decisions and are mere window dressing for the files. As appraisals became delinked from market clearing prices on the way up, they are likewise not reflective of either the market or the intentions of the real estate holder's assets on the way down. As Gibbons stated, there is a vast communication problem among the requirers, holders, and makers of appraisals.

In the absence of comparable sales data or even a market for property, it seems an appraisal must more and more focus on the holding power and intentions of the holder of the asset. An appraisal must reflect the most likely pattern of the market recovery over the term of the established holding period. An appraisal also must incorporate a business plan for continuing investment, repositioning, and marketing of the asset.

A final economic value may well be the calculated expected value of probable outcomes. Such a detailed economic model of a project would not be warranted for assets with a value of less than, say, $50 million. Such an appraisal would have a major impact on the holder of the asset's business decision.

Such an economic evaluation should provide lucrative employment for fellow real estate counselors (CREs). As Counselors, we must be concerned with the devaluation of valuation methodology. Whether or not we also serve as appraisers, Counselors cannot afford to allow major capital pools, such as pension funds, to consider our industry as unprofessional and chaotic.

Data Collection and the CRE's Role

A major inhibiting feature of real estate as an investment asset category is the deterioration of a reliable database. Pension funds, in particular, will not return to the marketplace until they are convinced that a credible database exists for real estate.

In the current marketplace, there is no coherent basis for determining demand for space or for determining true economic (net effective) rents. Thus, there is no coherent basis for determining value. Contract rents are meaningless in the welter of kickbacks, side payments, free services, and the like. Buildings are measured differently in different cities. Seemingly modern structures are technologically outmoded or riddled with asbestos.

A true moral hazard has been created in that many major institutional investors no longer trust real estate data. The current supply/demand situation will resolve itself temporally, as will the burden of past due and delinquent debt. The resonance from the lack of trust in real estate as an asset class will last longer. Here is where CREs can add clarity and professionalism to the process as advisers to financial institutions and by convincing clients that their long-run interests are best served by sharing and opening up their databases, heretofore deemed proprietary.

Notes

1. *Real Estate Newsline* (Kenneth Leventhal & Company), October/November 1992, p. 3.

2. James R. Cooper and Robert K. Brown, *Research Monograph 104* (Georgia State University, 1992), pp. 59–64.

3. James Gibbons, letter to author, October 8, 1992.

Source: *Real Estate Issues,* spring/summer 1993.

7 Price Differentials in Public and Private Markets

Do real estate practitioners really want a "perfect" market for real estate investment? Insofar as it would broaden real estate capital markets and reduce cyclical volatility, yes.

Pricing anomalies between the public and private real estate investment markets persist for a number of reasons. Academic observers like Anthony Downs, senior fellow at the Brookings Institution in Washington, D.C., and Peter Linneman, director of the Wharton Real Estate Center at the University of Pennsylvania in Philadelphia, tend to attribute such anomalies to timing divergences among cycles—the economic cycle, the investment cycle, and the real estate cycle.

Based on my own experience as a real estate investment banker, one of the most important reasons that prices differ between the two markets is that private markets occasionally offer investors a good reason to pay a premium. That reason is operating control (where it is available). In addition, certain investors may prefer single assets to portfolio assets, or put value on a demonstrably better asset management capability, a more conservative capital structure, or the like.

Price differentials are not a recent phenomenon. Market analysts have long noted the anomalies that obtain from time to time between the public and private markets for real estate investment.

The salient characteristics of a private real estate market, as contrasted with the public market, are as follows. It has fewer participants. Information flows imperfectly. Trading is not concentrated. It lacks standardized contracts. Supply and demand may be out of balance: Limited demand can create supply overhangs or excessive demand can create supply shortages. In the early 1990s, such imbalances resulted from a negative bias toward real estate and regulatory pressure to dump properties at fire-sale prices.

Private markets are negotiated markets. At times, prices may be driven by such imbalances between buyers and sellers or by asymmetric information. At other times, prices may be based on appraisals. Markets based on appraisals tend to be normatively conservative; their reliance on comparable historical data smoothes out potentially wide differences in valuation.

The salient characteristics of public real estate markets are as follows. There is a central trading place or places. Accurate information is broadly disseminated. Transactions are reported. Contracts are standardized. Under the best circumstances, public markets bring together large numbers of willing buyers and sellers. A sufficiency of willing buyers and willing sellers produces equilibrium pricing and mitigates against emotion and systematic error.

Pricing in public markets relies more heavily on the discounted value of projections of future earnings. In the view of some economists, public markets are "perfect" markets in which the equilibrium established between buyers and sellers tends to clear the market.

Liquidity is an implicit ingredient of the theoretical perfect market. So is information—as much as possible. Perfect-market theoreticians believe, in the extreme, that no information flows should be curtailed. There is, in their view, no such thing as "inside" information. Insiders who trade on privileged data contribute to the perfect market simply by helping to establish the market clearing price.

Practitioners may have a somewhat different view of public markets, observing that fairly often they also are subject to supply/demand imbalances that can make them illiquid. Examples:

- In the early 1970s, it was common knowledge that should J.P. Morgan, Wall Street's largest investor of pension funds, dump its large stock positions in the "nifty fifty" (the 50 most popular common stock investments at the time), the price that would obtain would bear no resemblance to the closing price for its portfolio quoted in the *Wall Street Journal*.
- The illiquidity of the New York Stock Exchange was clearly highlighted in the October 1987 market crash.
- Junk bonds lost their liquidity when Drexel closed in 1990.
- California municipal bonds lost their liquidity in the days following Orange County's (California) bankruptcy last December.

- Even real estate investment trust (REIT) equities that are listed on the New York Stock Exchange do not enjoy a high level of liquidity on days when mutual funds are selling their positions.

There are times when the private market operates almost perfectly, and sometimes the public market operates rather imperfectly. By and large, it can be said that real estate investment generally takes place in a market that is more imperfect than perfect: a market that lacks standardized contracts and a steady flow of accurate information and in which supply/demand imbalances are more the rule than the exception.

The Opportunities in Markets Out of Sync

The two markets—public and private—appear to move in and out of equilibrium with each other. The differentials offer certain opportunities.

At times in the 1970s, the private market was willing to pay much more for real estate assets than the public market. Morgan Stanley took advantage of this differential by taking several publicly traded companies private, and selling their assets to insurance companies, pension funds, or real estate operators. [See article 1 for details.] Thus, the Tishman Company, which was trading at $8 a share ultimately distributed $27.50 a share; Monumental Properties, trading at $18 a share, distributed $72 a share; and the Ernest Hahn Company, trading at $8 a share, distributed $52.50 a share. Each of these transactions took from one to three years to accomplish. Because the private real estate market was at that time even less linked to Wall Street, confidentiality could be maintained throughout (and the arbitrageurs, caught napping, were bypassed).

Twenty years ago, when the real estate portfolios of institutions were not as linked to securities as they now are, Morgan Stanley took advantage of a huge pricing anomaly that could not occur in today's markets. Interest rates were high. Bank and public utility companies, which would have had to pay 12.5 percent for financing in the public bond markets, were able—through private sale-leaseback transactions with the real estate side of insurance companies and pension funds—to obtain financing for 10.5 percent. The credit in support of the interest payments was exactly the same. What appeared as a Baa credit to the public bond holder appeared as a high-credit real estate transaction to the institutions, which were having trouble investing their real estate allocations. (Note: When the chief economist of one of the largest life insurance companies discovered this anomaly, he ordered all 22 branch offices to cease and desist from making corporate mortgage loans at a rate less than the daily posted rate in the *Wall Street Journal* for Baa rated public utility bonds. This crude early device for linking public and private markets effectively put Morgan Stanley out of business on that particular transaction.)

Even today, real estate transactions that could not take place in the public market could do so in the private market. A real estate investment trust focused on high-rise office buildings in central business districts, for example, may not be acceptable in today's public markets but similar assets could have appeal for private investment funds.

Why do these anomalies persist? Public markets respond quickly to events that may not always seem relevant to private real estate investors, particularly those who intend to hold on to property for a long period—based on their strategic control of the property—and thus can look through the "noise" in the marketplace. Public markets tend to respond more to changes in interest rates. Taking the view that interest rates and inflation rates will normalize over the long term, a private investor might not react as violently as the public market to daily fluctuations.

Institutional investors may well have medium- or long-term strategies for their asset allocations or portfolio balances that are out of sync at times with a short-term view of the real estate investment market. Some long-term investors are announced contrarians. When real estate is out of favor in the public market, some institutional investors stay in the marketplace and reap the benefits of favorable pricing and terms.

The sale of the Monumental portfolio provides an example of why private investors might pay high prices. Morgan Stanley designed packages of regional shopping malls to fit perfectly with the holdings of certain large institutions, packages that could provide individual institutions with desired market dominance. Paying premiums for these tailor-made investments was easily justified.

Some investors are more comfortable, given their experience over many years, in accepting certain types of risk not currently in favor in the public market. Some institutions might favor regional malls, while others might favor high-rise office buildings. Some provide construction lending. Some back developers with predevelopment funds. Particular institutions at particular times over the cycle have been able virtually to make the market for certain types of real estate investment.

Becoming Perfect?

Do real estate practitioners really want to remove the investment market anomalies that occur in each real estate business cycle? Those with knowledge of why and where inefficiencies occur, adequate capital to hold firm when market inefficiency is working against them, and the discipline to sell when it is working with them have learned to benefit from these anomalies.

However, it is the duty of real estate professionals to work to broaden the acceptance of real estate investment—especially among pension funds—so that real estate will enjoy access to long-term capital in the years ahead.

Pension funds offer the most promise. Their longer-term liabilities tend to be a good match for real estate loans and investments. Banks and insurance companies, on the other hand, tend to shorten the investment terms for their array of financial products.

Pension funds have not lived up to the expectations of consultants that real estate as an asset class would grow to 10 percent of their total assets. If the 10 percent allocation were achieved, the real estate industry would be guaranteed a future supply of long-term capital.

For pension funds to achieve a 5 to 10 percent position in private real estate assets, they will have to change their preference for "passive" investments and overcome their obsession with liquidity. "We cannot pay retirement benefits with appraised values," they say. In soft markets, the desire for liquidity exacerbates downward price pressures.

Pension funds tend to overvalue their need for liquidity (and pay a premium for the possibility of liquidity, even when it may not exist) and undervalue the opportunity to gain operating control of assets in the private markets. Pension funds must become good "control" investors, meaning that they must be willing to manage assets actively.

Pension funds increasingly are demanding either premium returns on real estate or an exit strategy that gives them the liquidity they think they need. The following paragraph provides another story to illustrate the real estate liquidity problem of pension funds as well as the delinking of public and private markets at times.

In 1971, Morgan Stanley set up Brooks Harvey Realty Investors, a private equity real estate investment trust. A major pension fund insisted that the institutional investors be provided with a quarterly valuation of the trust shares, which were offered originally at $20, as if they were traded on the public market. During the real estate depression of the mid-1970s, the stock prices for real estate declined, and Morgan Stanley's valuation group pegged the Brooks Harvey shares at $8. Brooks Harvey's protestations that the real estate was good, underleveraged, and worth far more than the valuation did little to ease the dismay of the shareholders. They insisted, in 1982, that Morgan Stanley sell the real estate and liquidate the trust, which it did at $28 a share. The investors then had cash, a diminished asset allocation to real estate, and, because they could not replace the real estate for the prices paid ten years earlier, a major reinvestment problem.

How can real estate professionals broaden the acceptance of real estate investment by institutions?

There is a real need for standardization in contracts. On the various financial exchanges, minimal standardized paperwork and a high degree of trust are all that is required to trade billions of dollars of securities daily. Real estate can never become this simple. But why must every major investment or lease contract be handcrafted at considerable time and expense? These contracts need not be all the same, but they should contain standard language for certain major points of the deal. This language should come from the broad agreement of a sizable number of market participants. The standardization of key documents would make the real estate investment market far more comprehensible to new entrants. Contract standardization is an area in which the Urban Land Institute, through its Capital Markets Task Force, is doing some work.

Easier price discovery is another basic criterion for a broader real estate capital market. New market entrants find real estate price discovery an arcane and mysterious business. The insecurity and distrust this breeds hinder investment follow-through. Pension funds as a class were disillusioned with real estate valuations in the early 1990s. Justifiably, their managers feel that the data the real estate industry provided then were neither timely nor accurate. (The valuations made in the late 1980s may have been equally defective.)

Part of the price discovery problem is that appraisals have become delinked from real market values both on the way up in a cycle as well as on the way down. In the 1980s, real estate assets traded for large premiums over appraised values. In the 1990s, they have traded at steep discounts under appraised values. Because of supply/demand imbalances, real estate proved not to be an inflation hedge, as it was always purported to be, during certain phases of the business cycle.

ULI also is working in the area of easier price discovery. It is studying the construction of a commercial market rent index for some key cities. A properly constructed index can give market participants a real-time window on what is going on.

Generally available systems for collecting and publishing rents and sale prices of commercial properties have not been developed previously for good reasons. Because each building is different, the development of useful pricing measures is difficult and costly. Furthermore, many real estate professionals benefit financially from the lack of broadly shared solid pricing information and so are reluctant to support its development and publication.

Conversely, many real estate professionals have been hurt by the same lack of information. Reconstruction of actual rents for office properties in general, before major downturns in the market, indicates that actual net effective rents start declining long before investment in new construction begins to be curtailed. The availability of actual sale and lease prices would force investors to be more realistic in assessing the income potential from new space in an already soft market. The tremendous losses suffered from cyclical overbuilding would then be avoided.

Another potential aid in price discovery is arising out of the attempt of pension funds to create a network among pension fund managers for trading partnership interests in previously illiquid pooled real estate funds. There is more than $40 billion invested in pooled real estate funds. Pension fund managers are seeking to develop reputable, standardized financial information in order to facilitate price discovery and thus stimulate the trading of interests in these pooled funds.

As banks and insurance companies continue to adjust their portfolios of real estate loans and investments to meet new regulatory guidelines, they present Wall Street with a good opportunity to expand the market for mortgage-backed securities (MBSs). But, it is the same old story: The growth and liquidity of the securitization market are inhibited by the lack of ongoing accurate and timely information on individual assets, information that traders need to evaluate and underwrite the risks associated with maintaining trading liquidity in commercial MBSs.

Real estate's plethora of locations, practitioners, and property types make unlikely the achievement of a truly perfect market for real estate investment. Nonetheless, this market needs to be brought into modern times. In an age in which data on financial assets are flashed around the world in standardized format and acted upon immediately, real estate remains too arcane and mysterious a process.

While all real estate practitioners also will never be perfect, they can aspire to a higher level of openness and trust in the interest of broadening the real estate capital markets and mitigating the volatility of the real estate cycle. It is important for all real estate professionals to become involved in the price discovery process by providing better data on the bare essentials: sale prices, net effective rentals, the property measurement characteristics used in calculating rents, the overhang of subleased space, and the like. At the same time, academic research into the divergences of the real estate cycle from the general economic cycle should be encouraged. Real estate professionals should work together—and ULI is the ideal place—to create the underpinnings of the real estate capital markets of the future.

Source: *Urban Land*, September 1995.

8 Why Foreign Capital Flows into U.S. Real Estate Are Drying Up

From today's perspective, the outlook for international investments in U.S. real estate in the 1990s is not good. The future rests on three factors:

- the degree to which real estate can be considered an asset class in modern portfolio theory;
- worldwide investment liquidity; and
- the health of local commercial property markets.

None of these factors currently favors maintenance of recent foreign capital flows into U.S. property.

The Problem of Valuation

In a global financial marketplace filled with increasingly powerful instruments by which baskets and bundles of financial assets can be traded across time zones in multiple currencies, the valuation of real estate remains essentially a handicraft. Ascribing a particularity and uniqueness to each individual asset detaches real estate from international financial markets.

Volatility is at the heart of the operation of modern financial markets. Since the commencement of financial deregulation and globalization some 15 years ago, the media have begun widespread reporting of raw economic data including consumer spending, production, employment, trade, money supply, and the like.

When the data are reported, markets tend to move. The trend toward more economic reporting has increased market volatility.

Small investors engaged in a multiplicity of trades once served to smooth out volatility. But the increased institutionalization of funds has taken smaller investors out of direct market activity. Playing financial markets is more and more an insider's game. With the trend to complicated computerized investment products moving full steam ahead, markets will become more unintelligible to nonspecialists. The consequent reduction in players will increase volatility further.

Volatility increases risk and thereby increases the return required on baseline investments like U.S. government bonds. This, in turn, drives up the returns required for secondary investment products such as real estate, because investors require a certain spread over baseline investment yields for these secondary products.

Investors in real property traditionally have counteracted capital market volatility by an appraisal process that smoothes out returns over a ten-year closed investment period. They struggle at the time of purchase to derive a mechanistic internal rate of return, which is used, at a spread off a baseline financial asset, to arrive at a price.

For the next ten years, they ignore daily and cyclic volatility—though they may perform periodic reappraisals.

But bank examiners, in their zeal to mark all the nation's commercial real estate to market (that is, to compel banks to value all their real estate assets at current depressed-market conditions), have ravaged this way of doing business. Real estate's current investment problem is the huge market overhang of fully leased, investment-quality property for sale at yesterday's values based on long-term rates of return. No one is willing to buy these properties at those prices.

The real estate appraisal process that smoothes an asset's valuation rather than settling in at a particular sale price that could reflect the high or low point of a cycle is in conflict with modern portfolio theory. Portfolio managers measure financial assets daily, including their highest and lowest prices over a cycle. Real estate investment value speaks in an arcane language that is hard to decipher in the noisy, volatile financial marketplace.

Globalization

Before they start prowling around the world seeking investment opportunities, institutional investors first fulfill fundamental domestic investment needs. Financial instruments that cross national boundaries are chasing the marginal dollar. As an ultimate step in the investment process, global investment requires worldwide excess liquidity. In an illiquidity cycle, international investments will be liquidated first, in a last-in first-out pattern.

Financial globalization, then, is a diversification move, often driven by episodic trade surpluses in national accounts. The brief-lived Italian foreign investment spree in the early 1960s was based on that country's white goods "miracle." Oil exports fueled Kuwait's investment spree in the 1970s. Significant trade surpluses were behind the Japanese tidal wave of foreign investments in the 1980s and the beginning of the 1990s.

Few financial products are truly global and sufficiently homogeneous to be tradable in multiple markets. Real estate is not one of them. Particularized and local, real estate is not easily analyzed from afar. Its arcane and chaotic pricing of rents and assets, its way of producing periodic windfalls and large losses keep it in the company of products that the global marketplace looks at last and gets out of first.

The global landscape is difficult to predict. Will the world of the 1990s become more stable or more volatile than it is now? Uncertainty itself—the risk premium—should keep rates for international investments relatively high.

The Soviets are exhausted, the Germans are preoccupied with their eastern sector, and the Japanese appear, for the moment, to have lost their way. Weapons of mass destruction—nuclear bombs, chemicals, ballistic missiles—are spreading to small states that may become aggressive. Does the United States have the will and the resources to be the world's SWAT team? How will a policeman's role affect our budget deficit, our interest rates, oil prices?

As for Japan, a year ago it looked golden. Today, in quite a reversal, Japan faces shrinking stock market values, problematic land values, higher interest rates and, for its banks and insurance companies, eroding asset quality. But the issue is not where Japan is now. It is where it will be a year from now

The U.S. trade deficit with Japan persists. The Japanese still hold lots of dollars and can roam wherever they wish in the global marketplace. Japanese investment perceptions tend to be group-driven and binary. The switch is either "on" or "off." It will remain on "off" for the near term, particularly because the environment is such that the Japanese cannot even determine the worth of the properties they already own.

Europe essentially will be looking inward. Changes associated with the events of 1992 will absorb western European capital. Guns are drawn in Lithuania, Albania, Yugoslavia, and (Soviet) Georgia. The economies in eastern Europe and eastern Germany will be absorbed in creating private property, privatized industry, banking systems, market pricing structures, and convertible currencies. Any marginal capital left over will be tagged for reconstruction in the Persian Gulf region and industrialization in Mexico and Latin America

In Sum: Unmet Conditions

It is not necessary to belabor the obvious, the sick condition of most U.S. real estate markets. In downtown Los Angeles, for example, a hefty office space oversupply is being augmented by construction to protect short-lived entitlements. The market could end up with a four- to six-year supply to work off, with no likely tenants in sight.

Commercial property supply and demand will remain out of balance in some markets for as long as three to four years. In some markets, where buildings sit empty and net effective rents deteriorate, there is no known "truth" of value. Four cash flow projections recently prepared by different firms for a major downtown Los Angeles office building, for example, vary substantially even in the initial year of the investment period. Investment-grade real estate has become illiquid and thus unlinked from the capital asset pricing system.

The 1990s look to be a period of full allocation of capital, not one of excess liquidity. In addition to the demands for capital already enumerated, the rollover of the debt binge of the 1980s looms. In the United States alone, $500 billion of corporate debt will require refunding over the next three years—two and one-half times the level of the previous three years. New mortgage capital is expected to contract from a peak of $100 billion in 1987 to nil over the next two or three years. New equity capital for real estate will contract from a high of $22 billion in 1988 to about $5 billion in 1991.

Thus, the market for foreign investment in U.S. property will be far from buoyant in the 1990s. None of the conditions—a valuation methodology compatible with financial markets, investment liquidity, or healthy local property markets—is met. The time has come to hunker down, size down, and manage assets.

Source: *Urban Land* (Viewpoint column), July 1991.

9 Does China Meet the Preconditions for Long-Term Investment in Real Estate?

As part of an Urban Land Institute study tour to China last spring, we visited three cities: Beijing, Xiamen, and Shanghai. This article summarizes the long-term investment prospects for China at the present time, with special emphasis on political, economic, and social factors, as well as an examination of market conditions. The data gleaned in this article from the study tour will prepare us to become "China watchers" in preparation for the Counselors' (Counselors of Real Estate) 1997 High Level Conference, "China Revisited."

The study tour program was developed by S.L. Chen, a U.S. citizen who was born in China. Chen has devoted his career to investment banking and management consulting involving China. He pioneered secondary trading in Chinese government debt, and he helped to reopen the Shanghai Stock Exchange. In the interests of full disclosure, the author wishes to acknowledge that one of his daughters is happily married to one of S.L. Chen's sons.

The choice of Beijing and Shanghai as destinations was obvious; they are the Washington, D.C., and New York City of China. We also wished to visit a second-tier city that was benefiting from strong development and was less dependent upon the central government. Xiamen (formerly Amoy) fit the bill. Not only is it located in south China (a long way from the central government), but it is the mainland deepwater port nearest to Taiwan, and it would benefit spectacularly if any rapprochement occurred. Other interesting information on Xiamen: The islands of Quemoy and Matsu lie offshore, and it is a city where Chen is quite active as an entrepreneur.

Preconditions for Long-Term Investment

Here is a short list of preconditions for long-term investment in any emerging-market country. We are studying real estate investment in particular, but these conditions might apply to any form of long-term investment. These preconditions are being evaluated here against political, economic, and social criteria prior to drawing a conclusion. I am indebted to fellow CRE (Counselor of Real Estate) Christopher Jonas for sharing some of these criteria at the High Level Conference in Scotland.

- There is a general perception of confidence about where the country is headed. No major conditions must be set. No major hurdles need be overcome.
- There is a broad diversity of investors who are interested. We will not be out on a limb.
- There is an ability to value investment returns, which is generally understood, professionally supported, and linked to the local currency.
- There is the prospect of a secondary market. There is a preexisting exit strategy—a way out.
- There is a professional database readily available providing comparable rents, costs, sale prices, and the like. (Query: Does such a database exist for real estate in the United States?)
- There is the ability to repatriate rents, dividends, or sale proceeds.
- The local currency is convertible externally. There is a free currency market, as well as ability to hedge the local currency.
- There are systems in place to manage the investment.
- There is a regulatory system in effect to regulate the marketplace from malpractice and corruption.
- There is a rule of law and an established process to resolve conflicts between international investors and local partners. The decisions of international arbitration agencies are enforceable in the local court system.
- Investment returns include a risk premium that will adequately compensate for all the risk. Investments in the emerging market will clearly outperform investments at home.

For many readers, the answers to these queries may be apparent without reading further. If all these conditions were met, China would be a mature market. This article attempts to utilize the following analysis as a means of conveying some of my impressions from the study trip. In the conclusion, I will attempt to indicate an investment strategy that might work at the present time in an emerging-market nation such as China.

Political Conditions

For those of us in the West who are trained to think linearly—or, since the computer age, binarily—the yin and the yang of the Orient, which is very much a reality, makes assessment truly puzzling. Commentators on China have come up with wildly optimistic as well as wildly pessimistic predictions for the evolution of the political system that must replace the current aged leadership.

A threshold query might be: "Who is Deng?" Deng is the ruler of China. Is he head of state? No. Is he head of the Communist Party? No. Is he generalissimo of the People's Liberation Army? No. The only title the *Los Angeles Times* could come up with for Deng is chairman of the All China Bridge Association (presumably contract and not structural). Identifying future leadership is a problem inherent for prospective "China watchers."

A more optimistic scenario might call for gradual change from the top. A continuation of Deng's "to get rich is glorious" policy has provided a vision and a relative stability since its promulgation in 1979. This has been one of the most stable political eras in China during the past 150 years. Certain economic zones and certain cities have enjoyed exponential growth and resulting wealth as foreign capital has poured in.

Economists insist that the only persistent underpinning for a free political system is an open- and free-market system. Sectors of China have headed this way for the past 15 years with the support and even the participation of the senior party leadership. Yet many commentators observe that China today is a system in which authoritarianism has fragmented. There are both vertical and horizontal bureaucracies, with huge power vacuums everywhere. Dissent is crushed, yet the taxes are not collected. It is a structure that is elaborate, but institutionally weak. Governance is personalized. It is a rule of men and not of laws. It is a government of relationship, bribery, and corruption. The nation-state is in a twilight zone, moving out of authoritarianism into some form of market socialism. The ideological vacuum at the core leads to individual bargaining instead of rule under law. Regulations are constantly changing, and they are seldom promulgated, giving great power to the bureaucrats who have a copy of the law.

Local municipalities compete with Beijing for foreign capital. Individual state ministries compete for foreign capital. There is chaos in central planning, fragmentation, regionalism, and wanton regulatory change. At the center is a cadre of old, weak leaders. There is no charismatic leader or an agreed-upon vision. What set of established institutionalized values will govern regardless of whether the current movement toward individual entrepreneurship persists or goes the way of the Cultural Revolution or the Great Leap Forward?

The optimistic theory of slow democratization from within flounders on the realities of having the will to reengage tens of millions of workers in new jobs, reforming state ministries and industries, providing a long-term vision to comfort the populace during the accompanying individual economic hardship, and democratizing the institutions without losing control. Other scenarios would include a Sun Yat Sen type of emerging charismatic leader from outside the present structure who would provide the will to manage change and the vision to comfort the populace during the hardship that will certainly accompany it. This, too, is one of the more optimistic turn of events. Less optimistic would be a military coup, a breakup of China into superregions, a fallback to the old warlord society, and the like.

From this brief and superficial analysis, we can comfortably conclude that the first precondition on our list is not met. China lacks an unconditional premise of political stability. Moreover, there is no clear rule of law, protection against corruption, regulation against malfeasance, nor a process that is enforceable in the local court system for resolving disputes with local partners.

The author has no basis for guessing at the political outcome. The military could certainly play a key role. Just whom is the People's Liberation Army (PLA) prepared to shoot? The people? There was some ambivalence in 1989, and there would probably be a great deal more today. Even the military is engaged in the economic boom. The PLA owns a few super-high-rise multiuse structures. A new form of neofascism? This is not as strange as it sounds. In Bhutan, the army has a monopoly concession to brew and sell malt whiskey to supplement its pension plan. The odds are that there will be an authoritarian government in China with accompanying human rights abuses, conscripted labor, lack of freedom to travel internally, and the like for as long as any prudent investor cares to project.

From this brief and superficial analysis, we can comfortably conclude that the first precondition on our list is not met. China lacks an unconditional premise of political stability. Moreover, there is no clear rule of law, protection against corruption, regulation against malfeasance, nor a process that is enforceable in the local court system for resolving disputes with local partners.

Economic Conditions

Buying Power

Deng predicted that national wealth would quadruple between 1979 and 2000. His goal will be exceeded. Foreign investment has poured in, and many Chinese have escaped from their own economy into the world economy. There is a sense of unreality. State cadre workers make about U.S. $30 per month. They pay $1 per month as rent for a small apartment in a seven-story walk-up that, although quite new, has the appearance of a low-rent building in the South Bronx. Such an individual has a bicycle, a TV, an electric fan, and a small refrigerator. The cooking facilities are one or two gas burners. There is no bathtub or shower stall. They probably eat two or three meals a day at the state enterprise. Both family members work, and their single child is cared for by a grandparent or through schooling and child care. They save 40 percent of their income. There are virtually no private automobiles, cellular telephones, and the like.

These luxury items come as perquisites for higher officials in state ministries or industries.

Yet there is also a veneer of much greater wealth. Some of it comes as remittances from overseas Chinese relatives. Some of it comes from true entrepreneurship in this boiling economy. Some of it comes from corruption. As the highly regulated local economy runs into the world economy, inflation runs rampant. Official inflation at present is 15 percent. Unofficially it is said to be 20 percent per annum, but it has been as high as 40 to 50 percent per annum. The state-controlled central bank runs the economy with rigidity, on a stop/go basis, turning on and off the credit lines to the local banking system. At present the economy is in a stop phase, due to excessive real estate speculation, and it is virtually impossible to borrow for working capital in the local Chinese currency.

Employment

China's employment in agriculture is about 73 percent, as compared to 5 percent as the Organization for Economic Cooperation and Development (OECD) average. If China were to mechanize its farms, there would be an underemployment problem for hundreds of millions of individuals. Yet, at present, it is problematic whether China will be self-sufficient in grain. It is said that 100 million persons are unemployed at present in the countryside and 10 million in the cities. Each major city has pass points, preventing those in the countryside from coming in. Yet there are said to be a couple of million floating countryside people in both Beijing and Shanghai. They are invisible, as otherwise they would be arrested on the street. It is said that state industry has 100 million employed, of which at least 25 million are not needed in their jobs. Thus, the unemployment potential for China is huge, and any restructuring of agriculture and industry will present very serious political problems.

Currency/Capital

The local currency is not convertible. Tourists can purchase RMB (local currency) at about 8:1 to the U.S. dollar. Estimates of the real market, if the RMB were fully convertible, range from 12:1 to 15:1. Thus, a free float would produce a situation far more serious than the one currently being suffered by Mexico.

There is a serious shortage of investment capital, even though China enjoyed the largest foreign investment inflows of any nation in 1994, when $30 billion of capital flowed in. About two-thirds of the capital inflows were Chinese (25 percent Hong Kong Chinese and 40 percent overseas Chinese). This amounted to about one-third of the world's foreign investment last year. As was very visible on the study tour, about two-thirds of the foreign investment went into real estate. This year [1995], foreign investment is estimated to drop one-third to $20 billion, partly as a result of overbuilding as well as the Bank of China crackdown on speculative building. Yet, at the same time, China's infrastructure is primitive. China has huge needs for roads, railways, airports, power plants, and port facilities. Much of the existing infrastructure is poorly constructed.

It has been suggested that Hong Kong will be kept as a market to the world by the Chinese for 50 years following 1997. It has also been suggested that the reason for this is the value of having the Hong Kong dollar as a currency. Further, it has been suggested that without the Bank of China having the resources to support it, the world currency dealers could overnight destroy the Hong Kong dollar.

Thus, the momentous problems facing the Chinese are unemployment and inflation. The following section will discuss in more detail the will required to sustain the populace through any economic transition. Looking at our initial list of preconditions for long-term foreign investment, we may now say that China lacks the following: returns linked to local currencies, repatriation of investment returns, and currency convertibility.

Social Conditions

Demographics

An incredible strength of China is the homogeneity of its populace. Of the 1.2 billion population, 92 percent are of Han ethnicity and share a 2,000-year history. Individuals living in the city are much better off than they were in 1979. There appears to be an energy and an optimism about the people. Having made five trips to China since 1984, this author is now more impressed by the disappearance of Mao uniforms, the color and ebullience of the street life, the local entrepreneurship, and the bustle of the retail stores. However, great challenges lie ahead.

Company Restructuring

One challenge is the 25 million workers who must be restructured from state industry. A woman we had lunch with talked of her father. He works in the Ministry of Mines where he does nothing all day but read the newspaper. When he comes home, he does all the shopping, cleaning, and washing, because his wife is working overtime for a foreign manufacturing company. Recently in the United States, companies such as Sears, General Motors, DuPont, AT&T, IBM, and others have restructured hundreds of thousands of jobs. Eliminating layers of management has resulted in sharply improved competitive ability and profitability. This occurred in a market economy, where it required a decade of needling by stock and bond analysts, leveraged buyout attackers, and Japanese competitors to overcome the inertia and get the job done.

I submit that it is not possible for us to understand what it will take for the Chinese bureaucrats to do the same. For those of us who have spent our entire lives enjoying and applauding a free-market economy, we have no sense of the mind-set of those who have risen to positions of wealth and influence by disdaining such a system. How can individuals who have lived their lives in such a different system be expected to have the will to face political instability by firing one in four individuals and emulating our system?

Family Life

Yet another challenge is the policy of one child per family, which has led to unprecedented abortion and infanticide of female children. The United Nations reports that the normal ratio of girl babies to boy babies is 115:100. In China it is 49:51. The demographic impact of this massive social "experiment" is difficult to comprehend.

As Chinese families move from the closed society of the Cultural Revolution to the global marketplace in a single bound, they are free to pluck whatever they wish from the consumerism shelf of the world without going through the 100 years of the industrial revolution that the West experienced. Preliminary Gallup polls in China indicate strong preferences for color TVs, washing machines, and VCRs. The automobile is a luxury, owned only by the state ministries, but within a decade or two aspirations will no doubt reach this level as well. In major cities such as Beijing and Shanghai, literally hundreds of high-rise structures are being built with minimal parking. When China turns away from the bicycle to the automobile, all these structures will be isolated from the then-preferred means of transport. Imagine also a nation of hundreds of millions of student drivers.

The key descriptive word in China today is change. Of course, China's social policies have embodied change throughout its history. I wonder how seriously the average citizen might take this sudden veer toward capitalism. Even with all the economic freedom, virtually every citizen is still the subject of a dossier that remains with them all their lives. They are not privy to the content until they require something of the central government or try to leave the country.

Some inquire as to the role of the church in China. On this visit the author saw far more use of the local Buddhist temples by worshippers than in previous visits. It is said that two or three new Christian churches are founded in China each week, and that Bible study is reducing rural illiteracy. My wife and I visited what appeared to be a thriving Christian church in Shanghai. Across the street was a former synagogue, turned into a state office, to which we were denied admission. It remains to be seen what role religion may play in influencing the major decisions that must be made in the immediate years ahead.

Revolving Door In and Out of China

A major choice for Chinese of influence today is to get rich or to help their people. Getting rich seems to be the current preference. We were told that all the rich and powerful Chinese want to get their children out of China and into a Western university. Ironically, at the same time, the overseas Chinese are stumbling all over themselves to get back inside China. Hence, $20 billion of overseas Chinese investment came back into the country last year.

Market Conditions

Office markets in Beijing and Shanghai are extraordinarily tight at present, with thousands of foreign firms seeking world-class office space where there is limited supply. Rentals are among the highest in the world, or as much as $100 a square foot per year. At present there are approximately 100 high-rise, mixed-use projects under construction in Beijing and almost 400 in Shanghai. In Shanghai, there will be about 40 million square feet of office space added in the next three to four years. Otis sold as many elevators in China in a month last year as it sold in the United States the entire year. Thus, there is classic overbuilding 1980s style against an imponderable market demand and office rentals will plummet to levels we cannot now predict; but they will go to at least one-third of their present level. As noted, the overbuilding is fueled by overseas Chinese money, international banking funds, and competing Chinese ministries. Likewise luxury style villas renting for $200,000 a year or selling for $500,000 and up are vastly overbuilt. They are a target of the Bank of China's credit restraint. In all the cities visited, we viewed half-completed hulks of such property. There appear to be at least ten retail megaprojects under construction or being planned in Beijing, including the infamous Li Kha Shing/McDonald's site. Some of them are several city blocks in size. All are bicycle- or street-accessed. One has to wonder if the overseas remittances, the foreign travelers, and the corruption payments will provide sufficient buying power to support these ventures.

The McDonald's Beijing site is a classic example of regulatory anarchy. All the land in the country is owned by the government. Most of it is granted land, which can be conveyed by the government. The rest is allocated land, which has been granted by the government to a state agency. In most cases, the agency itself cannot reconvey the land without government approval. McDonald's was on allocated land, and either did not know it or did nothing about it. Thus, the government felt justified in taking the land away from McDonald's and giving it to Li Kha Shing. What other arrangements may have been made, the author knoweth not.

There is a tremendous market for lower-class housing, running into the billions of square feet. The market for such housing today is the state ministries or businesses, which purchase such structures and then rent them to employees at a highly subsidized rate. This market is not quality or amenity conscious. One wonders how many U.S. developers would like to be pictured on the cover of their local Sunday supplement in front of their newly developed, South Bronx style seven-story walk-up. There is also a good market for industrial property and for all types of infrastructure.

The best market for a Western investor is a build-to-suit office or industrial property for a Western tenant who will pay rent in a hard currency and possibly put a year or two of rental payments up front as construction finance. These deals have been done, but the current overbuilding would seem to take away this market opportunity.

Construction costs come close to Western standards for high-rise buildings once all the indirect costs are figured in. A job requiring six architects in the United States may require 30 in Hong Kong and 300 in China. In some cases, construction workers appear to be dragooned off the farms, and they live in the building during the construction cycle. They have to be trained in all aspects of city life. Construction finishes are substandard by Western expectations.

Examples of Manufacturing and Market Successes in China

In a huge industrial tract outside Beijing, we visited the Motorola operation. They have doubled their original capacity in an attempt to keep up with the burgeoning market in China for cellular telephones. These sell for about $3,000 a copy, or ten months' wages. They cannot keep up with the market, which is mainly state enterprises and wealthy individuals. Of most import, Motorola has established programs to train and house its employees. A long-term Chinese employee of Motorola will own his own home. Training standards are the same as in any Western country where Motorola operates. Likewise for the Holiday Inn hotels I visited in Xiamen. The chain now has 54 hotels in China, runs a training university in Beijing, and continually trains its staff on site at each property. Holiday Inn opened in Xiamen with 44 middle managers, all expatriots; three years out, 75 percent of those jobs have been filled with local Chinese workers trained by the company.

If China makes the transition from within, it will be in large part due to the good work of Western companies making the kind of effort required to bring their employees as stakeholders into the market economy. Looking at our list of investment preconditions, we cannot determine from this analysis if those regarding database information and local management systems have been met. There are a large number of market participants, so you will not be alone; but it sure helps to be Chinese.

Property Investment

As already noted, one must be very careful about land transferability. Information is hard to come by, and locals will often give assurances that may not be true. The rule by man rather than by law makes legal certainty extremely difficult. Capital gains taxes may be levied ex post facto, if your speculative profits seem too high. A good hedge is to have a local partner. Yet, there have been cases where local partners collude with planning agencies as their proxy in negotiating what the local partner could not attain for himself.

Under current conditions of credit restraint, local finance is extremely difficult. Your project must be all equity, or it must stand up to the scrutiny of the international money and capital markets. As noted, a great deal of finance is from offshore-Chinese equity or prepaid rents or purchase options in hard currency.

Construction work is usually performed by huge state-owned construction companies with 50,000 or more employees, and there is much featherbedding and use of unskilled labor, which results in higher costs than one might anticipate. There will be no bidding process or critical path construction planning process.

Most foreign investors are drawn to Beijing or Shanghai. In Beijing, the acute shortage of top-grade office and residential space has resulted in high rental rates. In 1994, top-grade office rentals were about $90 per square foot annually, and top-grade residential rental rates were about $80 per square foot annually. As noted, a large number of office and residential projects are due to be completed in 1995 and 1996, which will make future rent levels problematic. Prime street-level retail rents are as much as $225 per square foot annually, with some 10 million square feet of retail due to be completed within the next three years. Beijing hotel occupancies are close to 80 percent, with average room rates in the five-star hotels around $170 per night.

Shanghai is little different, with perhaps a greater oversupply coming on the market. Street-level retail along Nanjing Road achieves annual rents between $130 and $250 per square foot annually. Residential property suitable for expatriate living would sell for between $150 and $300 per square foot. Presales of office space range between $180 and $350 per square foot, with about 30 million square feet coming on the market by the end of 1997.

Conclusion

It comes as no surprise that, in my opinion, most of the fundamental conditions for long-term investment are not fulfilled in China at the present time. So much for intellectual analysis. Why then did China receive one-third of the world's investment dollars last year? In part because of the offshore-Chinese affinity. Also, up until last year, it was still possible to receive a three-year investment payback on most major investments. Often the payback was in a hard currency as well.

The fact is that early investments in emerging economies are short-term investments. Discounted cash flow analysis is not appropriate. Money must come back in two or three or four years. Returns must run at 30 to 40 percent a year. Until the recent spate of overbuilding and the Bank of China negative reaction to speculation, China was a great place for short-term investment in real estate. Unfortunately, real estate is, by its nature, not a short-term asset. Liquidity must be provided by presales of office buildings, apartments, villas, and the like.

There should continue to be good investment opportunities in second-tier cities, particularly where a reliable Chinese partner is involved. Major U.S. pension funds may wish to place a small portion of their high-risk funds into Chinese real estate. A $30 billion fund might risk a couple of hundred million dollars against a 30 to 40 percent return.

As for me, while we were in Xiamen, S.L. Chen and I became proud grandfathers for the first time. My granddaughter's name is Katherine Yu-Ting Chen. I now have a long-term investment in China, and I love it.

Source: *Real Estate Issues*, August 1995.

10 Real Estate: Global or Local?

Why should whatever happens to the Thai baht affect the ability to finance local real estate?

Commercial real estate traditionally has been considered a local business, based upon locational characteristics and intimate knowledge of tenant needs. Transnational real estate investment in the 1980s, coupled with globalization of money and capital markets in the 1990s, has caused some to believe that commercial real estate is a fungible commodity that may be traded broadly, irrespective of local needs or characteristics.

Perhaps the leading query in our domestic markets is how much longer the longest sustained growth boom can continue without running into inflationary pressures. And there does appear to be a whiff of inflation in the air. Labor cost increases are disguised in part by bonus trips to Hawaii, annual cash bonus awards, stock options, and the like. Yet many localities are operating at under 3 percent unemployment, a statistic below traditional reckoning of frictional employment levels. The Federal Reserve Bank is practicing a balancing act between keeping interest rates low until the Asian crisis is resolved and moving to higher rates to avoid longer-term inflation. Most economists seem to be predicting good growth through the 2000 presidential election and a possible shallow slowdown the year following, caused in part by higher interest rates.

Meanwhile, the competition between public and private sources of capital continues. [See article 16.] Insurance companies and commercial banks continue to benefit from Wall Street's liquidity squeeze during the last half of 1998. Commercial banks remain aggressive on underwriting standards in selected cases. Insurance companies are aggressively marketing whole loans, syndicating such investments among two or three entities, and seeking to standardize mortgage documents.

In the public markets, real estate investment trusts (REITs) still represent a relatively small percentage of the commercial finance market. Although stock prices have moved up this year, large capital flows continue into Internet and media companies. REITs have become recognized as slow-growth vehicles, somewhat underleveraged from a real estate point of view. Commercial mortgage–backed securities (CMBSs) have not recovered to the values they represented a year ago. CMBS pricing spreads to ten-year Treasuries remain relatively high for each rating category, and especially high for the lower-rated tranches. The "bottom" pieces are priced at spreads to Treasuries roughly double those of a year ago.

Private equity in real estate continues to be aggressive. Private equity is priced differently than public equity because of the higher leverage tolerated and the perceived greater investment risk that is sought.

The phenomenon in U.S. capital markets that remains not fully understood is the link between domestic real estate capital pricing and the international capital markets. For instance, why should whatever happens to the Thai baht affect the ability to finance local real estate? It is a complex issue. Capital markets do not like surprises, and last year [1998] there were several of them in a row: in Russia, in Brazil, in Southeast Asia, and in New York and Connecticut, where Long-Term Capital Management, a large hedge fund, became illiquid. At such times of uncertainty, there is a flight to quality in the capital markets. Capital came out of emerging-markets debt, lower-grade corporate debt (junk bonds), and real estate debt, causing spreads to Treasuries to double virtually overnight.

Why is commercial real estate debt lumped with emerging third-world countries and junk bonds? It is because of the lack of transparency of real estate investment data, lack of solid comparable information, and lack of full disclosure. CMBS portfolios have not gone through a down cycle as yet. There is uncertainty as to how these portfolios will perform. What is a normalized ratio of past-due loans and delinquencies during a real estate recession? Who will collate and disseminate the data for these large portfolios? Who pays for such information? Will market makers for such securities stay around during a down cycle? Answers to these types of investor queries are not clear at the present time.

Real estate is still seen to be a local and a private business. The concomitant lack of transparency is also a deterring factor in U.S. pension funds making larger allocations to this asset class.

Turning to overseas markets, the Asian real estate problem has not been solved. There is an estimated $2 trillion of debt overhang in these markets. In the 1980s, the Japanese applied local valuation to global markets. The local valuations they used were, in effect, rigged prices, kept artificially high to keep the ruling party in power. The Japanese also took currency risks. In the 1990s, both the currency and the markets went against them. As a result of strong cultural preferences for not admitting mistakes and not acting decisively, little has been accomplished during the past eight years. In the United States, real estate problems were resolved in about five years. Windfalls and excessive gains were tolerated. Resolved real estate assets were estimated to amount to the equivalent of about 2 to 3 percent of one year's gross national product (GNP). A comparable figure for Japan is estimated at 18 to 20 percent. Moreover, the quality of unresolved Japanese real estate assets is poor. There also has been a criminal element identified with certain types of Japanese real estate assets. In 1998, Japan resolved $50 billion of real estate assets, or 4 percent of the estimated $1.2 trillion of bad paper outstanding.

In China, the potential is even worse. Many of the huge state-owned enterprises are effectively bankrupt. There is an excessive supply of high-rise office buildings. The state-owned banking system is filled with illiquid paper extended to state-owned enterprises and real estate projects. The state-owned banks are essentially financed by the savings of the country, including the huge peasant class. It is estimated that it will take as long as ten years to resolve the situation. If denied World Trade Organization membership and other international recognition, China may become even more insular. Along with this is the risk of devaluation of China's currency if the resolution of its economy becomes unsynchronized, resulting in still another Asian crisis.

Finally, there is the imponderability of a resolution to the problems in the Russian economy. Thus, one may easily predict further turmoil in the international capital markets from time to time. Real estate capital markets in the United States will suffer during such times of crisis, because real estate will continue to be viewed as immature and nontransparent. Private markets such as banks, insurance companies, pension funds, and private equity will benefit from such disruptions in the public markets.

Is real estate global or local? Essentially it is local and private, but financing costs are going to be driven by world events, among other factors. As a result, real estate is a local business in a global marketplace. A real estate owner/operator must think locally and act globally. Following are suggestions as to how to react to the increased complexities of the real estate capital markets.

- Have a long-term capital strategy, not the tactic of getting the cheapest capital available.
- Think locally about location, tenant needs and satisfaction, competition, and the like.
- Act globally in the sense of being able to interpret the impact of global events on financing costs and access to capital.
- Line up capital needs early.
- Have plenty of equity in your projects.
- Try to finance a couple of years ahead to prevent being in the capital markets at a time of crisis.
- Maintain good capital sources in both the public and private markets.
- Be certain that private capital financing sources themselves are not dependent on the public markets to lay off their own loans and investments.
- Be prepared to pay a premium, if necessary, for availability of capital.

No one anticipates, or even desires, a "perfect" market for real estate finance. That would take all the fun out of the game. But no one enjoys the capital crunches either, and—from time to time—they will be with us. Fasten your seat belts and enjoy the ride.

Source: *Urban Land* (Capital Markets column), October 1999.

11

The Withdrawal of Credit from Real Estate

Writing from his experience as chair of the second ULI Real Estate Credit Task Force but expressing his own—not necessarily the task force's—interpretation of the credit situation, the author explains why credit is not available for commercial real estate and suggests that the prospects for short-term remedies are dim.

The latest credit crunch is past. The capital market has a plentiful supply of credit available at attractive rates. It is just not available for commercial real estate. A number of factors contribute to this situation.

Overall, the real estate market has become exceedingly complex and confusing. It lacks essential information and predictability. It lacks an agreed-upon standard of value for its products. Often, arcane rules and procedures and practices within the financial industry militate against funding for real estate, and add to the confusion. This complexity—in conjunction with the usual plethora of rumor, hyperbole, and gossip—renders virtually impossible a coherent depiction of the current real estate market. Incoherence and complexity, along with market fundamentals, discourage the investment that could bring liquidity back to the industry.

Major Roadblocks

The major roadblocks to a return to liquidity in commercial real estate are listed in the following pages. Some of these concern the condition of the real estate market, some concern how the business of real estate is conducted (and perceived to be conducted), and some concern regulatory and institutional practices within the financial industry.

Oversupply. Although the oversupply factor is obvious, industry practitioners need to be reminded of it continually. When we blame the credit withdrawal on the regulators, the bankers, the accountants, the appraisers, and so forth, we are addressing the effects and not the causes of the problem.

The primary cause of credit withdrawal is too much product, which depresses rents, inflates vacancy rates, and thus ultimately undermines the ability of borrowers to service debt on income properties.

Lack of Statistically Relevant Demand Analysis. The investment capital system needs to be able to put a value on investment-grade real estate. But calculating value has become virtually impossible in certain markets. Practitioners, including ULI members, are unwilling to reveal true information on net effective market rents, building measurement comparables, and the like. Without true information on rents, valuation becomes impossible.

There are many other uncertainties in many markets. When and under what market circumstances will value be accorded to older, asbestos-ridden, technologically obsolete office buildings that now are worth less than the debt they are carrying? What will be the net effect of restructuring and downsizing in major office-using industries such as the financial industry? Will businesses be using more or less space per office worker? Lack of good demand information keeps large liquid asset pools, such as pension funds and foreign investors, out of the real estate investment market.

Development Professionalism. Major financial institutions perceive a lack of professionalism and self-discipline on the part of developers. Admitting the reality of the marketplace, developers have downsized by 50 to 90 percent and have created sharply altered business plans. Historically, such discipline has been lacking in the development business. Some observers point the finger of blame at Congress for having legislated, in the 1980s, very favorable tax incentives for investment in real estate—a specious argument in my view. To reestablish institutional confidence, the development industry must demonstrate the professionalism to develop to demand rather than to financial availability.

Lack of Confidence. Some serious-minded people—many are politicians—believe the whole problem is an "attitude thing." If we could somehow engender consumer confidence, everyone would go out and rent additional office space and occupy hotel rooms. While this view contains an element of truth, the market's structural problems are so severe that the fundamentals must change before any change in attitude can reasonably occur.

Investor confidence is what needs propping up. To restore that confidence, substantially all outstanding real estate debt and equity must be repriced to reflect market realities.

Related to the attitude problem (and contributing to it) is the tendency to consider real estate as all the same—and currently, all bad. Industry practitioners are as guilty of thinking this way as anyone. Investors should not lump together real estate assets and real estate operating companies. There are good real estate assets as well as bad. The story on well-located, well-tenanted properties also needs to be told, in this time of so much bad news on the real estate front.

Bank Reserve Requirements. Risk-based capital rules effective March 1989 per the Basel Accord with the Bank for International Settlements require banks to reserve 8 percent of capital on loans to businesses. No capital reserve is required against Treasury bills. Prior to the new rules, banks were required to hold 6 percent capital reserves against both Treasury bills and business loans.

However, it simply is not true, as has been thought, that these reserve requirements have curtailed the capacity of banks to lend. Bank loans have not been keeping pace with growing bank assets, while bank holdings of U.S. government securities have outpaced growth in assets. In early 1992, U.S. government securities constituted 16.3 percent of total bank assets, up 51 percent from 10.8 percent at year-end 1985. Had business loans kept pace with assets, they would have grown $26 billion instead of falling $24 billion between January 1991 and January 1992.

In light of this $50 billion gap in business lending in 1991, banks are quite liquid at present. Federal Deposit Insurance Corporation data indicate that, as of January 1, 1992, 97.4 percent of U.S. banks are complying with the 8 percent equity capital rule and that the banking system as a whole has about $33 billion of equity in excess of the required capital. That banks lack capital is fiction. We must look elsewhere for the cause of credit shortages.

Credit-Rating Concerns of Financial Institutions. Real estate exposure in this time of oversupply, diminished values, and unreliable data does not serve well the credit-rating concerns that financial institutions may have.

Banks and insurance companies may wish to issue commercial paper or medium- to longer-term debt instruments to fund their asset acquisitions. Rating agencies such as Moody's and Standard & Poor's rank the creditworthiness of such financial institutions on a relative basis. Those with relatively higher percentages of real estate mortgages and equities are accorded relatively lower credit ratings. Thus, real estate exposure can increase the cost of funds and limit the availability of funding even for large financial institutions.

Likewise, institutions may wish to issue common stock, and the higher the value of these securities the less the cost of raising equity. In such cases, the security analysts are the arbiters of values. They too are disenchanted with holdings of commercial real estate. Senior officers of certain large commercial banks have indicated that reducing real estate from 25 percent to less than 10 percent of assets could result in a doubling of the common stock price.

Financial Institutions' Accounting for Real Estate. It is merely a matter of time until all financial institutions practice mark-to-market accounting, as investment banks—and commercial banks for certain financial assets—now do. For reporting purposes, insurance companies do not practice mark-to-market accounting, but many use internal management information systems that provide mark-to-market data. Pension funds, on balance, avoid real estate as an asset class because they cannot mark it to market on a periodic basis and thus integrate it into their capital asset pricing models.

The issue, then, is when and how mark-to-market accounting for real estate assets will be adopted. Adopting it overnight in this depressed market would seriously deplete the resources of certain commercial banks and insurance companies. At this time [1992], it would seem wise for the regulators of banks and insurance companies to continue the current practice of periodic review of past due loans and periodic write-down of delinquent loans, while the earnings and reserves of institutions are bolstered over time by low interest rates. This approach—similar to how the less developed countries' debt burden was handled—does not seem to impair the liquidity of the banking system.

Pressure from the Securities and Exchange Commission, the Financial Accounting Standards Board, and security and credit analysts will result in mark-to-market accounting being required for institutional real estate assets at some time in the future. Until that time, the market will continue to be confused by the apples and oranges accounting practices of different financial institutions.

RTC Sales. The potentially adverse impact on property values of the Resolution Trust Corporation's aggressive sales of real estate and real estate mortgage loans has been of such concern to ULI members that ULI president Jim Klingbeil appointed a task force, under the leadership of Ron Nahas, to study the matter.

Finding in a case study of apartment and office sales in Dallas that the RTC program's contribution to changes in property value cannot be isolated from the many factors that are driving down value, the task force has reported that it is not possible to conclude definitively that the RTC disposition program has driven prices down more than they would have gone had the agency not sold the properties. In any case, as the RTC task force recognizes, RTC has been a significant player in only a few areas.

Appraisal Practices. Blaming real estate credit problems on the appraisal community is like blaming AIDS on the Surgeon General. That is not to say, however, that appraisal practices are not making the problem worse.

Appraisers are under considerable pressure to be conservative in their estimates of value. Thus, for example, they apply RTC liquidation sale prices of third-tier properties (the only available "comparables") in establishing book write-off values on second- or first-tier properties with delinquent loans. Or they use lengthy lease-up periods, low rents, and high expenses in their discounted cash flow models for income property and then add 200 to 300 basis points to the investment rate at which such property trades for today. Under today's conservative appraisal assumptions, a building with credit leases may be valued at a distressed sale capitalization rate.

Often, the problem is one of communicating the goal of the appraisal. Does the sponsoring entity want an appraisal that indicates the property's "liquidity" value in a depressed market? or its "normalized" value? or its "intrinsic" value? or some other value? Lack of agreement on what constitutes the basis for these various "values" confounds the issue.

Financial institutions, investors, and regulators all express growing dissatisfaction with the results of appraisal techniques under current market conditions. Not only do these techniques presume normal market conditions, but they also depend on unreliable data. Inadequate data on lease rates and on the supply of and demand for space, coupled with the increased complexity of lease—primary and sublease—transactions, limits the capacity of appraisers to estimate "value" closely.

Lack of confidence in the appraisal process is another reason that institutional investors are staying out of the commercial real estate market. The valuation problem is a serious one. The Real Estate Credit Task Force has made it a priority issue for its continuing work.

Remedies That Have Been Proposed

Some steps can be taken to ease the flow of credit to commercial real estate, but little can be accomplished until the market itself stabilizes.

Financing Solutions. Vulture funds, some small local financial institutions, REITs, and public offerings represent pockets of liquidity and investment interest.

Thus far, REITs have not been issued in the volumes predicted. Moreover, the taxation rules under which REITs operate implicitly assume that real estate is a passive investment, a concept that, in my opinion, is not appropriate under current market conditions.

Securitization, likewise, is a problematic solution. It is a concept that works extremely well for a broad asset class boasting a well-seasoned and reliable database of experience. Thus, it works for housing, but not as well for idiosyncratic commercial properties. When credit enhancement is available, securitization provides a means of broadening the investment market and thus lowering the cost of financing for a commercial property—a property that could probably be financed (at higher real estate rates) in the first place. Securitization is unlikely to make much of a dent in the large volume of commercial mortgages that must be repriced over the next few years.

The hard truth is that traditional real estate financing institutions—commercial banks, insurance companies, savings and loans, and pension funds—are (or want to be) out of the market. Marginal sources provide incidental help. But until these major sources regain confidence, there will not be enough capital to refinance the real estate debt coming due.

Forbearance. Forbearance—the relaxation of certain regulations or regulatory practices that diminish the ability of institutions to invest in real estate—is political suicide in the wake of FIRREA [the Financial Institutions Reform, Recovery, and Enforcement Act of 1989], the RTC, and the Keating Five. Although there has been much discussion of regulatory forbearance—by the ULI Real Estate Credit Task Force, among others—there is little likelihood that Congress will take any action that may be perceived as bailing out the real estate industry once again.

In 1991, the four federal bank and thrift regulatory agencies took steps to address the treatment of real estate loans and to support the renewal or extension of bank real estate loans under appropriate circumstances. Nevertheless, new war stories about roadblocks encountered in the bank regulatory process continue to surface.

Some people have suggested that the risk-based capital rules be relaxed to make it easier for banks to invest in real estate. But as the previously cited data on bank reserves indicate, such a step is not warranted. In fact, rather than the rules being relaxed, the opposite is occurring: The Federal Reserve is currently promulgating new risk-based capital rules for banks that would make real estate lending even more difficult. And the National Association of Insurance Commissioners is reviewing risk-based capital rules for the life insurance industry. Forbearance on these proposed new rules would be constructive.

In some respects, the Federal Reserve Bank's push for maintaining lower interest rates is a forbearance strategy. It has allowed commercial banks to finance more cheaply and to widen their spreads on consumer lending and other activities, and thus to build up their profits and create reserve capacity to absorb real estate write-offs.

Tax Code Changes. Any number of fairly minor and technical changes in the tax code have been proposed to add liquidity to the real estate market. REIT rules could be relaxed to allow investors to be more active and therefore more diligent, as well as to make it easier for pension funds to use the REIT format. If allowed to invest in taxable partnerships and use investment vehicles providing contingent interest or sale-leasebacks or participating mortgages, pension funds could be more active investors.

The foreclosure process could become somewhat less painful if phantom income recognition were deferred or if passive losses could be deducted against all income. A concerted effort to ease these tax barriers could assist in clearing the market of fore-closed properties and attracting new investment flows into real estate.

Other Public Policy Steps. Only if the real estate debt burden threatened a massive banking failure would Congress consider bailing out the real estate industry. It looks as if this debt burden, cushioned by higher bank earnings, will be absorbed over a multiyear period, preventing such a crisis.

The most we can hope for from public policy is the Federal Reserve Bank's continuing support of the overall liquidity of the banking system and continuing intra-agency attempts to smooth out the regulatory process and thus facilitate real estate write-downs.

This long-term approach primarily addresses the welfare of the banking system. It does not really help to increase the capital market's allocation of capital to real estate other than by reducing the burden of distressed real estate.

Other constructive measures within the realm of public policy include continuing regulatory support for the renewal and extension of real estate loans; a clearer and more realistic definition of appraisal standards; and cessation by the General Services Administration of office construction in favor of leasing or buying existing inventory at good value to house government workers.

One real estate financing area for which public policy initiatives and regulatory forbearance would appear to be indicated is in financing for the acquisition and development of lots for housing, to prevent a critical housing shortage from dragging down economic growth rates as the economy recovers.

How Long Will the Downturn Last?

In predicting time to recovery, it is tempting to fall into the trap of treating real estate as a single aggregated commodity. But, obviously, all real estate will not recover at one time, nor indeed is all real estate in trouble. Nonetheless the battle-weary slogan, "Stay Alive 'til '95" may be meaningful. In three years, commercial real estate will have endured a six-year downtime—long enough to cure many ills.

Logically, the problem needs at least three more years to work out. Approximately $340 billion of commercial mortgage debt must be renewed, reworked, or foreclosed by banks and insurance companies over the next two years. William B. Brueggeman, writing for Goldman Sachs, estimates that $185 billion of mortgage loans held by institutions must be repriced. Some industry practitioners estimate that realized losses on foreclosed property are running at 40 to 50 percent of initial valuations.

Some commentators think the crisis will last significantly longer, at least for certain classes of real estate. David Schulman of Salomon Brothers testifies that his firm's recent 50-city survey found evidence of a 12-year supply of office space. A recent survey by Price Waterhouse leads to the conclusion that office activity will not pick up for five or more years. The survey indicates that a renewal of retail activity needs three years, while industrial and housing activity will pick up within one year. Estimates of recovery in the hotel sector contemplate even longer time periods.

It took the relative values of common stock almost a third of a century to shake off the 1929–1933 catastrophe. The six-year credit crunch for real estate may be expected to have a similarly long-term resonance.

The period of retrenchment, renegotiation, restructuring, and failure will last for at least another three years. Next, we may expect to see a period of caution, conservatism, and debt aversion. Underwriting standards will be tougher. Major capital pools will reenter the market for new investments with extreme caution. Real estate capital will be repriced to account for perceived greater risks and for the higher cost implicit in risk-based capital.

Development will become more institutional. Development companies will be expected to be professionally managed, with sound company and project business plans, audited financial statements, and rigorous demand analysis.

After balance is restored to the commercial real estate market and the necessary repricing has occurred, commercial banks will no doubt come back into the market. But risk-based capital rules will likely keep them from the real estate lending excesses of the 1970s and 1980s. Many industry practitioners have often enough heard the banks declare loudly: "Never again"—only to thereafter embark on another lending binge. This time, however, the rules and the cost of capital have changed so fundamentally, and the pain has been so long and so deep, that the postrecovery conservatism is bound to last beyond the turn of the century.

Source: *Urban Land*, September 1992.

12 The Creative Destruction of Real Estate Capital Markets

Arising out of the destruction of real estate capital markets over the last four years are new market forms that may reduce the costs of real estate capital, if industry practitioners can solve some ongoing problems.

When I first went to Wall Street in the early 1960s, many senior corporate executives still carried with them an aversion to debt, an aversion they had developed during the economic depression of more than 30 years previous. Indeed, it took the publication of a book by Harvard Business School professor Gordon Donaldson, *Corporate Debt Capacity* (Harvard Business School Press, Boston, 1967), to reawaken corporate America to the positive characteristics of financial leverage. By the end of the 1980s, Donaldson's message had been broadly received.

This tendency to remember long-term lessons is part of what makes "long-wave" societal and economic behavioral patterns. Such patterns have been identified by economists and social scientists from Serge Kondratieff and Friedrich Hegel and Karl Marx to, in our day, historian Arthur Schlesinger Jr. and M.I.T economist Jay Forrester, who traces fundamental economic forces through history over 50- to 60-year cycles. In the 1930s, economist Joseph Schumpeter theorized about the "creative destruction" of capitalism, an idea that Michael Jensen, currently a Harvard Business School professor, applies to his analysis of the positive regenerative effects of leveraged buyouts and corporate restructuring.

My point in mentioning long-wave theories is to introduce the view that the period from 1990 to 1994 has ushered in a long-wave structural change in real estate financial markets. As a result of the destructive forces prevailing in this period, individuals involved with real estate financial institutions in the United States and Japan, in particular, have made radical changes in their business behavior that will last for the balance of their careers, far beyond the millennium. Their attitudes toward financial leverage, aggressive financial projections, megaprojects, developer profits, and related issues are resulting in the creative destruction and restructuring of real estate financial markets.

This will happen despite much peripheral noise in the marketplace from the financial press and others anxious to restart the real estate bandwagon. Articles encouraging real estate investment have appeared in the *Wall Street Journal*, *Barron's*, and *Fortune*. Many new real estate offerings for pension funds are in the market. Barton Biggs, Morgan Stanley's investment guru, has suggested that institutions might allocate up to 15 percent of their assets to real estate. Thus, even though banks and insurance companies hold billions of dollars of unresolved real estate assets, new and evolving investment funds are again beginning to push returns on newly acquired property to levels that current cash flows cannot support. This "noise" misreads the current conditions of real estate finance in commercial banks and insurance companies and on Wall Street. Commercial banks or insurance companies account for about half of all commercial real estate loans and investments. Until their real estate holdings conform to the demands of market arbiters and until new forms of real estate financing have been created, they will be essentially out of the market.

Commercial Banks

For banks, the key constraint on funding is not government regulation but access to the capital markets. Banks need to obtain funding at a cost that provides a competitive spread on their transactions. The more profitable the spread, the better the compensation, the better the ability to recruit high-powered managers, and the lower the cost of equity capital.

For debt capital, the higher the credit rating a bank gets from traditional bond-rating agencies such as Moody's and Standard & Poor's, the lower the cost of debt. And the rating agencies do not like real estate. Thus, the less real estate (and the less bad real estate), the cheaper the enterprise's funding cost.

Wall Street security analysts likewise have an aversion to real estate, which serves to augment its negative impact on stock prices and cost of capital. Stock and bond analysts have been as instrumental as government agencies in imposing mark-to-market accounting on commercial banks.

Risk-based capital rules requiring banks to carry an 8 percent reserve against commercial and industrial loans, while requiring no reserve for U.S. government bonds, have moved banks out of real estate and small business loans into government bonds in the past four years. It costs them virtually nothing to invest in Treasuries with low short-term interest rates, while it costs them 125 to 150 basis points to underwrite and reserve against real estate loans. Their loading up on Treasuries has produced the second-highest bank earnings in history. These earnings have been crucial in rebuilding bank reserves after real estate write-offs.

The U.S. Treasury has a keen interest in keeping banks as holders of government debt. Over 20 years, the marginal buyer of Treasuries has moved from the Middle East to Japan to U.S. banks. Should banks start selling Treasuries, the bonds would have to offer higher interest rates to attract a new class of marginal buyer. It has even been suggested that if banks start dumping Treasuries, federal regulators may raise the required capital cushion against commercial and industrial loans from 8 percent to 10 or 12 percent.

The possibility of further federal regulatory actions—for example, the application of risk-based capital rules to off-balance-sheet derivative securities transactions; rulemaking concerning the social investment goals of banks; and forthcoming decisions on several pending large bank consolidations—helps persuade bankers to favor Treasury securities over commercial and industrial loans.

At the same time, more farsighted bankers are beginning to imagine what new forms of instruments might be needed to bring them back into real estate financial markets. A few banks are cautiously reentering the real estate debt market—offering 75 percent loan to value (value figured conservatively) on recourse loans that include corporate style security covenants, and 50 percent or less loan to value on nonrecourse loans.

Japanese banks have all the same problems of capital access, funding, and rating agencies. Only recently has the Japanese banking system appeared prepared to face up to its real estate financial problems.

Insurance Companies

Insurance companies, generally speaking, are confronting the same array of problems as commercial banks, although two to three years later in the cycle. They are less likely to use the capital markets to fund their loans and investments, but when they do they encounter the same rating agency and mark-to-market constraints. If they happen to be publicly traded, their common stock is subject to the same scrutiny.

Insurance companies finance most of their transactions through the sale of financial products to consumers. Today's products produce funding with fairly short maturities, and the pressure for investment performance is high. Insurance companies are hurting from the movement away from group retirement plans to individually managed 401(k) IRAs, which tend to invest directly in mutual funds.

Fitch Ratings, A.M. Best, and other companies rate the investment quality of insurance companies for the consumers of insurance products. Higher ratings will, in theory, attract more customers. To obtain higher ratings, the insurance companies must lighten up on their real estate holdings.

And like banks, insurance companies face risk-based capital requirements, which are imposed by the National Association of Insurance Commissioners, a professional association of state insurance regulators (see "Real Estate Investment by Insurance Companies," *Urban Land*, March 1994). U.S. government bonds require no capital reserve; bonds rated A and higher require 0.3 percent; foreclosed property and delinquent commercial mortgages require 15 percent; and commercial mortgages in foreclosure, joint ventures, and limited partnerships require 20 percent. Reserves for the ten largest assets must be doubled. These requirements ring the death knell for insurance company joint ventures on single large projects.

A recent ruling by the U.S. Supreme Court that Employee Retirement Income Security Act (ERISA) rules apply to assets held in insurance company general accounts also adds to the woes of insurance companies. Among other things, this means that a tenant leasing more than 10 percent of a building owned by an insurance company becomes "a party of interest" in that investment.

The most obvious way out for insurance companies is the intermediation of their real estate assets through securitization. They can sell off concentrated holdings and buy back through syndicates only securities that hold an A or better rating. This will create unprecedented demand for commercial real estate syndication and necessitate finding whole new markets for those tranches of real estate assets no longer deemed suitable for investment by insurance companies.

Outside of special-purpose separate account funds, insurance companies are unlikely to seek nonconforming real estate loans or investments while the intermediation process takes form.

Wall Street

The nonconforming commercial real estate assets of banks and insurance companies thus offer Wall Street an unprecedented opportunity. The market for commercial real estate securitization is relatively undeveloped to date, with the bulk of the transactions having come from the Resolution Trust Corporation. Wall Street brings a trading mentality to real estate and is, generally, unwilling to commit the time or resources needed for adequate due diligence and testing procedures. This factor in turn opens up an opportunity for a new class of real estate practitioners, most likely public accounting firms.

Wall Street can participate in the commercial real estate finance process in a number of areas:

REITs. The $550 billion of commercial real estate assets held by banks and insurance companies dwarfs the $14 billion that REITs raised in 1993. REITs are yield-driven instruments. Investors look for roughly 8 percent current return and 12 percent overall return. The attractiveness of the current return that REITs offer is vulnerable in the long term to a rise in interest rates and the growth of more liquid money-market funds. Their appreciation and growth component is also threatened by competition from other REITs and investors bidding up prices of existing properties.

Although the quality of property held by today's REITs is far more attractive than that held in the last REIT cycle, REITs remain an awkward vehicle for owning real estate. The tax laws impose a degree of passivity on REITs that is not appropriate to real estate ownership and operation. Over their investment cycle, REITs favor dividend maintenance and growth over capital replacements and renewals. They are forced to pay out such a large percentage of cash flow as dividends that they cannot accumulate reserves for property enhancement. It is not likely that REITs will be the panacea of the real estate capital market.

Opportunity Funds. Opportunity funds have amassed several billion dollars of buying power from pension funds and wealthy individuals to take advantage of anomalies in market valuation in the wake of the sudden departure of traditional financial sources from the real estate market. In the last four years, returns of 30 percent a year were not uncommon. But the wholesale dumping of property by the federal government and financial institutions is about over, though Japanese banks may continue to engage in it. Owners are pricing portfolios much tighter and bidders are becoming more numerous. There is less spread among the bids. A prospective bidder can spend hundreds of hours and several hundred thousand dollars in due diligence, only to come up with a dry hole.

Many opportunity funds add significant value to properties by applying sound operating techniques and remedying previous neglect. Their spreads and returns are bound to narrow, but the funds will continue to be a good vehicle for owning and managing securitized property and investing in the riskier, nonrated tranches of real estate securities.

Mutual Funds. Mutual funds have burgeoned as they chase markets and yields around the world. Lower-quality, high-yield money-market mutual funds have been attracting individually managed IRA pools, and these funds are an obvious market for the riskiest layer, the so-called Z tranche, of securitized commercial real estate product.

Securitization. It appears that Wall Street will enjoy a unique opportunity to recycle bank and insurance company restructured securities, requiring as high as 20 to 30 percent risk-based reserves, into assets needing only 0.3 percent reserves. The recycling apparatus will be a massive securitization process. As much cash flow as required will be dedicated to a top investment tranche, which will be rated A or better and sold back in pieces to syndicates of banks and insurance companies. The bottom tranche will be sold to opportunity funds, higher-risk mutual funds, and other risk-oriented investors, including some pension funds.

The only limit to the size of this market is the appetite of the investment community for the Z tranche. Both packager and purchaser likely will misunderstand the investment characteristics of the Z tranche, which will at times be mispriced and thus produce both windfalls and large losses for the investors. Not to worry, however. The creative destruction of the current cycle will not have to be dealt with until the next cycle.

An act pending in Congress would stimulate commercial securitization. The Commercial Mortgage Capital Availability Act would expand residential secondary mortgage market provisions to commercial real estate conduits. It would:
- extend SEC shelf registration provisions to commercial mortgage conduits;
- exempt such conduits from ERISA; and
- allow banks to base their 8 percent, risk-based reserves on the participations they retain in commercial loans instead of on the entire principal of the loans.

The prediction of one prominent syndicator of real estate that commercial real estate syndication will grow to $1 trillion by 2000 appears exaggerated. Such an outcome would solve the real estate problems of financial institutions around the world. In any case, this market should grow rapidly in the next five years.

A major drawback in securitization is that the farther investment in real estate is removed from the potential for active and aggressive management, the more problematic the investment outcomes. Wall Street tends to avoid initial due diligence and, even more so, ongoing operating responsibility by relying on conservative debt ratios, corporate style covenants, and diversity in packaging. Growth in securitization will provide opportunities for purveyors of due-diligence services and individuals able to manage large pools of assets.

The Creative Part of Destruction

As the destructive slope of the current real estate cycle begins to flatten out, it is time to address some ongoing issues in order to define the future of real estate capital markets.

Valuation. It is extraordinarily difficult to value real estate under present market conditions. In some CBDs, the calculation of true net effective rents is close to impossible to perform because data are not disclosed on free rent, tenant improvement contributions, give-backs, and other payments or concessions; and we lack data on the overhang of sublet space. Thus, to predict the time required to retenant a project becomes extremely difficult. Original cost and replacement cost are meaningless benchmarks.

As securitization progresses, properties will trade on statistical assumptions regarding rent that will produce windfalls and losses—further demoralizing the market. Appraisals can be as delinked from values in the present demoralized market as they were in the speculative boom of the 1980s. To attract broader and deeper market participations to the real estate capital markets, we must be able to provide more reliable appraisals of commercial real estate. Pension funds, for example, remain relatively underinvested in real estate. Although they find it appealing as an asset class, pension fund managers remain dubious about real estate because of the unrealistic reporting and valuations they witnessed at the beginning of the real estate collapse of 1990–1991.

Reliable Databases. Standardized, nonproprietary information on rents, sale prices, supply, and changes in occupancy is needed to underpin the growth in securitization. A disinterested party should collect and disseminate data.

Several industry associations, including the Urban Land Institute, are looking into the feasibility of producing a statistically reliable rental index for key markets throughout the United States and for the country as a whole. For the first time, some major financial institutions—banks, insurance companies, and pension funds—have indicated their interest in sharing their real estate data.

Reliable data can help bring large financial institutions back into the real estate capital markets. Securitization in a statistically reliable market offers these institutions the liquidity they need for trading their positions.

Looking ahead, one might even contemplate the arrival of derivative real estate securities that would allow investors to buy a basket of options on particular geographic markets or property types, going long or short at any particular time.

We need reliable data to better forecast real estate cycles. Better data will bring more players into the market and lower the premium for real estate capital. Then, all real estate practitioners will share in the challenge of creating the real estate capital markets of the future.

Source: *Urban Land*, June 1994.

13

Commercial Real Estate Finance Trends

Required over the next five years will be intelligence, creativity, the willingness to invest in management information systems, and longer-term relationships based on trust.

Over the next five years [starting mid-1997], economic conditions most likely will normalize with a growth rate of 2.5 percent a year, calculated as an average annual growth in population of 1 percent and an average annual growth in productivity of 1.5 percent. Because of globalization, the transfer of manufacturing to lower-cost producers, and corporate downsizing, inflation should not be a factor over this period. No five-year projection ever includes a recession, yet one is likely in this time frame. In any event, such a slowdown in the economy should have far less impact on real estate than usual. The excesses of the late 1980s will have been worked out, and significant overbuilding should not yet have occurred.

Service businesses will no doubt remain sluggish in terms of ultimate productivity. Shortages of skilled labor will occur in such sectors as airframe production, software engineering, chip manufacturing, and the like. The government deficit and especially entitlements will remain major issues throughout this period. Interest rates should remain historically high because of the global demand for capital. Once again, speculative building of products such as industrial facilities, hotels, suburban office space, and apartments will be underway.

Longer-Cycle Impacts

Even a five-year time frame fails to take true long-term trends into account. It may be useful therefore to review briefly certain factors that may ultimately play a major role in the pricing and availability of real estate capital.

"Unconventional" retail sales (through catalogs, home shopping, the Internet) today have replaced about 110 regional malls. The average fully occupied office floor is 25 percent vacant at all times. Hoteling and personal data and communication packages will cause office use to become far more efficient. A 6 to 10 percent adaptive use and efficiency gain on the $3.3 trillion of commercial real estate in place could produce a dividend of several hundred million dollars. Despite such opportunities, significant quantities of retail and Class B and Class C office buildings must be completely reconfigured.

The securitization of commercial real estate is being held back chiefly by lack of better and more available data. When such data become available, as they will, there will be easier valuation, greater trust in the secondary-market pricing of securities, and even greater recycling of assets among financial institutions. Synthetic securities will allow both short- and long-term investment in various property types and geographic markets, as well as in the real estate market as a whole.

The continued globalization of money and capital markets will provide immense opportunities for investment capital.

The computer will further drive deinstitutionalization of investment capital. Insurance companies must totally reposition their balance sheets, as defined contribution and 401(k) self-administered pension plans continue to gain momentum. There will be public market access to real estate debt and equity through real estate mutual funds and worldwide trading over the Internet.

Demographics will drive the intragenerational transfer of hundreds of billions of dollars of post–World War II wealth. Retirees will hold a greater percentage of the nation's invested wealth, and their preferences will change patterns of retailing, entertainment, and the like.

At some point it would seem that inflation will become a factor in the face of potential shortages of commodities, agricultural products, oil and gas, and highly skilled human capital.

Clearly, issues such as capital gains tax reduction, indexing of capital gains, or reinvestment rollover provisions (free of capital gains tax) could have a major impact on the liquidity of the real estate capital markets.

State of the Capital Markets

When analyzing the probable reaction of individual players in the capital markets, it is useful to look at the flow of funds through each of the major types of financial institutions. What is the nature of the institution's liabilities? How is it funded? To what regulatory pressures is it subject? What do security analysts and bond-rating agencies take into consideration when evaluating its debt or equity securities? How does it make money? For what behavior are its senior executives likely to be rewarded? How can financial offerings be designed to help solve its internal problems and meet its objectives?

Commercial Banks

In recent years, commercial banks have moved into spread pricing of funds at a premium over their cost of capital. Such a spread should account for the cost of underwriting the loan as well as the inherent risk that the loan may be delayed in repayment or go into default. Risk-based capital rules force banks to allocate more higher-cost equity capital to real estate than they do, for example, to government bonds. Mark-to-market accounting (which may spread over the five-year period to "off balance sheet" derivatives and hedges) further increases the amount of higher-cost capital a bank must carry. Third-party market arbiters such as bond-rating agencies and Wall Street security analysts put further pressure on banks to sustain a fairly high rate of return on equity capital. As a result of all these pressures, many banks have become intermediaries themselves, packaging portfolios of real estate investments to sell at a spread or a fee to smaller banks or other financial institutions. Other banks have substantively withdrawn from real estate business as a result of their losses in the early 1990s.

Banks will continue to be a major player in the real estate finance business. The issue is whether they can resist competitive pressures to lower underwriting standards. At present, loan-to-value ratios remain conservative, with significant equity and pre-leasing required. Other types of underwriting standards are beginning to slip, however, such as tenant improvement allowances, the number of months required to re-rent space, rent "spikes," and the like. As the real estate cycle stabilizes and new construction gains in volume, it is likely that lending spreads will continue to deteriorate and that underwriting standards will weaken. The commercial banks will, no doubt, once again be the engine that drives new real estate construction. A new generation of construction loan technicians will have to be trained, and on-the-job training in this field tends to be costly. Probably fewer banks than ever will engage in this process. Several large money center banks will be in real estate only to package and resell securitized products to others.

Insurance Companies

Insurance companies were the perfect long-term lender for real estate when their liabilities consisted of 20- and 30-year-pay, whole-life insurance policies. Now that their liabilities are term insurance and a range of other short-term products, they can no longer survive as long-term investors. In addition, insurance companies have been subject in recent years to rigorous risk-based capital rules that harshly penalize their traditional real estate investments. The joint venture financing of a large single asset in a partnership with a major developer would now be subject to a 30 percent capital hit under the new rules, whereas a high-grade bond would have a capital hit of 0.3 percent. Thus, many traditional real estate investors, including Aetna, Prudential, and Travelers, are drastically shrinking their real estate portfolios.

Pension fund separate account real estate investments remain a potential source of long-term capital for insurance companies to invest, although one may question the willingness of pension funds to commit their capital to an insurance company that has retreated from the real estate business for its own account. Securitization also remains a major commitment of insurance companies. They are recycling their old portfolios through Wall Street and buying back the investment-grade "top" pieces, which offer augmented liquidity and have a nominal capital requirement. Several insurance companies, such as Northwestern Mutual and Teachers' Insurance, have remained strong participants in real estate investment, so it is difficult to characterize the entire industry. It is safe to predict, however, a greatly diminished capacity to serve the real estate industry with the traditional forms of capital. Real estate investment will become less a principal business and more an agency business, as insurance companies intermediate the investment funds of others.

Real Estate Investment Trusts

REITs have played a powerful role in the recapitalization and re-equitizing of many important real estate businesses; consequently, the current generation of REITs benefits from property holdings that are much higher grade than was the case in the 1970s. In addition, for the most part, current REITs are less leveraged. Indeed, about 20 percent of current REITs enjoy investment-grade bond ratings on their debt. Taking these real estate assets into the public market has created cheaper capital and a much better public flow of information than was the case when these properties were held privately.

However, certain generic questions remain concerning the structure of REITs. Is there such a thing as passive real estate? Is something not lost when the ultimate investor is so removed from the properties themselves? How do REITs provide the growth that Wall Street calls for as acquisition properties revert to replacement or greater-than-replacement cost? REITs cannot retain significant capital due to the tax laws and investor preferences for a high dividend payout. Can the properties support a continually growing dividend payout throughout the real estate cycle? Where do funds come from to provide necessary property replacements and renewals? After the third or fourth year, there is mounting pressure on REIT trustees to trade off between required capital expenditures and dividend payouts.

Over the next five years there will be growing consolidations among REITs. One requirement for an investment-grade bond rating is a significant capital base. Questions also will be raised about the tradeoff between low leverage and an investment-grade rating and the higher leverage that is more traditional for real estate assets. Mounting pressures to pay dividends and investor dissatisfaction with slow growth and relatively lower investment yields will cause REIT values to trail the market in general. This in turn will produce situations in which real estate shares are trading at a significant discount to the inherent underlying real estate value, thus causing firms to de-REIT, liquidate, or go private.

Commercial Mortgage–Backed Securities

The CMBS market has grown rapidly in part because of the requirement for commercial banks and insurance companies to hold investment-grade real estate securities in order to benefit from the lowest requirement for risk-based capital. The process reallocates cash flows from large single assets or portfolios of properties so that the investment-grade "top piece" enjoys healthier cash flow support and the more speculative "bottom piece" becomes riskier and more volatile. The market for top pieces is virtually unlimited, although a limiting factor is the investment community's appetite for bottom pieces, mispricing of which is not uncommon and with which both buyer and seller can anticipate unpredictable windfall gains or losses.

CMBS pricing is following the same path followed by highly leveraged "junk" corporate debt in the 1980s. CMBS spreads began quite high and then narrowed considerably, falling below spreads charged on comparable debt by banks and insurance companies as investors became more comfortable with the characteristics of the security. The investment market then broadened.

There is at present perhaps an illusion of liquidity, as market makers in the secondary market are few and limited principally to the original issuing house. Other factors inhibiting the growth of this market are the lack of ongoing reliable data to support secondary trading and the issue of who pays for such data. Once these problems are resolved, as in the case of REITs, there will be much more data available for CMBS assets in the public market than was the case when they were privately held. That in itself should add validity to the market.

It is likely over the next five years that there will be unanticipated gains and losses from these securities, especially during the next down cycle. The major requirements for the sustainable growth of the market are a broader investor base for the bottom pieces and a major improvement in the secondary-data dissemination required for price discovery. Despite these problems, this market should continue to grow dramatically, unlike REITs.

Mutual Funds

Despite the huge increase in investible funds from 401(k) plans, mutual funds have not been a significant factor in the real estate capital markets. As these funds continue to grow—and as individuals become less sanguine about the equity markets—it is quite possible that a family of real estate mutual funds, or tradeable closed-end funds, will come into being. Such funds could hold unleveraged commercial properties, especially if investors do become dissatisfied with the REIT format. They could also provide debt funds for various types of participating or short- or medium-term mortgage instruments, much as the mortgage REITs attempted to do in the 1970s. Finally, higher-yield and riskier mutual funds might become a home for the bottom pieces of CMBS originations.

Opportunity Funds

Opportunity funds have served to replace the equity funding of real estate that traditionally came from the life insurance companies. They were viewed as short-term vehicles, initially benefiting from the real estate fire sales of the early 1990s. They are probably here to stay, however, as they provide an opportunistic approach to the real estate markets that many investors prefer as a portion of a diversified portfolio. The relatively short-term payback of these funds allows a new look at rapidly changing investment conditions.

While returns are clearly less than the windfalls of a few years ago, such funds should be able to continue to generate returns at a significant premium over normalized equity returns in the stock market.

Opportunities will continue to include insurance company portfolios as they adjust their balance sheets. Investment opportunities for these funds will include insurance, banks taken over by others, incubator REITs, REITs going private, raw land, incubator land for homebuilders, real estate operating companies requiring a capital partner, and distressed portfolios overseas.

Foreign Investors

Japan and Western Europe are dealing with internal deficits and capital problems—with the exception of the Dutch, who continue to invest in U.S. real estate, particularly REITs. At the moment, mainland China is the largest beneficiary of surplus cash flows, about a third of which are coming in from overseas Chinese. Large amounts of investment capital will be required in Eastern Europe and the former Soviet Union, as well as in developing market economies such as Southeast Asia, Indonesia, and India.

It thus seems less likely that the United States will benefit from foreign capital flows in real estate over the next five years to the extent that it did in the 1970s and 1980s. Real estate seems to come late in the foreign investment cycle because of the lack of available data, lack of trusted third-party advisers, lack of liquidity, and possible lack of an investment return that compensates for all of the above factors as well as currency risk. The two areas most likely to attract foreign investment are REITs and CMBSs because of relatively better data disclosure and relatively better perceived liquidity.

Pension Funds

Pension funds have not yet lived up to the expectation that 10 percent or more of their assets might be invested in real estate. Current investment in real estate is less than a third of that amount. Returns on real estate over the past decade were the lowest of any major asset class, although recent returns have compared favorably with historical results. (Nevertheless, they are nowhere near as favorable as stock market returns up to the end of 1996.) Probably no class of financial institution is coming out of the past ten years more disoriented about real estate—or more capable of being the major capital provider to the industry. Pension funds remain the only major long-term investor left. The duration of their liabilities is perfectly suited to longer-term real estate investment. As stock market returns revert down to their mean (and as real estate returns revert up to their mean), it would seem appropriate to expend major efforts to rebuild pension funds' confidence in the real estate investment process.

The loss of confidence goes deeper than disappointment over stated investment returns. The intellectual underpinnings of real estate have been lost. It clearly is not an inflation hedge when markets are overbuilt and there is no significant inflation. It may (or may not) be a separate asset class. While pension fund advisers were uniform in their rationale for real estate investment in the 1970s and 1980s, they themselves now appear disoriented and they lack a consistent rationale as to why pension funds should invest in real estate. For example, there is debate even on what constitutes "core" real estate—single-asset transactions or securitized offerings.

Confidence in valuations and price discovery was eroded both on the way up in the late 1980s and on the way down in the early 1990s. Many pension fund portfolios appear to lack a basic strategic orientation, instead resembling a series of brokered deals with no sell-side strategy. In some cases, there appears to be no basic alignment of interests among pension plan sponsors and their advisers. Pension funds feel they have been subjected to high risk, high fees, and low returns. Some significant pension fund advisers are reluctant to have their performance benchmarked on a basis comparable to that employed in the fixed-income and equity asset classes. Software support for real estate is lagging that provided for other asset classes. There is a multiplicity of systems, inconsistent reporting of results, and massive amounts of data provided with little analysis to assist decision making.

Many of these service-provider issues are being addressed. New fee structures are being proposed, along with co-investment. Benchmarking systems are being adopted by certain plan sponsors. National property management companies are being formed on the premise of delivering lower-cost service with superior management information systems. [See article 17.]

Along with securitized offerings from Wall Street, pension funds should be a major supplier of capital to real estate over the next five years, especially as they reallocate assets from the U.S. equity market into alternative asset classes. In order to free up this capital for the real estate sector, however, more work needs to be accomplished on the intellectual underpinnings of real estate investment.

Underpinnings of Real Estate Investment

The somewhat simplistic rationale for investing in real estate—as an inflation hedge—simply does not work anymore. Inflation is not as worrisome as it was a decade ago, and real estate has not performed. Securitization techniques such as REITs and CMBSs have only made the debate more confusing. Do REITs trade like small-capitalization stocks? Is the value of physical real estate altered significantly when it is included in a REIT format? Is there some alchemy that can make an asset yielding 6 percent become one yielding 10 percent? How long can the financial levitation last? These queries may become less significant as REIT relative payouts and growth begin to decline.

The further development of real estate derivatives and financial hedges will allow sophisticated investors to rotate in and out of real estate, property types, or locations on a basis that would be impossible when trading physical assets. The major impediment to their development is the lack of broad, consistent availability of data.

The price anomalies between public and private real estate markets continue to confuse potential investors, many of whom believe the best deals trade to insiders. [See article 7.] As mentioned above, such anomalies surely will occur once again when REITs decline in relative value because of lower-than-expected growth in cash flow and dividends, while the values of the underlying real estate increase along with rents and decreased vacancies.

What is the appropriate return for real estate held in an institutional investment portfolio? How does one know whether the return is good or bad compared with that of other financial assets, especially in cases in which real estate seems to command high fees, is essentially handcrafted, illiquid, and based on imperfect data and price discovery? Some have suggested that real estate, on this basis, should return around 500 basis points over the ten-year Treasury bond. Such a spread may be intellectually consoling, but can such returns be sustained on investment-grade commercial real estate?

How does one obtain consistent, reliable data on which to base sound real estate investment decisions? It turns out that office buildings are measured on different bases in different locations. The calculation of economic rent varies from purveyor to purveyor, and often important components are left out. How is vacancy to be calculated? How about a downsized tenant paying above-market rent on untenanted space?

Pension funds will not meet their potential as real estate investors until these types of queries are resolved. Growing exposure to the public markets should serve to support the development of consistent and reliable data. Those individuals who deliver the data freely and openly, rather than keep it sequestered in the hands of the privileged few owners and brokers, will end up controlling the real estate investment industry.

Over the next five years, many previous conditions will reoccur. On the margin, there will be too much capital flowing into real estate—primarily from commercial banks, Wall Street, and pension funds—carrying with it the continual threat of overbuilding in certain markets and locations. However, the economic downturn that can be anticipated over this time frame will mitigate the severity of any overbuilding in this cycle.

An unusual degree of functional obsolescence in real estate will occur. Probably several hundred regional malls already are ripe for adaptive use. In certain cities, high-rise downtown office structures will continue to give way to suburban offices with cheaper transportation and other costs. Hoteling will further change office use and the demand for square feet per capita. High-rise office structures in formerly attractive locations, which may be filled with asbestos, already are becoming economically obsolete.

Particularly among pension funds, fee pressure on advisers will continue, along with ever increasing demands for sophisticated services. The public markets will become more important, more liquid, and more heavily traded and also the source of ever improving information about the underlying real estate.

Above, all, what will be required over this period is intelligence, creativity, the willingness to risk investment dollars on management information systems, the ability to see the problems of the financial institutions as readily as one's own, and the ability to develop longer-term relationships based upon honesty, integrity, and trust.

If the self-discipline the industry was forced to acquire in the early 1990s can be maintained, together with improvements in the flow of real estate data, the millennium could prove to be a golden age for commercial real estate investment.

Source: *Urban Land*, May 1997.

14 Irrational Exuberance

Ample evidence was available in the late 1980s to convince any regulator that there was significant overbuilding.

A recent [1998] missed luncheon that Federal Reserve Bank chairman Alan Greenspan was scheduled to attend called to mind a time in early 1991 when the Urban Land Institute Credit Task Force met with Greenspan. At that time he challenged ULI to provide the Federal Reserve Bank with clues to when the commercial real estate economy was heading into an overbuilt cycle. He expressed the notion that the Fed was not prepared for the overbuilding in the late 1980s and the real estate depression that followed in the early 1990s. As a result of his challenge, the ULI Credit Task Force (now the ULI Credit Symposium) has remained in business ever since.

Several of those involved with the ULI Credit Task Force felt that ample evidence was available in the late 1980s to convince any regulator that significant overbuilding was occurring in the commercial real estate sector. All the signs of "irrational exuberance" were there, including the lowering of underwriting standards, making loans in excess of cost, and speculative building with no preleasing.

There were classic structural problems that almost always occur during a time of economic excess, for instance, a serious blurring of the roles of principals and agents. Those who reaped the rewards were not held accountable for the problems resulting from excessive development. Such mismatches were prevalent in commercial bank lending, where bonuses were paid on loan production, with no accountability for actual loan performance a few years later. A grand game of musical chairs was played, with Japanese investors in many cases ending up as the "winner" of partially leased buildings in overbuilt markets and the developer and financial intermediaries walking away with the money. The Japanese "conquest" of certain urban markets turned out to be a hollow victory, for which the price continues to be paid.

As long as the money flowed, everyone was "entitled" to build in an already over-built market. The motivation, in the kindest terms, was the conviction that the newest building would dominate the market and take tenants away from weaker ones. In the most negative terms, stubborn building in already weak markets was an example of excessive greed for development fees and a lack of any sense of final accountability for the multiyear devastation such overbuilding could cause. In any event, many knew, or certainly ought to have known, that substantial overbuilding was occurring.

Perhaps the most serious structural problem was the lack of political will in the commercial real estate industry to do anything about it. Had the Federal Reserve Bank, the Comptroller of the Currency, the FDIC, or any of the other regulators been at all successful in restraining the flow of funds into the industry in the late 1980s, one may be certain that the industry would have lobbied Congress relentlessly for protection from such interference in the marketplace—to such an extent that it would have made the savings and loan lobby of the 1980s look like amateurs. Thus, while the real estate industry complained loudly about the curtailment of credit in the early 1990s, it showed little inclination to operate with prudence or self-discipline in the years preceding. The combination of the lack of political will to take responsibility as an industry and the propensity to operate as an unrestrained group of free riders caused the real estate cycle to be more pronounced than it had to be and rendered the appeal for protection in the down cycle somewhat less convincing. Ultimate responsibility lies with the real estate industry itself, not with the financial institutions or the regulators.

An interesting and seldom expressed consequence of the severe real estate depression of the early 1990s is that it forced the Fed to keep interest rates low to protect financial institutions, primarily the banking system. Despite the protests of the inflation hawks still remaining on the Open Market Committee, Greenspan kept rates low for a sustained period of time, allowing commercial banks to rebuild their reserves while moving their investment portfolios out of distressed real estate loans and into government securities. The Fed was able to keep the yield curve sloped to such a degree that the banks could pick up a considerable spread over their cost of short-term borrowing and yields on Treasuries.

While Greenspan deserves credit for keeping rates low for a long period of time and fueling one of the longest sustained growth periods in the nation's economic history, in an ironic sense the real estate industry gave him the rationale for doing so by crippling the financial system to the extent that he had little choice. An amazing statistic is that the rest of the economy was growing so well that, despite the real estate depression, there has not been a quarter in the 1990s that did not show overall positive economic growth. In fact, it is highly likely that, without the real estate depression, the Fed would have been forced to raise rates earlier, which no doubt ultimately would have caused the current growth phase to have been shorter-lived. The real estate industry has not yet been given its share of credit for this classic example of the law of unintended consequences.

The following factors might be considered indicators of overbuilding of commercial real estate. They all are based on common sense; recognizing them requires no unusual amount of insight, and they all were plainly present in the late 1980s.

- Developers putting up space with little or no preleasing.
- Developers "financing out" on new projects with little or no financial risk to themselves and not having the discipline to subordinate their development fees. Without financial risk there is little to restrain the developer from overbuilding. Generally speaking, there should be at least 15 percent developer equity (not counting developer fees) in a project and substantial preleasing.
- Rental concessions to tenants, such as reduced rent, free rent, generous tenant improvement allowances, and payment of moving costs.
- Increasing vacancy rates. High vacancy rates in Class B buildings may indicate overbuilding before vacancies show up in Class A buildings.
- Aggregate loans to commercial real estate growing at rates faster than that of the general economy.
- New space being created faster than the local economy is growing; real estate as a driver of, rather than a responder to, the local economy. If real estate becomes a key support of the local economy, it is going too far.
- Compensation in financial institutions being driven by loan production rather than risk-adjusted returns on capital.
- Real estate financial products being sold to buyers of last resort, that is, retail customers or new market entrants.

One may inquire what impact such recent trends as securitization, technology, and consolidation may have on the ability to predict commercial real estate cycles. Securitization has had the benefit of providing a great deal more public information about real estate to the marketplace. Real estate investment trusts (REITs) and commercial mortgage–backed securities (CMBSs) have perhaps drawn more sophisticated clients and a higher level of skill and knowledge to the markets. Technology has increased the availability of information and heightened competition. Consolidation among real estate developers, REITs, and real estate practitioners should allow for better-capitalized real estate companies, a higher degree of professional management, increased funding for technology, and a management approach more like that of an industrial company. Along with such possible improvements, however, comes a moral hazard—public markets and increased technology may become nothing more than newer packaging around an industry in which the old practices simply perpetuate themselves. These newer trends produce another list of warnings concerning the real estate cycle:

- Who is buying the "B pieces," the risky tranches of CMBS offerings? Are they sophisticated buyers? Are these pieces priced correctly on a risk-adjusted basis? Is there a buildup of such pieces in bank and life insurance company portfolios?
- Are more conservative debt ratios of public REITs beginning to deteriorate, especially due to increased unsecured lending to REITs?
- Is a tradeoff developing in REITs between dividend maintenance and capital expenditures? Are dividends being maintained at the expense of the properties?
- Are large CMBS portfolios being underwritten to obscure the performance of individual properties? Is the benefit of diversification being overplayed; that is, do 100 bad properties somehow become one good portfolio because of the diversity of cash flow?
- Is there solid, ongoing due diligence regarding the individual properties in large CMBS portfolios? Is due diligence being performed by true third parties?
- Is secondary market making in large CMBS portfolios diverse? Are these real markets, or are they "trades by appointment," with only the issuing underwriter standing by to make quotes?
- Are the technology and database advantages accruing to the larger, well-capitalized firms being made available to investors across the marketplace, or are they being deemed as proprietary, thereby preserving the insider nature of the real estate market?
- Are the larger consolidated firms continuing to rely on true third-party validation of values, or do such megafirms remove the checks and balances from the real estate investment process?

Real estate disclosure has benefited greatly in recent years from broader access to public markets. Information requirements of the Securities and Exchange Commission (SEC), the rating agencies, security analysts, market makers, and investors have made available much more data on assets held in REITs or in CMBS portfolios. As more and more assets are captured in the public markets, it may become possible to construct national and local indices of rental rates and vacancies that are more reliable than previous indices. The existence of such data may eventually mitigate the volatility of the real estate cycle.

As more reliable data enters the public marketplace, one might even envisage the construction of property indices that could be traded, much as one trades the Standard

& Poor's 500 Index. If such indices existed for both the national and local markets, and by different property types, an investor could take a long or short position on any particular property type or location. A prospective large office tenant, for example, could hedge the possibility of rising rents by purchasing an index to hedge the risk.

As more real estate meets the rigorous reporting standards of the public markets, confidence will grow in real estate as an investment asset class and demand for real estate will increase in the public markets. There may be a day when "perfect" information will be available online on each significant market and property type.

When that day arrives and there is an overload of information and data, keen minds and wisdom will still be needed to make sense of it all and to protect us from our unlimited propensity to "irrational exuberance."

Source: *Urban Land* (Point of View column), June 1998.

15 Tragedy of the Commons: Will It Be Different This Time?

The excesses of the real estate development market of the late 1980s may be compared to the "tragedy of the commons." The tragedy describes the circumstance where a village common is overgrazed to the point where there is no fodder left for the village animals. This occurs because individuals feel an entitlement to their share of the common good and no collective sense of responsibility to conserve or renew the food supply. The result is that no one individual destroys the common, but that individuals as a group devastate it—and trust in the institution of the village is lost.

Overbuilding Is Overgrazing

In the case of real estate development in the late 1980s, each project was deemed in the eye of its beholder as being very special, having unique appeal, and coming on the market at precisely that window of time when the last full building would be executed and before the devastation of overbuilding. Lost in the analysis was the devastation caused to all buildings in a specific locale by the serious "overgrazing" that resulted from a number of seemingly isolated and innocuous decisions to build.

Real estate development has traditionally been a local business, played chiefly by insiders with information not always readily available to the financial marketplace, where individual entrepreneurs attempt to gain windfalls by getting an edge on the market in general. The lack of broadly accessible, accurate, consistent data on real estate has helped to preserve this insider's game, as it has also contributed to the volatility and amplitude of the real estate cycle. The more transparency, the greater the depth of accurate information available to all players in a market, the less chance there will be for such wide swings in real estate as occurred over the past ten years.

It is entirely possible that 1998 will be regarded in retrospect as the year of equilibrium; the year when aggregate supply and demand for real estate came into balance; the year in which virtually no new developments caused excessive capacity or declining rents. Along with the achievement of market equilibrium have come the beneficial results of several recent trends—such as securitization, technology, and consolidation. A rising tide lifts all boats, so it is difficult at present to assess whether or not these newer trends in real estate will provide greater stability to the industry. The answer will come only as we swing into yet another real estate recession caused by overbuilding. At the end of a complete economic cycle we will better be able to assess the significance of these new trends. Meanwhile, the issue is: Have these new trends in real estate served to dampen the volatility of the real estate cycle, or is the real estate development game just the same old game being played out in a new wrapper?

The Moral Hazard of Rewards and Punishments

One of the problems with real estate, especially in the late 1980s, is the moral hazard that resulted from a delinking of rewards and punishments. Those who piled on production in financial institutions, especially savings and loans and commercial banks, were rewarded handsomely for meeting or exceeding targets. Bonuses and longer-term incentives were not tied to the outcome of the investment. There was no linking of the rewards for production with the risk involved in the transaction. There was little or no concept of risk-based capital or of risk-adjusted return. This led to loans being made at 100 percent or more of cost to developers with no equity stake or risk in the project, often with all their development fees being paid out on the front end in cash instead of staying at risk in the transaction.

A further moral hazard occurred when entrepreneurs played the RTC [Resolution Trust Corporation] game and achieved, in the early years, windfall profits as a result of the federal government's capital being at risk. The positive side of this event was that we cleaned up the mess in a hurry; a fact that our Japanese friends do not appear to have caught on to. As a result of astute management by Alan Greenspan, our banking system survived the test quite well. Bank executives were also a beneficiary of this delinking of rewards and punishments. The Federal Reserve Bank kept rates low, allowing the banks to build up their reserves. Certain bank stock prices initially fell to 20 percent of previous values and then increased eightfold, giving the bank officers windfall profits on their stock options.

How Can We "Fix" the Real Estate Cycle?

Without the transparency of timely and accurate data on rents, it is unlikely that any system will be developed that will cause punishment to occur prior to overbuilding. The kinds of systems that might produce data in time to prevent overbuilding are probably too draconian to withstand the political and regulatory process. Examples of practices that might prevent overbuilding and truly mitigate the real estate cycle would include a national rent index, quarterly finance reports, and quarterly rent reports.

Rent Index. A national rent index with various local components could help. The Urban Land Institute made some significant progress on this front in the early 1990s, but industry support lagged and then collapsed as the real estate markets improved and it became every institution out for itself once again. Such an index could be derived statistically. It would cost a few million dollars—a cost that could be shared by several of the major financial institutions in the real estate business. The ultimate value could far outweigh the cost. Developers, financial institutions, and tenants could go long or short in various individual geographic markets and product types, smoothing out cycles in local markets.

The index must be monitored by an independent fiduciary in which there is a high degree of trust. The Urban Land Institute could be such a body, as could any one of the major universities involved in real estate education. Such an index would be organized by geographic sector and by major property type. The moral hazard here is the industry's lack of willingness to make real estate a public utility and share the formerly inside information so broadly. Each player feels advantaged to "get an edge on the market." In so doing, they increase the volatility of the cycle and are thus each a cause of the major windfalls and catastrophic losses that occur in the industry with embarrassing regularity.

Quarterly Financing Reports. The Comptroller of the Currency could require each major bank to report on a quarterly basis the details of each real estate financing in which it has engaged, including accurate data with respect to volume of construction lending, loan to value, true equity, degree of risk taken by the developer, rental concessions, amount of preleasing, and the like. As one who is fundamentally antiregulation, I find little appeal in this draconian tactic, but reporting out such data to the public on a real-time basis, i.e., on the Internet, could provide a basis for mitigating the cycle.

Quarterly Rent Reports. The Securities and Exchange Commission could require each publicly traded real estate operating company, real estate investment trust, originator of commercial mortgage–backed securities, etc., to report publicly on a quarterly basis net effective rentals on all of its properties on a consistent basis. Such data could be fed by the Internet to all interested parties, including a public or quasi-public utility, which would construct the rental indices referred to above.

What Is Different This Time?

In theory, the securitization of a significant amount of real estate, primarily through real estate investment trusts and commercial mortgage–backed securities, provides the marketplace with a much greater pool of data than was the case when such assets were held by private institutions. Punishment seems more directly linked to the negative event. For example, if a REIT persists in overdeveloping a particular market, the word gets out quickly, and the public and the financial institutions will sell the shares of that particular REIT, increasing its cost of capital and most likely making it a takeover candidate. The public disclosure required of publicly held firms provides for a much more rational market, although the punishment does not occur until after the over-building has occurred.

Likewise, one may surmise that properties controlled by opportunity funds are likely to be more closely scrutinized and more aggressively dealt with than those financed by large financial institutions, which, at least at the beginning of a cycle, have traditionally stretched out problem loans, quarter by quarter, hoping to avoid a write-off.

In general, the current real estate industry structure has more monitoring devices than before. The imposition of risk-based capital rules have forced commercial banks and insurance companies to become more rigid in their real estate analysis. Wall Street common stock analysts as well as credit analysts are quick to punish a public company for a missed earnings forecast, excessive leverage, nonaccretive acquisitions, or overbuilding. These stock and bond analysts ride herd on the publicly held financial institutions as well, such as commercial banks and insurance companies; and they are quick to punish excessive financing to real estate on the part of these firms.

In general, real estate benefits from the consolidations and the larger-sized real estate firms, both public and private—(especially if their larger size allows them to make the investment in technology that is required to attain efficiencies in operations). Most larger, consolidated firms also have a more conservative debt structure than was the case in the 1980s, as they wish to gain the advantage of an investment-grade bond rating and lower-cost capital. The consolidations will truly benefit real estate if they can bring off the benefits of professional management, discipline, and scale to an industry that has been highly customized and handcrafted for too long.

What Is the Likely Outcome?

It has been said that "disciplined, speculative" development is an oxymoron. This is somewhat surprising, given all the newly developed risk management tools in the financial markets. If this is true, then the only real discipline in the real estate markets is the flow of capital. So long as the financial sources maintain discipline, the real estate cycle will be moderated. In the late 1980s, the financial institutions became part of the problem themselves as they contributed to the overgrazing of the public commons.

The larger real estate firms need to develop discipline. A truly mature industry should not be relying solely on capital sources and regulators to keep it from excessive behavior. It will be difficult for real estate firms to develop such discipline, however, if a significant portion of new development continues to be carried out by local entrepreneurs who have no incentive other than to get and keep an edge on the market. Such behavior, which is always rational in the individual sense, creates an imperfect and distorted market overall. It is impossible to punish such behavior in advance of overbuilding.

Thus, in the absence of some draconian moves to produce transparency of markets and information, it is highly likely that the real estate development market will remain imperfect; i.e., the same old business in a new wrapper. The major difference at present is that the punishment is likely to come faster and be harder. Those who avoid "overgrazing" and keep their powder dry will be there to mop up the pieces at substantial discounts and take ultimate advantage of such imperfect markets. The tragedy of the commons will continue with all the concomitant windfalls and losses. Perhaps that is the ultimate reason why so many of us find real estate such an entertaining and stimulating place to make our living.

Source: *Real Estate Issues* (CRE Perspective column), summer 1998.

16   When Markets Clash

There will be money to be made.

Recent events in the real estate capital markets may be seen as part of the evolving clash between public and private markets for real estate. Back in the 1970s, the two markets were almost completely separate. Public real estate companies traded at times as much as 80 percent below the net asset value of the real estate carried on their books. This was borne out by the liquidation of Tishman Realty & Construction in 1976 for approximately three-and-a-half times the price of its common stock; Ernest W. Hahn Inc. in 1980, for three times the value of its common stock; and Monumental Properties in 1979, for almost four times the value of its common stock. [See article 1 for details.]

In the 1970s debt markets, investment bankers could place mortgage securities secured by the headquarters properties of regional banks or public utilities at as much as 250 basis points below the rate at which the public debt of the parent company was trading. This prompted the chief economist of Equitable Life to publish an edict to all field offices stating that no corporate mortgage could be issued at a rate less than that quoted in the daily *Wall Street Journal* for publicly traded debt of public utilities; thus, capital market links were born.

The 1970s also saw the initial formation of real estate investment trusts (REITs), which were primarily mortgage-oriented, and equity trusts, which, for the most part, lacked the quality of property seen in today's REITs. A number of factors, including higher interest rates, poor management, and small lot size caused most of these trusts to disappear by the early 1980s. Several real estate companies went public during the early part of the 1970s, but most of them returned to private status later in the decade when private real estate assets were valued much more highly than public companies.

Securitized debt also made an appearance in the 1970s, although it was limited primarily to tranched debt of high-quality issuers, secured by a lease to their headquarters building. The debt tranches were structured to take advantage of a positively sloping yield curve and bore little resemblance to the slicing and dicing of today; thus, the public markets for real estate debt and equity securities emerged in the 1970s, but the preponderance of commercial real estate finance was private, dominated by insurance companies.

Private financing sources continued to dominate the real estate capital markets in the 1980s, with insurance companies prevailing in the debt and equity markets, including large joint ventures. Pension funds began to allocate capital to real estate, and the pension fund advisory business grew rapidly. Commercial banks became increasingly aggressive throughout the decade, lowering spreads and underwriting standards to create market share. Even savings and loans, which had been traditional housing lenders, participated in syndicates of commercial real estate ventures. Private foreign investors came into the market in a big way as well. The real estate capital markets were flooded by private financing sources, and the quality of investment portfolios deteriorated as a result of the concomitant overbuilding.

Regulators placed stringent pressures on private financing sources in the early 1990s, including the imposition of risk-based capital rules on commercial banks and insurance companies. Many savings and loans were beyond salvaging. Pension funds lagged several years in marking their holdings to market. Credit and common stock analysts made it clear that real estate was anathema. In the early 1990s, the funding of financial institutions with large real estate holdings became problematic. The private market for commercial real estate finance had dried up.

REITs—especially after the tax-efficient up-REIT ruling first given to Taubman Centers Inc.—became an excellent vehicle to raise equity capital to pay down the banks. Developers who had never considered a REIT were encouraged by their lenders to do so, and the quality of real estate placed into REITs far exceeded that of the previous round. In the mid-1990s, REITs benefited from the repricing of real estate, coming out of the recession of the early part of the decade, and investors were lured by annual returns of 30 percent for two years back to back. As a result, REITs were viewed as a growth stock, not the income security they were designed to be.

Commercial mortgage–backed securities (CMBSs), formerly purchased chiefly by savings and loans, came into the fore as other lending sources dried up. A series of problematic investments could somehow achieve stability by being pooled, and the disparate cash flow characteristics of a hundred loans proved a more reliable financing vehicle than individual whole loans.

Disproportionate cash flow was dedicated to the "top" piece, and the rating agencies provided investment-grade ratings to such tranches. A market developed for the "bottom" piece among opportunity funds and those willing to take higher risks. Issuances ballooned, and the public debt markets drove many commercial banks out of the business. Underwriters of CMBSs evolved from the role of intermediary to that of principal, extending their own capital when necessary, and holding unsold, often riskier, pieces in inventory. By acting as principal, they could issue a competitive quote to a borrower and make as much as a 150 to 200 basis point "inside spread" by slicing and dicing the pooled securities. This worked fine as long as the market was receptive. Otherwise, inventory backed up, and investment banks began to have the same problem that commercial banks had experienced early in the decade.

By the first half of 1998, the public debt markets had pretty much taken commercial banks out of the business. Because of their inside spread, investment banks could undercut commercial banks in pricing their loans. Commercial banks could not compete with Wall Street on spread and sustain an adequate return on their capital. Underwriting standards began to deteriorate in the banking system, as banks attempted to remain competitive. In midsummer, Federal Reserve Board chairman Alan Greenspan cautioned commercial banks on their lending practices to real estate. It looked like the public markets were here to stay, while the private markets were losing significant market share.

Some analysts also raised questions about the possible fragility of the CMBS market. The rising tide of repriced real estate in the mid-1990s was lifting all boats and possibly masking the performance of many of these loans over time. An investment-grade rating could obscure the nature of the assets in the investment pools. Large CMBS pools had not been fully tested in a real estate recession. There was no good statistical record of loans past due and delinquent during adverse times. Ongoing due diligence on individual loans in pools in the secondary market was problematic, and it was unclear how such diligence should be funded or who should perform it. Liquidity in the secondary markets could become a fiction. An investment-grade rating did not mean there was a depth of market makers; often the only market maker was the original issuer, and the trades were "by appointment." This was especially true when investment banks were bulked up on inventory. Thus, in many ways, large CMBS pools were unseasoned, untested, immature securities. They would need to go through at least one full economic cycle to test how they would perform over time.

All this came to a head, of course, in the liquidity crisis in the debt markets late last summer. Problems in Russia, Latin America, and Asia caused liquidity to dry up in the emerging-markets' debt market and created a flight to quality—primarily to U.S. government and high-grade corporate bonds. A debt security was either high grade or low grade; there were no shades of gray. CMBS issues were swept up along with high-yield and other lower-quality debt issues. The real estate financial community was puzzled as to why real estate debt was regarded as so risky when the supply and demand characteristics of commercial real estate probably were as well in balance as at any time in recent years. The reason soon became obvious: Investors regarded CMBS paper as unseasoned and immature and dumped it into the illiquidity hopper.

The real estate public equity markets, in the form of REITs, also took a battering in 1998. With commercial real estate repriced, it became apparent that REITs no longer were growth stocks. The process of moving equity securities from one class of investor to another can be expensive. Despite a few ups and downs, the stock market throughout 1998 continued to place a higher value on growth stocks than on income stocks. This resulted in a decline in value for virtually all REIT shares, with some classes of real estate suffering far more than others.

Taking advantage of the misfortunes of the public market, the private market came roaring back in—more strongly than earlier in the decade—and quickly attempted to regain market share. Some insurance companies made 80 percent of their annual mortgage commitments during the last third of the year. Commercial banks, while cautious in their lending standards, found the widened spreads far more to their liking.

The wake-up call of 1998 was that public securities markets can dry up quickly for reasons that have absolutely nothing to do with the quality of the underlying real estate assets. This potential delinking of the capital markets from the underlying assets should motivate all major users of real estate capital to have multiple sources available, in both the public and private markets. In fact, a case can still be made that real estate essentially is a private market business.

The future of REITs will be driven by the state of the real estate economy. For the next two to three years, leases will continue to roll over due to below-market-rate rents, allowing some REITs to experience double-digit store-to-store growth. Although such growth is typical for this stage in a recovery from such a severe real estate depression, expectations will be created that will not be sustainable in flat or declining rental markets. As this cycle of REITs grows more mature, there will be increasing pressure to rob properties of desirable or even critical capital expenditures to maintain investor expectations regarding dividends. Over time, taking away these expenditures will degrade the portfolios of many REITs. Come the next real estate recession, dividend growth will cease to meet investor desires, and stock prices will fall. When they fall to a certain level—say around 65 percent of net asset value—opportunity funds and real estate operators will begin to take REITs private, much as they did with public real estate operating companies in the 1970s. For those attuned to arbitraging anomalies between the public and private markets, there will be money to be made.

Differentiating among CMBS issuers will be difficult until a downturn shows how individual portfolios fare. As these securities mature, there undoubtedly will be "branding" distinctions made in the marketplace among issuers, based on the support of secondary-market trading activities, ongoing due diligence on individual loans over the cycle, the quality of follow-up information provided to the marketplace, and the diligence and tenacity applied to past-due or delinquent loans. If true secondary markets develop in terms of information flow and trading activity, there should be substantial continued growth in the CMBS market.

If, over time, public markets dominate real estate finance, real estate markets will become far more transparent, with copious amounts of public data available on individual properties. In this event, it is likely that the long dreamed of national rental index will become a reality. With enough public data on hand, various indices of property types and locations could be traded long or short, and hedge markets could develop for major users of space.

Despite the transparency of the public markets and the better flow of information, such markets ironically could still become highly volatile and delinked from underlying real estate assets. Recently, Greenspan warned of the risks of the new international financial architecture. The increased volatility of the markets can, in effect, cause lower growth because of the anxiety created, which is exactly what occurred in the debt markets late last summer.

On the other hand, many may not really want a fully public, transparent real estate capital market. Detailed real-time market knowledge is not broadly shared. The industry wants the world to be predictable, while it remains unpredictable. In a thoroughly predictable, transparent world, profits are limited. Obviously, the entrepreneurial talent that makes this business so entertaining and adventuresome would not be drawn to such an environment. So, as much as some may yearn for perfect markets and a broad public market for real estate, we had best keep the private markets alive and well. Without the clashing of the public and the private markets, the industry would lose much of its unique character, as well as many of its opportunities.

Source: *Urban Land* (Capital Markets column), February 1999.

17

Pension Funds' Investment in Real Estate: A New Model

Any entity that takes the leadership to streamline and enhance the flow of information will not only open up institutional real estate investment to much broader acceptance, but will also control the process.

The institutional real estate industry has been plagued by low returns over the past ten years. Returns on real estate were less than returns on short-term cash for the past decade, and it has now been proven that real estate is not a hedge against inflation when markets are overbuilt. The intellectual underpinnings of real estate as an asset class are flawed.

The theory of the 1980s appeared to be that real estate was a separate class of assets and that investors would not get enough of it. Pension funds were therefore advised to buy and hold property until their allocations approached 10 percent of their assets. In fact, the funds never reached that level. With rising values for financial assets and falling values for real estate assets caused by the real estate recession, pension funds actually lost ground. And a monolithic, hold-only model based on core assets consisting of large, high-rise urban office buildings and super regional shopping malls caused many large plan sponsors to buy high and sell low if they desired liquidity in the 1990s.

Advisory firms suffered as well. As their staffs remained geared to the high acquisition levels of the late 1980s, their fees were under enormous pressure. Meanwhile, they faced ever-increasing demands from clients for added reporting, valuation, and property and asset management workouts. The consolidation of the pension fund real estate advisory firms, currently [1996] in progress, is the result.

Consultants and advisers appear confused about how to position real estate investments by pension funds; some suggest that real estate is simply another industry sector, like oil and gas, and that the sector should be rotated periodically. Implementation of this idea appears impractical for large funds, however, at least until synthetic securities are developed for real estate investment. Others talk of the four quadrants of real estate investment (public debt, private debt, public equity, and private equity), suggesting that astute plan sponsors will adroitly rotate among the four sectors as anomalies occur in the market. Once again, easier said than done.

Basic information, valuations, and appraisals have come under increasing scrutiny as plan sponsors have lost their trust in information about real estate investments. Appraised values were too low in the 1980s and too high in the early 1990s, and advisers were accused of being too slow to bring values down at the beginning of the real estate depression. The practice of basing advisory fees on appraised values came under increasing pressure. The loss of trust in information will remain a serious impediment to restoring confidence in the real estate investment process.

Even if the plan sponsor gets the investment process right, it still must face significant restructuring of the advisory business—as well as other pervasive issues such as valuation, information flow, and alignment of interests among real estate pricing, risk, and fees that are not yet resolved.

The Plan Sponsor

An ad hoc partner and I recently completed a study of one of the larger public pension fund's processes for investing in real estate, hoping to streamline them. While this particular fund has done a good job of investing in financial assets and has become a leader in certain practices, it has a rather poor reputation in the institutional real estate industry for its bureaucracy, politicized investment process, and lack of alignment among the various parties—staff, consultants, trustees, and advisory firms. These factors have kept the fund from enjoying the economies of scale in real estate it could otherwise achieve.

Unless an overall strategy for investment is rigorously followed, unless the investment process is free of bureaucratic obstacles and political bias, and unless the measurement of performance is disciplined, a major institutional portfolio can easily come to resemble a random collection of brokered deals. Furthermore, staff must work with the pension fund consultant to determine appropriate market rates of return for real estate and the correlation of various classes of real estate with risk-adjusted returns.

In this case, my partner and I focused on the real estate investment process and not on particular investments or investment strategies. There are two absolute requirements for successful investment in real estate by a large plan sponsor: a competent, motivated staff and benchmarking of performance. Advisers must be rewarded— or not—on the basis of such benchmarking.

The assignment dealt with a large pension plan that had a large board. One of the first recommendations made was that the board form a small subcommittee to take leadership of real estate investments. This subcommittee would include the chief investment officer and would receive significant input from the staff and outside consultants. The team would shape the real estate investment strategy, formulate the annual real estate business plans, and make recommendations to the board's investment committee about the engagement and retention of real estate advisers.

The hope was that by breaking down a larger group (the board) into a smaller team, the board could be depoliticized. Moreover, it was hoped the team would be a catalyst for getting the staff, board, consultants, and advisers to work together. The suggestion was also made that a small group of industry leaders without conflicts of interest—a real estate advisory council—be formed to act as advisers to this policy-setting team and to bring a real-world point of view to its proceedings.

It was recommended that a team be created with existing staff to rework the large existing portfolio. Subcommittee members would work out tight parameters for each existing property, deciding whether to hold or sell the property, whether to invest additional funds in it, and so on. Another suggestion was that greater discretion be given to existing managers to make investment and property decisions affecting the existing portfolio, within established parameters. The subcommittee would benchmark and evaluate each manager and reward the manager accordingly. Managers could be penalized for poor performance by moving their properties to other managers or to outside service providers and by withholding additional investment fund allocations.

Another recommendation was that new investments be made in time to take advantage of existing market opportunities, but only after the existing portfolio was reorganized. Also favored was giving more discretion over new investments to the managers, within tightly drawn parameters. Two-thirds of new investments were to be made in "core" properties (apartments, industrial facilities, suburban offices, and selected retail space, for example) and one-third in cutting-edge investments, such as incubator REITs, venture capital, securitized real estate instruments, operating companies, and the like.

The recommendation was made that the client pay essentially break-even advisory fees, with meaningful incentives. We tend to calculate fees based on net operating income rather than on appraised values. Some advisers felt comfortable with a break-even fee of around 7 percent of net operating income, capped at around 35 basis points annually; others did not. But type and size of properties managed are just two of the variables to consider in determining fees. Workouts, for example, require far more effort than stable properties.

We suggested an incentive fee of 25 percent of returns over a base return of 5 percent real return over inflation (measured over the consumer price index) for core assets and 35 percent of returns over a base return of 8 percent real return for cutting-edge investments. Another recommendation was that such incentives be paid out on a three-year rolling basis, so that after a three-year initial lag, an adviser could receive incentive fees in each year of a contract. Other issues affect fees: coinvestment, acquisition and sales, and broken deals. Each adviser will trade hard for the fees he or she deems appropriate.

Performance benchmarking is undoubtedly controversial. Advisers claim that industry standards for benchmarking are statistically flawed, that investing in different time periods (the late 1980s versus the early 1990s, for example) makes comparisons invalid, that different types of property or different locations cannot be compared, and so on. Nonetheless, comparison of results over time is mandatory, especially if advisers are to be given discretion over their funds. It was suggested that the client implement a system of weighted average benchmarking for particular properties that might include several factors: a targeted real rate of return, a targeted internal rate of return, a targeted initial cash return, and a targeted stabilized capitalization rate spread over the ten-year Treasury interest rate. Advisers' overall performance could also be compared against a weighting of several benchmarks, including a targeted real rate of return for the portfolio; a comparison to a basic index such as that of the National Council of Real Estate Investment Fiduciaries (NCREIF), plus a spread over it; a comparison to the initial pro forma forecasts; a comparison to other advisers' performance; and a comparison to other classes of assets.

Some advisers refuse to participate in a comparison of their performance. While one could advance many arguments against benchmarking, pension fund advisers must be willing to be rated and live with the results. Rebuilding trust in a system that might well be imperfect is essential to regaining substantial participation by pension funds in real estate investment.

One of the client's weaknesses was advisers' reporting of real estate assets. In part, the client created this monster by insisting on stringent reporting standards for data (most often raw and unanalyzed data) in a form that advisers did not normally use. Naturally, the client received mountains of documentation with little analysis and no prioritization of items it ought properly to review. It was recommended that reporting be radically simplified and that it provide information to management by exception. Attempts were made many times to dissuade staff from re-underwriting transactions. Giving discretion to the advisers and then exercising management's prerogative to hire and fire means that much of the reporting can be eliminated. The sponsor's focus should be on making certain that it is receiving appropriate risk-adjusted rates of return for the various categories of real estate and not on absorbing minor details about property.

The provision of timely data about property to the sponsor in a uniformly acceptable format is vital to the future of institutional investment in real estate. Property data were being passed to the client in an unanalyzed state from property manager to asset manager to portfolio manager to adviser to consultant through two or three different computer software systems. Each participant seemed to favor a different color for his or her book of information, so the plan sponsor would end up with as many as seven differently colored books containing substantially identical data on his desk. This is a costly and inefficient process that is not particularly useful for conveying information to the property owner. The institutional real estate industry suffers from a lack of uniform data presentation and analysis and from the use of multiple computer software systems for reporting. Any entity that takes the leadership (and spends the capital) to streamline and enhance the flow of information will not only open up institutional real estate investment to much broader acceptance but also will control the process.

Some plan sponsors get bogged down in real estate, perhaps because of its tangible nature. In some cases, trustees of multibillion-dollar portfolios argue over $3 million in capital improvement items or over how many trees should be planted on a particular property. This aspect of real estate keeps many plan sponsors from applying the same type of focus and discipline to real estate that they conventionally apply to their financial assets. In the case of real estate, if it becomes everyone's business, it ends up being no one's business.

The Pension Fund Adviser

It was surprising to find that, in addition to the problems the client had in dealing with real estate, much of its difficulty emanated from the still somewhat immature status of the pension fund advisory business. Rather than a cogent portfolio strategy, we identified too often a series of brokered deals that emphasized the buy side and had a too-little or too-late emphasis on selling. Risks and rewards were not analyzed adequately. Often the client took high risks with low returns for what appeared to be high fees. Especially with the current spate of consolidations, advisory firms end up with a long list of clients and the potential for conflicts of interest. In the client's case, clear examples of the client's interests being placed behind those of the advisory firm were found.

The chaotic conditions the client created were made even worse by the behavior of some pension fund advisers. When the client had no clearly defined investment process in place, many advisers used the situation to their own advantage by manipulating such process as existed. This lack of good process caused some advisers to behave differently than they may have elsewhere. Bad practice drove out good—to reword Gresham's Law—engendering a breakdown of trust among all parties.

The advisory business is undergoing a transition, and many advisers have begun to work on some of the problems underlying pension funds engaged in real estate investments. For example, there appears to be lack of agreement about the various roles being performed in the pension fund real estate business. We identified at least seven distinct roles: property management, asset management, portfolio management, pension fund adviser, pension fund consultant, pension fund staff, and pension fund trustee. The fact that the roles are not clearly defined means that plan sponsors are confused about the value of these separate services and how much they should pay for them.

When an adviser performs all tasks, including property management, plan sponsors become even more confused about the cost of separate services. Fees are not broken out in all cases, particularly for property management, where certain expenses can be passed to the owner or the tenant and thus become buried in expenses for the property. Our experience indicates that certain newly formed national property management companies are attempting to bid away portfolios from advisers by claiming to replace all these functions for as low as 35 to 40 basis points a year. In some cases, pension fund advisers are part of very large financial institutions, where overhead costs are allocated on the basis of formulas that might or might not reflect independent market conditions. These factors confuse plan sponsors even more and breed further distrust of advisers and confusion about actual costs.

Pension fund advisers must restructure their fee schedules to rebuild confidence among plan sponsors that fees are equitable in terms of risk, returns, and services. Appraisal-based fees are sometimes arbitrary and always lag current conditions. Fees based on current net operating income appear to serve both parties' interests much better. Capping such fees at an approximate break-even level, with a tangible incentive in the early years, also seems appropriate. The many other aspects of fees, such as for origination, sales, and broken deals, need to be tailored to an adviser's particular assignment.

A constant state of tension often exists between pension fund advisers and the plan sponsor's consultants. While consultants are the gatekeepers of the pension funds, plan sponsors and trustees may rely too heavily on them to make decisions they should make themselves. In some cases, especially with public funds, it is easier to pay large fees for consultants than it is to pay the salaries required to recruit and retain talented staff. At least a portion of the power placed in the consultants by plan sponsors is a result of lack of trust between plan sponsors and advisers, who are at times considered little more than high-powered brokers. Our model of an overall investment strategy—discretion within strict parameters, benchmarking of performance, fees aligned with services performed—is meant to restore the trust that ought to exist among the various parties in the institutional investment business.

Industry Issues

Lack of a clear focus on the role of real estate in pension funds adds to the confusion of institutional investors. How does one reconcile the difference in prices between public and private markets with the process of appraisal? Huge apparent windfalls created out of distressed properties add further to the distrust institutions feel toward real estate valuation and pricing. Often institutions believe the good deals are picked out by knowledgeable insiders before they come to the marketplace.

What is the expected rate of return from institutional-quality core real estate under present market conditions? How is it best expressed in the pricing model for capital assets? How does the advisory industry restore trust? How can we derive better information to establish prices? At this time, the real estate process remains much too mysterious. It is extremely difficult to obtain consistent data about true economic rents, sale prices, square feet of rentable area, vacancies, and the like. Insiders control the database, and the data are not commonly shared. The broad sharing of all relevant data, most likely over the Internet in a few years, is the only way to truly broaden institutional support for real estate capital markets. Lack of consistent, good data is the primary barrier to pension funds' taking their real estate allocations to 10 percent or higher. Lack of good data is also an inhibiting factor in the growth of public markets for commercial mortgage securities, especially in the secondary markets.

Pension funds would appear to be the ideal investor for real estate. The longer-term nature of pension fund contracts provides a good match for the longer-term flows and rental contracts that support real estate assets. One pension fund paradox is the reliance on quarterly benchmarking of relative performance, which causes the advantages of a long-term source of funds to converge with the volatility of financial assets. The implicitly private nature of real estate should allow pension funds the luxury of investing in an asset class that need not correlate to the daily volatility of financial markets.

Much remains to be done to broaden the appeal of institutional investment in real estate. Forward-thinking pension fund sponsors, advisers, and consultants must work together to develop the information base for capital markets in the new millennium.

Author's Note: The author wishes to acknowledge his partner's (William M. Kahane, principal of Milestone Partners) input on the consulting assignment referred to in this article. Kahane shared equally in the findings and conclusions of this report, but any errors, omissions, or misapplications of the findings are solely the responsibility of the author.

Source: *Urban Land*, September 1996.

18

Public Process Counseling

An earthquake rumbled across Los Angeles early in the morning hours of January 1994, bringing extensive damage to the entire city, including the 70-year-old art deco city hall. After the dust had settled, files, furnishings, and employees were relocated and seismic damage teams called in to determine what was needed to return the building to its function. Under closer scrutiny, it was discovered that the damage was more structurally pervasive than first thought and, to complicate matters, continuing aftershocks made additional tiles topple from 27 stories above. Estimated repair costs mounted, and a panoply of options was advanced. Pending resolution, a shroud of black plastic was wrapped around the top of the flaking tower.

Twenty-four months and $26 million in consultant fees later, the process is stymied. The project budget has grown to about $240 million for this 750,000-square-foot structure, and there are indications that it could increase to as much as $300 million. The mayor becomes alarmed as project costs soar to more than double the original budget, and he names a pro bono citizens panel to undertake a fresh look at the project and seek more cost-effective solutions. Your name is on the list, and if you agree to serve, you will find yourself in the midst of a public process counseling assignment. So hold on to your hat; it is going to be a wild ride. This is a highly appropriate assignment for a CRE (Counselor of Real Estate), because it calls for one of the highest forms of ethical decision making: the preservation of the public trust.

My experience in serving on six such counseling assignments in the past few years does not render me the ultimate authority on this subject, but each assignment has given me new insight into the process. I write this article to propose a possible framework for approaching public process counseling and to stimulate discussion, within our professional area, on a process that could profoundly impact public/private land use in this nation. I write so that we might be the beneficiaries of such increased discussion and thereby better serve our clients.

Public Process Counseling Indicators

Public process counseling is most generally indicated when a public entity experiences a breakdown of its legitimate process for decision making. Most often, the focus of the political process has become diffused and uncoordinated, weighted down with all the normal political baggage: diverse constituencies, multiple objectives and overlapping jurisdictions, divided councils, weak mayoral positions, and budget constraints. Proposed legislation can become so packed with a grab bag of issues from everyone's social agenda that the legitimate process is rendered unworkable. Sometimes wise leadership has no other choice but to seek the counsel of qualified outsiders.

Sewer Permit Allocation Ordinance—Los Angeles

In 1988, the mayor of Los Angeles, Tom Bradley, convened a citizens review committee to comment on a proposed sewer permit allocation ordinance. This less than romantic task would affect the pace and location of development in the city over the next several years. It was, in fact, a prism through which we could justifiably look at transportation issues, neighborhood issues, urban sprawl, edge cities, and each of the inputs in the urban development process.

The political process had loaded every wish list imaginable on the sewer ordinance, including the ratio of commercial development in the city to housing and the implementation of water-saving devices in commercial buildings. A draft proposal of the ordinance stated that permits would be allowed on a priority basis for the following: homeless shelters, affordable housing, projects that achieved a 35 percent net reduction in wastewater, economic enterprise zones, approved redevelopment areas, projects within one-half mile of the nearest mass transit, commercial projects providing child care for 30 or more children, and homeowner remodeling of less than 1,500 square feet. The focus of the proposed ordinance had been lost. Instead of sorting out the issues and setting priorities, an arbitrary laundry list of social justice issues, without debate or prioritization, had brought the allocation process to a dead halt.

Often, by the time the focus is lost, the news of the dilemma has also become public. The public entity can be under siege from constituents and the press.

(Counselors' opinions, conclusions, and mistaken judgments may end up in the local paper or in the *Wall Street Journal*.) Involved individuals, elected and salaried, are probably experiencing personal distress. Things have become desperate, and there are no face-saving means for closure.

Our minority report stated that the proposed ordinance was unfair, inconsistent with the city's general plan, and far too stringent. We estimated it would take a developer two years just to clear the sewer permit process hurdle. We further recommended a sunset clause for the ordinance.

Convention Center Site—Denver

Ten years ago [1986], the city of Denver and the state of Colorado were locked in a vise grip when they asked the Urban Land Institute (ULI) to provide a panel to choose the location of a proposed convention center. This project—along with the then-proposed new airport—had been bogged down for years in bitter disputes between city and state (each which felt it had jurisdiction) and among the more powerful members of the Denver real estate community. A new convention center was sorely needed to bolster the declining tourism business, yet the city's leaders and developers could not unite around this worthy objective. Feelings ran so high that our panel of ten was sequestered the entire week of deliberation.

Sequestration is not uncommon in such endeavors. It serves as a tangible reminder that a public process counselor is subject to a high standard of behavior. In performing most of my assignments, without sequestration, I find myself opportuned fairly often to attend functions or to meet with influential and popularly attractive individuals as guests of parties with interest in the assignment. Like it or not, a public process counselor must sustain, throughout the assignment, the detachment and independence of a true senior counselor.

Los Angeles Finance Task Force

In other, less emotionally charged instances, the counsel of outside advisers is sought as the basis for planning. I had the opportunity to serve on a public pro bono finance task force for Mayor Bradley. Our task was to review the city's economic condition and financial structure, to identify operational and capital requirements to maintain appropriate levels of service, and to examine conventional and alternative revenue sources to maximize capital formation and funding. The task force worked extremely well together. It was a stellar group, including future state treasurer Kathleen Brown and future state controller Kathleen Connell. In fact, in each of these assignments, I personally have found the quality and dedication of the private citizens involved one of the primary benefits of the experience.

The Charge or Assignment

Rarely is the charge of public policy counseling to arrive at a bottom-line solution. (The Denver Convention Center panel was unusual in this regard. The city and the state agreed to abide by the location decision of the ULI panel.) Herein lies the greatest contrast to private transaction counseling in a normal business environment. Indeed, there may not be a bottom-line, hard-nosed solution to the dilemma. There is room for softer type decisions, as well as purely utilitarian decisions, and the impact can be just as forceful within the area of conflict:

- The focus might be on the process for decision making or administration, identifying and bringing in good practice from the outside and reinforcing good practice where it is found in the client organization.
- The focus might be to identify bad practice or condition, not by being overly critical but by pointing out why another administrative process might be more effective.

Finance Task Force

In Mayor Bradley's finance panel, previously discussed, we came face to face with the problem particular to Los Angeles and certain other locales: the multiplicity of jurisdictional authorities operating in the same area, including federal, state, county, and city, together with a weak mayoral position, a strong but internally divided city council, and the lack of any cohesive regional planning authority. In particular, this assignment demonstrated the severe price paid at all government levels for failure to have a longer-term planning process and vision.

The essence of our findings was that the city utilized an extremely short time frame for planning purposes, engaged in an excessive amount of deferred maintenance (thus understating current budgetary requirements), and was lagging in its mandate to privatize operations. The lack of a planning cycle much longer than a year rendered the city ineffective in resolving key issues for Los Angeles, such as air quality, wastewater treatment, etc.

We concluded with a set of ten recommendations, including an increased local gasoline tax to fund deferred street maintenance. An increased gasoline tax appeared on the ballot and was defeated. Funding was provided for a portion of the deferred maintenance. An interdepartmental process was initiated to improve management of city facilities and, most important, the city council committed to develop a strategic financial plan and engage in multiyear planning. (This well-intentioned response did not materialize.)

Leasing of Office Space for State Agency

A more recent assignment involved advising a state agency on purchasing or leasing significant office space in downtown Los Angeles, which currently has one of the highest vacancy rates in the country. An obvious private transactional decision would incorporate price weaknesses in untenanted modern structures. Yet the state was willing to take part of its space by rehabilitating outmoded buildings in less than desirable locations. Using state funds to rebuild the decaying urban core had considerable appeal to certain private businesses which were also trying to hang on in the older inner city. Thus, a public process counselor must be tolerant of ambiguity and open to a multitude of stakeholders.

Suggested Process for Counseling Decisions

Regardless of the nature of the charge, public process counselors must actively seek and process large amounts of pertinent and often conflicting information with great precision. Indeed, the underlying cause of political logjams is often a failure to seek and see, to hear and listen to all the critical data. It is from this data that stakeholders can be identified and assigned relative value, that existing conflicts can be dissected and potential ones perceived. It is through this information that creative solutions are found that are cost effective and yet serve the people of the targeted area.

The gathering of this information can be a formidable task and may take some unconventional forms. One must move beyond the controlled presentations that are usually proffered to a truly investigative and proactive role. This type of interviewing is obviously more painstaking and time-consuming, but the payoff is there. The Denver experience is a good example.

Denver Approach

Our panel of ten spent a week there, sequestered the entire time, because varying city leaders were convinced that one of the developers would attempt to buy us off. We conducted interviews with about 100 citizens, politicians, and developers. The crux of our panel's decision making entailed my interview partner for the week, Nick Trkla (who passed away far too soon just this year [1996]), and me walking from the busiest intersection in downtown Denver to each of the proposed sites. We arrived at our recommended site in eight minutes. One of the other favored sites took us 43 minutes to reach. None of the others took less than 16 minutes. This was not a particularly sophisticated or trying process. We recommended a site in the center of downtown Denver, with compactness to nearby hotels and an easy walking distance for conventioneers during inclement weather. This rather simple-minded approach taken by Nick and me provided clarity and focus to the assignment and unpacked the decision of patronage, favoritism, and ancillary issues that had rendered the decision-making process cumbersome and unmanageable.

Pension Fund and the Interview Process

A very recently completed paid assignment called for an expanded and much more rigorous form of the interview process. My charge on this assignment was to make recommendations to improve the investment process in real estate for our client, a large public pension fund with roughly $5 billion in various real estate assets. I was fortunate to have an excellent partner on this assignment, and we performed our task over seven months.

We conducted approximately 100 interviews with trustees, staff, advisers, consultants, and many disinterested pension funds and pension fund advisers throughout the real estate industry. It was our goal to identify bad practices within our client and the industry and hold them up for critical comment as well as to identify good business practices within our client and the real estate pension fund industry and hold those up to our client as a new model. We knew there would be little impact if after all these interviews we only came up with a long list of new practices for the trustees and senior staff. From the beginning we needed to have impact on the process and the actors. That is, we should utilize at least a portion of each interview to begin influencing behavior in the direction it was assumed we would be heading. Thus, the assignment itself became a process for change, and we became agents of change during a portion of each interview. Just to be assured, early in the assignment I checked out our game plan/technique with a couple of senior friends at McKinsey & Co., and they validated this approach.

The assignment terminated in a five-hour off-the-record workshop with the pension fund trustees. Interestingly, all the good practices we recommended came from the interviews with the pension fund advisers. It now appears that we will have some impact on our client. The extent to which this is borne out in future practice will, in our opinion, owe as much to the proactive interview process we adapted for our counseling, as it will to the final workshop and written recommendations. [See article 17 for more details on the pension fund assignment.]

Los Angeles City Hall Seismic Project

Los Angeles City Hall is a designated historical monument and a cultural icon (which means it has been featured on *Dragnet* and in Batman movies). Our panel was handed a list of seven options. The instructions from the office of the mayor were to undertake a comprehensive fresh look at the project and seek more cost-effective solutions. Because of the cumbersome move-ins and move-outs of tenants and the working and reworking and reworking again of the same space, some portions of the seismic rehabilitation were costed out at as much as $600 a square foot. Following initial consultant presentations, which felt more like indoctrinations, the panel opted to be sequestered for the balance of its discussions. One unfortunate result of this process was that we had no opportunity to engage in a comprehensive counseling process. Our report was issued to the mayor and city council; it became public immediately, and we became adversaries to the project team as well as others within city hall.

The project suffered from a governance system led by a strong but divided city council, an equally strong mayor with very limited mayoral power, and a somewhat independent Department of Public Works. Responsibilities were blurred; focus was lost. There was no organic process to gain closure or consensus. As usual, the project became packed with Christmas tree ornaments from every participant, including deferred maintenance, the newest fire and safety regulations, and the most modern office setups (on 7,500-square-foot floorplates in the upper tower). Lack of control of the budget and the process provided a field day to the consultants, project managers, architects, and engineers who piled project upon project, ripped out leasehold improvements, evicted office occupants into other space, and labored profusely over three or four layers of plans. Indeed, the project had come under the control of the consultants who obviously resented the panel and, subsequently, may have attempted to discredit its recommendations. It seems they have even held off the repair of superficial wall cracks in the offices of city council members as a form of daily psychological reminder of the presumed inherent danger in the structure.

Our findings were comprehensive. In general we agreed it made sense to save the building as a cultural icon, but that no more than $165 million maximum (a bit over $200 a square foot) should be spent on the project. As a frame of reference, this is in a market where Class A buildings can be procured for $40 to $100 a foot or for as little as one-third of current reproduction costs. We also offered detailed advice on the governance process for the project. Our ultimate impact is not yet apparent, but the process of debate and discussion among key decision makers is well underway.

Suggested Criteria for Public Policy Counseling Decisions

The following criteria are suggested as a possible model for real estate counseling in the area of public policy:

- *Identify relevant stakeholders.* In many cases the public policy process identifies a huge list of potential stakeholders and then lacks the will and process for setting priorities and assigning values. In the public arena, this list ought to be drawn with awareness and imagination. Although the list of stakeholders may become long, being on it does not assure priority.
- *Identify potential conflicts.* Stakeholders must be heard and respected. However, rather than decorating every decision with a conceivable social goal, the public

process must begin to develop a context for decision making that focuses on a cost-effective solution to the basic problem, be it locating a convention hall, repairing a structure, allocating sewer permits, or leasing office space.

- *Seek creative solutions.* Too often the political process becomes binary. You are either for me or against me. There is a need for more awareness of the ambiguities and uncertainties in decision making. Room must be left for open exploration of other options. Perhaps a project can be staged or deferred to spread out the costs. Perhaps there are other options for cleaning up downtown rather than reducing the effectiveness of government workers.

- *Maximize long-term benefits.* This utilitarian concept is self-evident, but it is often lost in the political process. Short-term solutions produce greater long-term problems. We saw this in the Los Angeles finance task force as well as the City Hall seismic project. This is an extraordinarily difficult process for politicians. Perhaps not quite so difficult for statesmen. We need only look to our federal government, which appears fundamentally lacking in long-term budgeting, capital budgeting, and the multitude of short- and long-term policy tradeoffs.

- *Respect the public process.* Public servants deal with their own kinds of problems: conflicting objectives, multiple stakeholders, and intense political pressures. Many governmental activities are interconnected and cannot be isolated. Sometimes government requires soft judgments, rather than pure business judgment. Political pressure is not an evil. It is a reality in the public sector and in its best sense embraces public interest and public trust. Too often we denigrate the public servant who must come back every day to deal with massive problems, insufficient funds, and an often hostile press. In the meantime, we journey back to the suburbs with a self-righteous glow from a week of service to the community. Extremely capable, intelligent, and caring men and women represent our interests in the day-to-day workings of government. They deserve to rest confidently in our trust as well as our scrutiny.

- *Be a consensus builder.* Consensus building is possible only when all participants in the assignment trust and respect the real estate counselor's unbiased desire for success in their individual roles. The proactive multiple interview process can be a more potent vehicle for developing that trust and respect than the final written document or presentation. It is possible to employ the suggested criteria and still not attain consensus in your assignment; conversely it is impossible to reach consensus without employing them. Our goal as real estate counselors is to leave behind a cohesive unit of government, empowered by trust in and respect for each other.

Criteria Application

The Los Angeles City Hall seismic assignment is evaluated here utilizing the proposed criteria.

- The *stakeholder* issue was immense. When one considers the tremendous cost of rehabilitating a pop-culture icon against the immense needs of the city for public security, health, education, etc., it is easy to trash the structure. Yet, the city needs a centering structure in the downtown, but at what cost—$100, $200, $400 per square foot?

- The *conflicts* were overwhelming: city councilmembers' safety and comfort, public access, seismic engineers, consultants, historical preservation. The list goes on and on.

- The *creative solutions* included purchasing a modern structure with no civic identification, closing off 80 percent of the tower structure, demolition of City Hall, or building a modern structure.

- What would be the *long-term benefits* for the city? What would be the tradeoff between $200 million for health, safety, and education today versus a cultural icon a half century from now?

- Our *respect for the public process* exposed us to attack from the city council, the Department of Public Works, various consultants, and the local media. An ad hoc group of advisers can be made impotent in the face of such ingrained interests. Yet, how is the public voice to be heard?

- Perhaps our sequestration was incorrect for *consensus building*. Yet we felt we had to perform as independent agents. There was too much self-interest in the programmed presentations. Perhaps we should have overridden the imposed agenda and the schedule so that we not only made our independent evaluation but, perhaps, also reached consensus.

Conclusion

I have established two personal conditions for accepting a public process counseling assignment: 1) Can I tell the truth as I come to understand it? 2) Can I have an impact? Although I have encountered some rough spots along the way, the first condition has been met in each of the public service assignments described in this article. The second issue is problematic. Coming from the business world, my idea of having impact is much more concrete than anything I have experienced in the public process counseling arena. I would say that my own efforts in this area are mixed to date, but they are not without some impact in each assignment.

Process counseling is far more complex than transactional counseling. As is the case with any type of business practice, the only way to master it is by doing it and learning from your successes and failures. The role of a real estate counselor in public process assignments is to help clear away the debris and focus on the primary issues. It is to develop an orderly procedure for prioritizing important issues; to evaluate, admire, and defend good practice and to critically and objectively evaluate bad practice; to create an atmosphere of professionalism and calm in the midst of controversy. It is, as usual, to help guide our clients to do the right thing.

Source: *Real Estate Issues*, December 1996.

19 My Computer and Me

The profound impact of the computer on our daily lives is probably more pervasive than we know. That little gate, which is always either open or closed or an "0" or a "1," has the potential of converting our psyches into binary instruments. Everything becomes overly simplistic: either "go" or "no-go," "yes" or "no." There is little room for ambiguity or paradox.

Yet, we may have overestimated the computer's impact on society's productivity. One of my friends, an economic historian, writes of long waves of productivity from innovation, with true productivity gains occurring at the end of the cycle. He likens the computer to the electric motor, saying that a quarter century after its invention, the electric motor was utilized in the manufacturing process to shed illumination on steam-and water-driven shaft and pulley systems of production. The true harnessing of electrical power in the factory system did not take hold for 50 to 75 years.

Likewise, the impact of the computer on productivity is a long time coming. In the service sector, in fact, the computer may have become antiproductive. As new hardware is developed with 35 percent annual improvements in processing efficiency, new software must be designed. By the time someone has mastered the current configuration, it becomes outmoded. The endless process of change continues. There is hardly a steady state when one can master the equipment and its countless applications.

I have no doubt that, early on in the millennium, we will arrive at more standardized systems for processing information, and the true productivity gains, which occur at the end of a long-wave productivity cycle, will be achieved. Control of the information base will afford dominant power in a business segment. Businesses that spend the capital and the effort to master this change cycle will be in control.

But why wait for the millennium? Indeed, some businesses already are experiencing these productivity gains, e.g., the air transport reservations systems. Therefore, I share with you the following story, hoping that you, too, will be one of those dominant powers.

I've Always Been Online

I had always considered myself to be somewhat computer literate. My initial exposure to the computer began more than 35 years ago when I started my banking career at Morgan Stanley. There were 16 of us in the corporate finance department. We spent most of our time operating Friden electromechanical calculators in the machine room, running present value investment calculations for oil pipelines and hydroelectric power schemes and even England's then-proposed Channel tunnel. It would take us days to perform a simple 30-year set of pro forma income statements, cash flows, and balance sheets. The air was heavy, without air conditioning (and we smoked) and filled with the clatter of a dozen machines chugging through endless long division. Out of that inefficient and low-pay cacophony came future CEOs of Morgan Stanley, First Boston, Smith Barney, U.S. Trust and the chief investment officer of the state of New Jersey. It also produced enough complaints that soon—even though we did not yet merit private telephones—permission was granted to hire a consultant and commence developing simple programs (later termed proprietary software), which we would run in the evenings at the IBM service center in midtown Manhattan. Later, when we were advising on Singer's acquisition of the Friden business, all the pro forma ratios were calculated by the client on its computer. I was summoned up to the old partners room, handed the computer printout, and told to check each computer calculation on an electromechanical Friden. So much for productivity.

Those early years of modeling project finance on the computer served Morgan Stanley in good stead. A decade later, when I was responsible for the real estate unit, we did, in fact, have proprietary software on in-house mainframes, which we utilized to calculate investment returns and model real estate assets and projects. In that regard, we always thought we had an edge on our competition. Overspending on computers and proprietary software became a strategic direction for the firm, and it resulted in keeping the edge on such esoteric items as geometry trading and multiple currency clearing. The multiple currency clearing software provided the firm with a significant strategic edge when the seat became available on the Tokyo stock exchange.

My continuing exposure to the computer in the early years came by osmosis from my then-spouse who worked as a systems engineer for IBM. She was part of that powerful customer-support system that IBM developed and ascended upon. I recall her story of the mail-order customer who wanted to computerize accounts receivable for the first time. The elderly lady who was in charge kept the records handwritten on yellow ledger paper locked in her desk drawer. My wife dropped by several afternoons a week to visit with her and drink tea (with a lemon drop added). After several weeks the lady finally trusted my wife enough to unlock her drawer and give her the records, another breakthrough for innovation. A great benefit from the IBM experience was that our three children became at ease on the computer while they were in primary school. Two daughters ended up on Ph.D. tracks, and one is a professor of physical chemistry at Ohio State.

Throughout my 27-plus years at Morgan Stanley, I was beautifully supported by an efficient administrative staff, including an increasingly powerful computer group. And finally, at the end, I had a terminal on my desk, which I used continually for data retrieval—stock quotes and news stories online. I recall talking on the telephone with the CEO of a communications company and reading him a broad tape announcement regarding his business, which he didn't know was out.

On My Own

It was in 1990, when I retired from Morgan Stanley and became an independent real estate and business counselor, that I realized how extremely dependent I was on having clerical support service. The terminal on my desk was not indicative of computer literacy. I had never become adroit on the computer beyond retrieval usage.

After considerable deliberation, I opted for a single office in a high-tech executive services building, which provided mail processing, telephone answering with voice mail, and word processing with desktop publishing services. The cost for all this, including the office space and parking, was less than engaging a good full-time executive assistant. I had rapidly downsized to an office staff of only one, me; and I was going to be totally dependent upon others, whom I did not know, for important functions of my business existence. Only they had the needed technological knowledge and skill. It was a rather vulnerable position. I could almost see the buzzards circling.

I had mastered voice mail. In fact, I lived by it, wished I had thought of it first, and actually was disdainful of messages that only asked for a call back without including the reason for the call. My typing skills were excellent. I still used my old electric Royal at home for certain tasks. (I have come to regard typing, along with public speaking, as one of the high school courses that best prepared me for life.) I could always call on that skill if the word processing function at the office became tedious or inconsistent. Typing skills would serve me well if I ever decided I had to get on the computer myself; but, this was not the time in my life to welcome another major project. In addition to starting a new business, I was committed to a challenging array of volunteering, teaching, and professional tasks. Besides, I could afford to hire as much computer support as I needed. I would make it work.

Happy Birthday Baby!

In the first part of 1994 my wife went with me to an Urban Land Institute meeting in Scottsdale where we attended a lecture by Jennifer James, a behavioral psychologist from San Jose State, on the importance of staying in touch with the rapidly changing technological world. The audience appeared to be mostly 50ish. James said we probably would live another quarter century, and if we did not have the will to master the computer, we would be left hopelessly behind, missing out on a rich and most exciting phase of our professional life. Six months later, on the morning of my 57th birthday, my wife gave me a beautifully wrapped box of computer disks and informed me about the day and hour the remainder of the gift would be delivered. She had retained a consultant to design the package which included the newest, fastest CPU, fax, laser printer, CD player, software and, most propitious, nine hours of one-on-one instruction from a computer coach whose office was just down the hall from mine. The buzzards had landed. Technology had caught up with me. I was being forced to master the computer. For one who had successfully avoided such intimacy, it was not a happy birthday.

Being naturally compulsive and having a relatively light summer schedule, I inhaled deeply and set about mastering my new gift. I bought a dozen manuals on Windows 3.1, Word, Excel, PowerPoint, the Internet, CompuServe, etc. I sadly and quickly came to the conclusion that for me the best manuals were *Windows*, *Excel*, and *Internet for Dummies*. I scheduled my private instruction for three hours at a clip, two weeks apart, so during the in-between time, I could master what I had learned.

My instructor, Fleichelle, started at the beginning, granting me no credit for my independent study. Even then, all did not go smoothly. My sense of exploration and adventure got me in big-time trouble. I attempted to master mouse clicking and FileMaster simultaneously and blew out all the installed software by clicking and dragging much of it into the netherworld of computerland. This cost me an additional six hours of reinstallation time. I had vowed that I would never allow the PC to turn me into a typist. My speeches and articles would continue to go down the hall for desktop publishing. Despite this vow, I attempted to compose an article. After several afternoons of fruitlessly chasing consummate prose around and about the page and then losing it in the hinterlands of computerdom, I went home, poured a glass of Jack Daniels, and glared at my spouse. She is a fine woman, but she certainly misread me on this one. I wondered what kind of return policy she had negotiated.

But, Fleichelle did not give up so easily, and I am extremely grateful. Gradually, I began to experience some victories. The file I had saved the day before was still there the next morning. The words on the screen settled down. I was beginning to have some fun. Indeed, occasionally I was being chastised for making furtive clicking sounds on my computer keys while talking on the telephone. I graduated my nine-hour course with honors and reluctantly bid my instructor farewell, feeling comforted that she was available to me by phone if I had any problems.

By the end of summer, I signed up for CompuServe. In the beginning, I tried out some of the forums; simple ones like the topic of religion. When I broadcast my desire to communicate with someone on the great German theologian, Dietrich Bonhoeffer, I learned it was not always so easy to talk in forums. Someone obviously did not want to discuss Bonhoeffer when I did, and I was "flamed" off the religion forum. Now I depend on CompuServe for news, weather, e-mail, and stock quote updates throughout the day.

A bit later I attempted to get on the Internet. As recently as two years ago, this was still an adventure. Neither CompuServe nor AOL had Internet access. I had to go through a local supplier where access was controlled by a heavily accented gentleman who appeared to be completely self-assured and thoroughly antibusiness. After he had canceled my account several times, I was overjoyed to see CompuServe had developed direct Internet access. Now I can easily access such organizations as Morgan Stanley, Harvard Business School, the *Wall Street Journal*, the SEC filings, the Urban Land Institute, and the Counselors of Real Estate. Every day new names are being added to this list.

Now, two years later, I compose all my speeches, reports, and articles, as well as lists, messages, travel schedules, and the like, on my computer. I can prepare slides on PowerPoint, compose a document on Word and then WinFax it anywhere in the world. I get special satisfaction WinFaxing my cigar man in Hong Kong. I am truly operating in the 24-hour global marketplace.

E-mail is an absolute delight. People who before would never write or fax me and would seldom call respond to an e-mail within the hour. My address book is growing by leaps and bounds. Sons and daughters of friends have found me lurking in forums and e-mailed their surprise and congratulations. I e-mail my daughter at Ohio State almost every day. I can honestly say e-mail has brought us even closer together. When our pastor traveled to a church-sponsored hospital in Malawi, we e-mailed through his laptop from each location that had a phone line.

My favorite CD-ROM is *Monty Python*. I enjoy *Bible Soft*, which gives me a bible literacy I hardly deserve. After a trying day of dealing with crustaceous secretaries and floating margins, it's a joy to turn to computer solitaire. Nothing is so fulfilling as the animated cards arching over the screen when I win the game. One of my manuals actually has instructions for cheating at computer solitaire.

I only allow myself to commence my browse of the Internet around 4:30 p.m. when I am in my office. It turns out that I am a bookmark junkie. I have a couple of hundred exotic and fascinating sites logged into my bookmarks library. I have visited them only briefly, to date, but they are all there for when I have the time. It is compelling to have at one's fingertips the latest Stanford women's basketball scores, the program for next year's New Orleans Jazz Festival, the Los Angeles freeway speed table, a prayer for the day, and *Time* magazine. It is exciting to see the current state of flux in all this and to imagine how it will all evolve, especially with bona fide credit card security on the net.

Conclusion

So why do I tell this story? For me, it is my celebration that after 35 years, I am finally "online." I am constantly amazed that the computer is such an incredibly powerful tool. It has made me vastly more efficient in some tasks, but I am also totally nonproductive when I take a spin on the Internet. The stretch of learning I've experienced has been personally rewarding. I am proud to be among the 2 percent of those age 50 or above who operate on "the Net." My self-esteem, having suffered innumerable lows, has regained its hopeful equilibrium.

For us professionals in the real estate industry, I am more convinced than ever we will see incredible productivity gains from all this over the next 10–15 years. Massive databases of rentals, costs, comparables, and the like will be developed. As usual, the firms that make the investment and master the productivity cycle will control the business.

As for all of us aging sole proprietors, with a quarter century to go, I can only echo the good advice that I received. Jennifer James says we can no longer leverage off others. Now is the time for us to master the computer. If we continue to procrastinate, we will be left hopelessly far behind.

Source: *Real Estate Issues* (New Technology column), April 1997.

PART 4

Real Estate Capital Markets in the 2000s

Investment As Affected by 9/11

A Maturing Asset Class

Note to readers: In part 1 of this book, the author summarizes the key issues and points covered in the individual articles, and offers additional commentary to provide context and a longer-term perspective. Commentaries on articles 20 to 28 may be found on pages 21 to 25.

20 Clouds of Uncertainty

The next move most likely will be into a trading market, with new development becoming very difficult to finance.

As a result of the terrorist attacks of September 11, today's real estate capital markets are filled with clouds of uncertainty. It is a time to be cautious; although for risk-taking opportunities, it may be a time to buy.

The rippling economic effects have pushed the country into a recession, which may affect the economy for as long as two years. It will be an unusual worldwide recession, with Europe suffering relatively less, and Japan suffering relatively greater, economic stress.

Ironically, the terrorist attacks have forced the federal government to take the correct actions—for the wrong reasons. Monetary policy, as has been shown by Japan's experience, becomes increasingly less effective as the limit of zero-interest rates is approached. The federal government's response to September 11 created the fiscal stimulus and deficit spending that could never have been achieved before the terrorist attacks, and that may end up being the correct policy response to the recession.

Although in general, real estate markets are in much better shape than they were in recent economic downturns, the level of uncertainty about the near-term future has caused widening gaps in sales pricing and the costs of capital. What is considered normal will change. Even before September 11, it was difficult to determine true net effective office and industrial rents in areas like San Francisco and Washington, D.C. There likely will be a permanent change in the dynamics of tourism, the largest component of world GNP (gross national product), which is spending that is easily canceled or deferred. This negative change will severely penalize industries such as hospitality and airlines, which leverage high fixed costs with high debt ratios.

Commercial banks have been more cautious about lending this year, as the regulatory agencies have criticized their portfolios for certain corporate loans, especially in the communications sector. Hotel and airline loans will create increased pressure and conservatism on the part of lenders. Only a handful of banks continue to make construction loans, and the underwriting standards are conservative. The banks' willingness to continue to make such loans depends on the performance of the commercial mortgage–backed security (CMBS) market, where spreads have widened since September 11. A critical factor in the evolution of the CMBS market will be the ability of trustees of large multiloan portfolios to restructure individual loans to meet current conditions.

Real estate investment trusts (REITs) have fared well this year. The best news since September 11 is the proposed inclusion of Equity Office Properties Trust (EOP) in the Standard & Poor's (S&P) 500 Index, which will create additional buying support for the shares. This marks the acceptance of REITs as a standard investment vehicle, and it will probably increase pressure to base accounting standards on "generally accepted principles" rather than on "funds from operations."

Pension funds, ironically, find their asset allocation percentages in real estate moving up as the value of their equity portfolio moves down. This could reduce, on the margin, new money allocations into real estate.

Opportunity funds likely will move a portion of their allocation targets back into the United States—and out of Europe and Japan—to take advantage of perceived buying opportunities. A risky, yet interesting target of opportunity would be the debt of distressed hotel companies. Another opportunity for some is the need of many closed-end, specific-duration funds to liquidate their investments into a distressed marketplace.

For those entities with financial flexibility, now is an opportune time to restructure debt. It is advisable to move from short- and medium-term debt into long-term debt, and to move from floating-rate debt into fixed-rate debt. This is very much a time in which the strong get stronger and the weak get weaker.

We most likely will move into a trading market, with new development becoming very difficult to finance. There will be premiums for equity capital, and the market will become even more a tenant's market.

The new economy is not over. Broadband-width communication constitutes at present only about 10 percent of its potential. When it achieves 50 percent of its potential, in a few years, the new levels of connectivity will be a major driver of economic growth.

Source: *Urban Land* (Capital Markets column), November/December 2001.

21 Will It Ever Be the Same Again?

Finance symposium participants are divided on the nature of the economic recovery.

At the eighth annual McCoy symposium on real estate finance, held in New York City last month [December 2001], there was general agreement that the economic slowdown will last until at least the middle of this year. The consensus was that during the next six months there will be few transactions in the real estate market, very little new product will get built, and many projects currently on the drawing board will be deferred. The economy will show either negative growth, or growth below that of normal population growth. A significant number of businesses still will be growing, but a greater number will be flat or will have declining revenues. The financial system remains highly liquid, and there is plenty of excess capacity.

The major disagreement among symposium participants was the nature of the economic recovery commencing during the second half of the year. The group of 25 real estate finance practitioners was divided about evenly between those who believed a sharp recovery would occur and others who felt the recovery period would be prolonged. Those believing there would be a sharp recovery also felt that the economy would adjust to the possibility of further terrorist activity, while others who felt recovery would be sluggish held the view that the events of September 11 would have a prolonged negative impact on consumer confidence. Forum participants also commented on the $5 trillion loss of wealth in the securities markets, and predicted the unemployment rate to increase to above 6 percent.

In either case, the majority of forum participants agreed that the United States is in a period when the determination of net effective rents is problematic, causing tenants to choose to wait before signing new leases. For the time being, the transaction market is "frozen," with wide spreads between perceived values by buyers and sellers.

Those who believed that the terrorist attack on New York City would produce more permanent changes in the economy also predicted permanent changes in the real estate industry. They realized that building security and insurance costs will rise on a long-term basis. Certain types of tenants, such as government offices of countries reported to harbor terrorists, will no longer be desirable. Parking will be seen more as an expense than as a revenue item. Many businesses will avoid high-rise buildings. Large businesses will avoid concentration and will attempt to spread their headquarters operations over different communications networks. Furthermore, some businesses will pay for redundancies, flex space, and duplicate facilities.

The state of the insurance markets was the subject of a focused discussion. Without adequate terrorist insurance, capital availability may be greatly restricted. At the time of the symposium, Congress was considering some form of federal backstop for the insurance industry. The issues include the length of years covered, the proper definition of an act of war, and the amount of deductibility. Some felt that without adequate insurance to protect against terrorist risk, the commercial mortgage–backed securities (CMBS) market could shut down. It was predicted that underinsured commercial mortgage pools could be downgraded by the rating agencies.

Equity Markets. Owners of property will have to face up to a valuation issue at year-end. It is likely that assets in general will have declined in value 3 to 4 percent. Cash returns in general are about 8 percent, so investors still would have a real return of 5 percent, which does not look bad compared with other asset classes.

Pension funds are seeking a high-return area in which to invest assets. Real estate continues to have issues of transparency, pricing, and liquidity. Some pension funds have reached their real estate allocations because of the decline in stock market values. It appears that new money will be aimed more toward hedge funds and private equity rather than toward real estate.

Real estate investment trusts (REITs) lost market share in 2001. Apartments, in particular, were capitalized by Fannie Mae and others. REIT stock prices were up in a down stock market, but they have been flat since September 11. Hotels and airlines most likely will snap back in a recovery, but, as tourism is indefinitely postponable, the timing of the recovery for that sector remains problematic.

It remains difficult to raise new money for private real estate venture funds. As a result of the difficulty of price discovery, it is hard to buy or sell property. Many funds have gone abroad. The European business is driven by corporate, and some government, restructuring. Basically, there are five U.S. firms bidding on most larger European property sales. The smaller firms, however, cannot afford the due-diligence process, especially if they lose the property in question. Japanese markets remain inefficient, providing opportunities for the funds.

Debt Markets. The year 2002 will have extraordinarily low rollover of mortgage loans from the early 1990s, making it more difficult for insurance companies to meet their allocations. Insurance companies are losing debt market share to CMBSs and short-term bank lending. The slowdown in real estate sales transactions also has a negative impact on the demand for debt capital.

Lending criteria continue to be tightened. There is further increased emphasis on the creditworthiness of tenants and higher reserves for vacancies. Because of terrorism issues, lenders are concerned about concentration of assets in certain urban cores—New York City, Washington, D.C., Chicago, and the like. Life insurance companies' loan-to-value ratios are 60 to 65 percent, creating a large market for mezzanine finance funds. The large issues are underwriting a single tenant and insurance. Delinquencies are currently less than 1 percent. Even considering further corporate bankruptcies at the depth of the recession, the worst case anyone could state was a 4.5 percent delinquency rate, compared with a 14 percent rate in 1991.

After the events of September 11, will it ever be the same again? Yes and no. Issues such as insurance, security, concentration of personnel, communications, travel, and the like will be influenced for some time to come. Attempts must be made to separate out the long-term impact of terrorism from the negative impact of the recession. The recession shall pass; and it will pass sooner than the terrorist impact. For at least the next six months, developers should stay as liquid as possible, conserve their assets, trim their overhead, heap attention and goodwill on their tenants, and establish a thoughtful business plan for operating once the economy grows again. Over the medium to long term, the U.S. economy promises significant real growth, especially as compared with that of almost any other industrialized nation. Such growth will provide ample opportunity for developers who are sensitive to changes in tenant needs and preferences, who are willing to put hard equity at risk alongside investors, and who have a thoughtful and disciplined approach to the market.

Source: *Urban Land* (Capital Markets column), January 2002.

22

Disconnected Markets

Real estate developers should use the current attractive financing markets prudently, retaining an ample supply of equity in their projects.

According to participants in the ninth annual McCoy symposium on real estate finance, held in New York City in December [2001], there is a disconnection between what is occurring in the real estate capital markets and what is happening at the property level itself. Real estate capital market players are awash in cash and intent on making new investments in property, especially during a multigenerational period of low interest rates. Property operators, however, are encountering weak rental conditions and high vacancies. It is important, therefore, in discussing real estate markets, to distinguish between the two perspectives—that of the investor and that of the developer.

Paramount is the direction of the economy. As was the case at last year's symposium, participants were divided on whether 2003 will be a year of slow growth or of further recession. The consensus was that the current year will be one of slow, partial recovery, but that the economic recovery period will last longer than was thought to be the case last year.

On the negative side, the economy has many weak sectors, including capital spending in manufacturing and large deficits and layoffs in sectors such as telecommunications, technology, finance, airlines, and state and local governments. Even firms with robust unit sales are having difficulty preserving or gaining pricing power. Eroding margins are appearing for products such as personal computers and DVDs, as well as new automobiles for which sales are financed for prolonged periods at zero-interest rates. With interest rates so low, monetary policy can do little more to stimulate the economy. Weakened economies in Europe and the Far East are resulting in a decline in export trade. Labor problems are occurring in ports and airlines. Malfeasance has reduced trust in financial markets. And overhanging everything is the threat of war and terrorism.

Those with a more positive outlook are focusing on the longer-term positive demographic and technology trends in the United States, which should produce a minimum of 3 percent annual growth in the gross national product (GNP). Inflation is low. Interest rates are as low as they have been in 50 years. President Bush's fiscal stimulus plan should produce job growth. Real estate did not overbuild during this cycle. Even in the down cycle, real estate was protected by the large equity infusions in the 1990s and by low interest rates. The general consensus is not to bet against the U.S. economy.

Real estate fundamentals are weak and will most likely deteriorate further. Hotel markets have been weak since September 11, 2001. In certain high-tech areas, such as Boston's ring road and Silicon Valley, commercial hotels will not recover for several years. The same is true for office and tech-oriented industrial developments in similar locations, which may remain depressed for as long as three to five years. Corporate lay-offs have created vacant space—which remains unoccupied, but on which rent is still being paid—in virtually all markets. This "shadow" vacancy will further depress office markets as bankruptcies occur or leases expire. Low interest rates have encouraged renters to step up to homeownership, creating pressure on apartment rentals. In many areas, rent concessions of one or two months on a one-year lease were noted. Real estate will lag behind recovery of the general economy, and it will be negatively affected by the anticipated rising interest rate environment that the recovery will spawn.

The primary real estate capital markets' disconnect occurs in the equity markets, where rents are declining, the amount of "phantom" occupied space cannot be determined, and operating expenses are increasing while capitalization rates are declining. Operating expenses are increasing in part as a result of higher security costs, as well as state and local governments' search for augmented tax revenues from commercial property.

One driver of lower capitalization rates is the perception that "trophy" buildings can be purchased at less than replacement cost. This reasoning does not take into consideration the fact that such structures would not be built in today's economic environment. Unless the buildings are leased to "bankruptcy-proof" (a phrase whose meaning currently is clouded) tenants on long-term leases at rents above present levels, such transactions would seem overpriced.

One reason for the higher prices paid is that investors expect lower returns, in part due to lower interest rates and in part to the belief that returns from the stock market will remain depressed in the intermediate term. Free and clear unleveraged returns expectations have dropped from 8 to10 percent to 6 to 8 percent.

As always, real estate appraisals lag behind market conditions. Institutional investors in real property likely are reporting returns in the 8 percent range, which if marked to market value would net a positive return of 4 to 5 percent, still relatively positive when compared with interest rates or the stock market. A significant amount of investment capital appears to be patiently awaiting a period of greater stress for property owners, in a year or so, when pricing power will move from sellers to buyers.

Real estate investment trusts (REITs) will be under greater pressure to defend the quality of their earnings and their ability to maintain dividend payout levels. The president's economic stimulus package, if adopted with full tax relief on corporate dividends, will make REIT dividends relatively less attractive. There will be increasing pressure for consolidation among REITs although sponsors will resist the trend.

Benchmark returns for opportunity funds have drifted down in recent years from 25 to 20 to 18 percent, and to a current level of around 15 percent, as yields on alternative investments also have come down. Holding periods on more recent funds no doubt will lengthen, as fund managers will have to work harder for lower returns. Most funds have reached overseas for higher returns in recent years, but those markets also are becoming increasingly competitive. The investment climate in Japan is less favorable to foreign funds than was previously the case.

Even though there is plenty of debt capital available, the fundamentals are deteriorating, and institutions have maintained underwriting discipline. Stressed operating fundamentals have been masked by low interest rates. The new development pipeline is off by as much as 40 percent. There is more risk in the system than is apparent, as owners and developers are hoping the low interest rate environment lasts long enough for rental rates to recover. Many symposium participants believed this was a bad bet. Balloon maturities are risky. Real estate debt also trails the corporate market, where in recent months $150 billion of debt has been downgraded below investment grade. The commercial mortgage–backed securities (CMBS) market is new and has not yet been stressed. Expect downgrades, delinquencies, and defaults in this market in the year ahead. Procedures must be established to determine which entities are responsible for working out the assets and how they get paid. Special servicers of CMBSs may not be able to fulfill their responsibilities. CMBS underwriting spreads have deteriorated to the point where they may not compensate for the risk that originators must take in warehousing inventory.

There was general agreement that interest rates will rise, and that the country is enjoying a "full moon and high tide" in liquidity. The irony is that the economic recovery that will drive the stock market and investor returns, and ultimately rental rates, will bring with it higher interest rates. Higher interest rates will increase costs and reduce loan amounts, putting pressure on balloon and bullet loans that will mature in the near term. Real estate rental rates will lag behind the economic recovery and the return to higher interest rates, putting further stress on owners and developers of property financed at short or intermediate term. Such financial stress also could spread to new homebuyers who have used low interest rates to stretch the amount borrowed. Thus, temporary lower interest rates can be a mixed blessing unless prudent debt management techniques are used.

The recent adoption by Congress of terrorism insurance was both discussed and appreciated by symposium participants. Also discussed was the impact of the Sarbanes-Oxley Act on corporate governance, including nonpublic real estate firms. The broad adoption of more conservative accounting rules will affect real estate accounting. Synthetic leases probably will have to be done over in the form of sale-leasebacks and reported on balance sheets. Many types of guarantees, such as environmental cleanup, which have formerly been footnoted, may have to be valued and included on balance sheets.

Real estate investors regard periods of stress and low interest rates as opportune times to purchase property. Participants in the seminar believe that the period of stress will outlast the period of low interest rates. Investors and speculators who count on low interest rates to justify their investments may be taking on a higher degree of risk than they anticipate. Nevertheless, the current abnormally low interest costs should be taken advantage of. Perhaps one way to play the market in today's environment is to borrow as much as possible, with the caveat that the loan amount be limited to an amount that can be supported in an environment in which interest rates are 200 basis points higher.

Certain capital market players at the symposium pointed out that they were borrowing as much as possible at short-term and floating rates and then fixing the interest rate with a longer-term interest rate swap. Their theory was that when rates turn up, they can unwind the swap, with the profits derived from it offsetting the higher interest rates they would then pay. Such techniques are only for the most sophisticated. When markets are in shock, as they were with the collapse of Long-Term Credit Bank (Japan) and the Russian debt crisis, swap spreads do not behave as predicted.

Caution must be taken against adding too great a financial risk to the risks already inherent in real estate investment.

Real estate developers should use the current attractive financing markets prudently, retaining an ample supply of equity in their projects. Tenant credit-worthiness is at a premium. More stress is to come in terms of lease defaults and unoccupied space. The mere passage of time aggravates current vacancies. There is a limit as to how long tenants can pay for unoccupied space. The expected prolonged nature of the economic recovery will cause increased stress in the real estate system. Operating costs will rise because of increased security, fuel costs, insurance, higher local taxes, and the like. As always, tenant retention comes at a premium that places an increased burden on tenant services. Staying power and a conservative financing structure are of paramount importance. Avoid speculative projects, and enjoy the productivity gains and economic growth anticipated for the middle portion of the decade.

Source: *Urban Land* (Capital Markets column), February 2003.

23 New Conditions? Suggestions for Dealing with the Possibility of a Deflationary Environment

Around the country, real estate owner/operators currently [2005] are having to think about both deflation and disinflation—conditions many have not faced before. Deflation, properly defined as a sustained decline in the general price level, occurs when and if money and credit growth falls short of real gross domestic product growth for a prolonged period of time. The sustained strong money and credit growth policy of Alan Greenspan and his predecessors (and his likely successors) is most likely to prevent this situation from occurring. The Federal Reserve Bank has made it clear that it stands ready to take measures to boost liquidity if necessary before the economy enters deflation. The likelihood of a general deflationary cycle similar to Japan's recent experience, or to this country's experience in the 1930s, is probably less than 15 percent; some would peg it at zero.

Nevertheless, deflationary conditions can be experienced in certain industry segments, or even in specific geographic areas, in the absence of a general deflationary cycle. This was true during the early 1990s in the case of commercial real estate, which experienced far worse economic conditions than the country in general. Certain geographic markets, such as downtown Atlanta in the 1980s and downtown Los Angeles in the 1990s, suffered much worse economic conditions than the real estate industry in general. Many real estate owner/operators have significant previous experience dealing with falling demand, lack of pricing power, and the need to manage debt and control costs.

The general conditions encountered in a deflationary market segment include the following: declining rents, layoffs affecting the need for space, loan defaults (especially on the part of those who have overborrowed), an unwillingness to commit to medium- or longer-term leases resulting from tenants' expectation that future rents will be lower, a repricing of for-sale real estate, a requirement to prepare pro forma forecasts showing declining income streams, a need to provide even more tenant services while controlling costs at the same time, and a premium on protecting free cash flow.

In a disinflationary environment, debt becomes an intoxicating siren. Rates lower than those that have been seen for a generation or two can lure borrowers into a potential liquidity trap. Unless borrowings are backed up by locked-in, long-term credit leases providing a positive spread of investment returns to the equity, even lower-cost debt can become difficult to service. Furthermore, there is a tendency to overborrow at lower rates. As rates rise in the future, values will fall and loan-to-value ratios that were conservative at lower interest rates will become very risky at higher interest rates, with the potential of wiping out the equity in a project. It is likely that an improving economic cycle will cause interest rates to rise earlier and faster than rental rates, especially for office space, where there are lags in the marketplace.

Disinflation, defined as a decline in the rate of increase in average prices, has been the state of the U.S. economy for several quarters now. It breeds many of the same conditions caused by deflation, and it would be prudent to apply many of the same planning techniques to both.

Following are some suggestions for dealing with the possibility of a deflationary environment; many of them could prove beneficial even if a deflationary cycle never materializes.

- *Develop an action plan.* Have a business plan based on the scenario of deflation occurring. Develop pro forma sensitivity models examining the effect on individual properties of various percentage declines in rents and vacancies as well as a 200 basis point increase in interest rates. Deflation may not affect all geographic sectors or property types. Strategize using multiple scenarios of falling rents across individual portfolios. Consider how various categories of tenants will be affected. Explore opportunities for extending leases. Take into consideration how much rent can be reduced or how much inducements increased to renew expiring leases rates. Contemplate whether "equity leases" with shared ownership make sense in certain cases in order to hold onto larger credit tenants. Consider what portfolio-augmenting properties are likely to become available at opportunistic pricing. Analyze suppliers with an eye toward cutting costs and inventories. Take a close look at staffing needs.

- *Reduce inventory.* Order smaller amounts in shorter cycles to take advantage of decreasing prices.
- *Avoid commodities.* Move out of products and services that are commodity priced or drastically reduce costs in order to become a lower-priced option to customers. Be the low-cost producer—or get out.
- *Increase productivity.* Deflation may provide an opportunity to purchase technology products and services also suffering from declining prices. Those businesses with liquidity can increase their productivity by making technology investments at reduced prices.
- *Cut costs.* Deflation means lower wages as well as lower profits. Consider sharing equity with employees in return for reduced wages. Cut operating costs down to the bone. Wait for lower prices before buying. Relatively higher expenses increase the operating leverage of a business. In a capital-intensive business such as real estate, where there can also be high balance sheet leverage, the combination of the two can be devastating, as is the case at present in the airline and hotel industries.
- *Review contracts.* Negotiate longer contracts with tenants. Anticipate lease rollovers of credit tenants with offers of lease extensions at lower than the contract rate. Provide shared-equity inducements if required in certain cases. Take to heart the new adage, "Stay alive until 2005!" Avoid being locked into longer-term supplier contracts during a period of declining prices for goods and services.
- *Conserve cash.* Liquidity is king. Run businesses as tightly as possible, even if a liquidity problem is not perceived. Use "excess" cash for technology improvements and opportunistic buying.
- *Reduce financial leverage.* A deflationary cycle can trap owner/operators into loading up on low-cost debt in order to take advantage of the opportunity to buy distressed properties or properties held in weak hands. For those with well-run businesses, excess cash, and unused borrowing capacity, such economic cycles are "once in a lifetime" opportunities. Those not quite so well off who plunge into the property market and use up reserves may be taking a bigger risk than initially realized. In a typical economic cycle, growth resumes and regulators do an abrupt switch, worrying about inflation once again. Typically, interest rates will rise rapidly, coming out of a slow-growth or deflationary period, while, as usual, real estate rental rates will lag the recovery. By the time tenants begin to think of leasing additional space, putting upward pressure on rents, interest rates will already have spiked. Thus, overleveraged entrepreneurs can find the cost of debt and reduced loan-to-value ratios unsustainable. A cautionary rule of thumb might be for borrowers to internally underwrite their own loans as if interest rates were 200 to 300 basis points higher than at the trough of a slow-growth cycle and reduce the amount borrowed accordingly.

Real estate continues to be a classic market sector in which to play the arbitrage opportunities between private and public market pricing and between general economic and interest rate cycles and the discontinuous real estate cycle. Such strategies are probably best pursued by only the most sophisticated market players. For the typical real estate owner/operator, the best advice always is to tightly manage and plan businesses—and run a little bit scared.

Source: *Urban Land*, October 2005.

24 Toward Greater Transparency

The McCoy Finance Symposium—an outgrowth of the ULI Credit Task Force, which dealt with the serious crisis in the real estate capital markets in the early 1990s—gathers together about 30 leaders in the real estate capital markets annually for discussion of current conditions and issues.

As real estate becomes integrated into world capital markets, it must do better.

In a discussion of real estate capital markets in the 21st century, Peter Linneman, Albert Sussman Professor of Real Estate and Finance at the Wharton School of Business, led off the sixth annual McCoy Finance Symposium, held in New York City in December [1999], by outlining major trends that will affect capital markets in the next 20 years. For starters, he said, social security systems in the United States and parts of Europe will be funded, eliminating the current "pay as you go" plans. This will provide an enormous pool of fiduciary capital seeking investment, noted Linneman, and such funds also will be on the lookout for transparency and large, liquid trading markets. Later in the century, retirement plans will be funded more broadly in Europe as well as in Asia. Once again, he said, this will raise savings rates globally and create a drive toward greater information flows, or transparency. At the same time, individuals in developed countries will continue to shift to 401(k) self-administered retirement plans.

As a result of these trends, real estate will cease to be thought of as a separate asset class with unique pricing of capital and disclosure requirements, continued Linneman, and will increasingly be subject to the more rigorous disclosure and competitive forces of the money and capital markets. In addition, said Linneman, the Internet and communications technology will create borderless economies, increase globalization, and further establish English as the international language.

As real estate becomes increasingly integrated into capital markets, it must provide greater disclosure and transparency, said Linneman. In the past, real estate was viewed as a separate asset class, and institutions allocated separate capital to it and tolerated pricing of real estate loans and investments that at times was out of sync with the overall capital markets. As real estate becomes integrated into world capital markets, it must stand on its own and compete for capital along with all the great companies, he urged. Relative to the overall economy, Linneman predicted that real estate will erode in importance as technology and communications gain investment market share. Real estate, however, will remain important, and land use per capita may actually increase.

Discussion following Linneman's remarks focused on current conditions. The increased transparency in the public real estate markets in recent years has caused real estate to be priced where it is currently. Many investors are positioning themselves for the next down cycle in real estate. Lending institutions are being far more selective. Real estate investment trusts (REITs) are selling at discounts to net asset values. The times to make money in real estate investments are when assets are being repriced upward out of a down cycle or when real estate capital is mispriced because it is viewed as a separate asset class. Under conditions of market equilibrium between supply and demand, real estate will produce lower returns than other financial assets, especially compared with sectors such as technology and communications in the current market.

The topic of applying the Internet to commercial real estate was raised by John Stanfill, president of propertyfirst.com based in Alhambra, California. He noted that the ten largest commercial brokers constitute only about 15 percent of the brokerage industry, which is highly fragmented. Stanfill also characterized the brokerage community as holding information private, thus putting the client at a disadvantage. The Internet will break down this system and provide transparency to the brokerage client, he said, noting that those brokers who try to survive by hoarding information will fail, while those who focus on analysis, interpretation, and client service will succeed. The Internet, Stanfill continued, will provide more and more information and data, which will lead to accelerated transaction times and continually updated information.

Not only leased space but also for-sale properties will be shown on the Internet. Everyone will have market information at their fingertips, he said, which will reduce marketing costs. Stanfill predicted that the real estate industry will create a NASDAQ of commercial real estate, leading to national and local rent indices, which would allow tenants or investors to hedge and go long or short on baskets of property types or locations. Such products have long been a goal of the ULI Credit Task Force as well as of the McCoy Finance Symposium.

Stanfill commented on additional trends resulting from the Internet. Fees will be compressed, there will be more transactions and fewer qualified brokers, he said, and value-added property management will become more important as a means of controlling leasing. In the mortgage business, there will be a power shift from lender to borrower, noted Stanfill. Tedious mortgage applications will be eliminated, as well as front-end points. Borrowers will be in a position to auction off on the Internet their need for capital. There will be a short-form standardized application process, he predicted. Finally, the Internet will allow for benchmarking of asset returns, will become more and more international, and will provide a marketplace for much greater efficiency in accomplishing tax-deferred property swaps.

General discussion included comments that transparency to this degree is moving quite slowly. Currently, real estate markets are separate because of lack of data. Real estate debt markets are continually mispriced because investors do not have the data to price risk adequately. The Internet ultimately will solve these problems and create far greater market efficiency. It also will allow larger real estate operators to create integrated networks with their customer/tenant base.

A discussion of commercial real estate equity capital markets, which focused on REITs, was moderated by Mason Ross, chief investment officer of Northwestern Mutual based in Milwaukee, Wisconsin, and the symposium chair. At this point in the cycle, with no major asset-pricing anomalies, REITs should trade like public utility stocks did prior to deregulation. The reasons they do not include the high volatility experienced in REIT stock trading in the past few years and the perception that a downturn is ahead. Generally speaking, the REIT industry is in need of consolidation, better corporate governance, and better management. It is difficult for management to add great value in a REIT because so little of the cost structure is controllable. The fact that REITs, in substance, leave too little for management to influence will, over time, make it hard to keep good people in the industry. Concern was expressed throughout the symposium on how to attract and retain the best and the brightest to real estate. The industry lost an entire generation in the 1990s, and now technology has become far more attractive than real estate. The reason more REITs have not gone private include unwillingness to overleverage properties, tax issues in unwinding REITs originally established to defer taxes, and discrepancies concerning the "real" net asset values, i.e., lack of transparency. Moreover, a "going private" transaction requires cheap and plentiful debt, which is not readily available.

Pension funds are avoiding the public real estate markets. They see a cap in asset values, and they are not aggressive. Some funds believe they were sold another bill of goods in that the public market provided volatility instead of the liquidity they were expecting. It was also pointed out that the use of somewhat stale appraisal data to measure performance puts institutions late in the cycles, causing them to buy high and sell low.

Alternative investment opportunities on the Internet make real estate appear much less attractive. The Internet is subsidized by the lack of sales taxes and by the almost zero cost of capital. One event that might curtail capital flows into Internet stocks would be significant inventory problems, for example if e-commerce vendors were to experience warehouses filled with unsold goods.

Because private equity investors are running out of opportunities in the United States, they must go overseas. Yet a significant percentage of institutional investors does not wish to invest overseas. The opportunity funds, however, will begin to invest more heavily in distressed properties in Japan and Korea.

ULI's senior resident fellow of finance, Stephen Blank, moderated the discussion of debt capital markets for commercial real estate. Commercial mortgage–backed security (CMBS) originations were off sharply from 1998. There are fewer transactions in the market, interest rates and spreads have moved up, and the large volume of bank refinancing coming out of the early 1990s has been accomplished. There is uncertainty about interest rates, which will most likely increase. Spreads over Treasuries have remained high since the debt crisis of 1998. The private debt markets have gained market share over the public debt markets. There is a much narrower market for both the bottom piece of a CMBS origination as well as the mezzanine, or first-loss position. There is evidence of some CMBS activity beginning in Europe and Japan.

REIT debt also is expensive and trades similarly to high-yield corporate bonds. The volume of unsecured REIT debt issued in 1999 was down 50 percent from the year before. There is discrimination among REITs of the same investment rating, with a difference in pricing as great as 100 basis points. REITs of the same investment rating trade at 20 to 60 basis point premiums over similarly rated corporate debt. Commercial bank financing can be as much as 50 basis points cheaper than public debt for the same REIT. REIT debt will probably get more expensive.

The institutions see lower mortgage volumes in 2000 because of reduced transaction levels and the absence of a large volume of refinancing, as well as upward rate pressure. This is a continuation of the trends seen in 1999.

A discussion of significant policy issues facing the commercial real estate industry was moderated by Stan Ross, chairman of the Lusk Center for Real Estate at the University of Southern California in Los Angeles. Such issues included recent proposals to eliminate pooling-of-interests accounting in acquisitions, the proposal to consolidate joint ventures that previously were allowed to be off the balance sheet, the elimination of restrictions on financial institutions to engage in certain activities, and proposals to mandate telecommunication access to buildings (rooftop antennas) through eminent domain.

In the REIT sector, activities in which a REIT can engage have been further liberalized, including the possibility of a taxable REIT subsidiary that will allow REITs to provide competitive services (broadband access) to tenants. There was general discussion of several unique methods REITs use to measure income, including FFO (funds from operations). Symposium participants felt that REITs should not continue to attempt to position themselves as something separate, but that they should report on the basis of generally accepted accounting principles (GAAP), along with all other corporate entities. The market will figure out the unique aspects of real estate, as it does for all other industries.

The mandate of the ULI Credit Task Force, to which the McCoy Finance Symposium is a successor, was to provide an early warning to the industry of negative trends in the real estate industry. The industry itself appears to be in excellent shape at present, close to a supply/demand equilibrium. The major issue is the impact of recent attempts to integrate real estate into the global capital markets. Increased scrutiny of real estate loans and investments by the public markets has resulted in a characterization of real estate as having relatively less transparency than the capital markets have come to expect. In turn, this has resulted in restricting the volume of investment funds in the real estate capital markets, and in a risk premium in pricing real estate capital.

Standardization and increased disclosure will cause these premiums to disappear over time. Technology, in particular the Internet, should be extremely useful in providing the information and disclosure necessary to remove real estate as a separate asset class. Broader availability of standardized data will place a premium on overall capital market knowledge, on analysis and judgment, and on value-added services, while less value will be placed on secretive withholding of market data.

Overall, symposium participants were generally supportive of trends toward broadly available data and the linkage of real estate to the global capital markets, as such trends will result in greater capital flows into real estate and a cheaper cost of capital to the industry.

Source: *Urban Land* (Capital Markets column), February 2000.

25 Capital Constraints

Institutions are reverting to the single-asset, core real estate private market.

Predicting a continued slowdown in the economy, especially in the second half of 2001, Peter Linneman, Albert Sussman Professor of Real Estate and Finance at the Wharton School of Business, led off the seventh annual McCoy Symposium on Real Estate Finance, held in New York City this past December [2000]. Linneman emphasized that the first half of the year should be relatively solid but that the second half will face a "growth recession" in which growth is positive but below that expected from normal economic forces. Linneman also noted that the U.S. economy currently is in a period of asset-price deflation. While the overall economy should be free from inflation, certain sectors, including construction, should experience continued inflationary pressures.

Financing sources, especially construction loans and commercial mortgage–backed securities (CMBSs), have dropped notably in volume—as has commercial construction—in the past two years. Commercial construction peaked at about 15 percent above the previous peak in 1985, but the U.S. economy currently is 50 percent larger than at that time. Making the office market significantly vulnerable is the fact that perhaps as many as 500,000 tenants are working for firms that have a negative cash flow. As these firms go out of business for lack of capital and new funding opportunities, they will take with them jobs in banking, finance, accounting, legal, and other services. While most of these people eventually will find new jobs, the loss could cause a notable slowdown in demand.

The greater transparency called for at last year's symposium has yet to materialize. Market pricing mechanisms and benchmarks continue to differ in public and private markets. The NAREIT [National Association of Real Estate Investment Trusts] real estate investment trust index can decline, for example, while the NCREIF [National Council of Real Estate Investment Fiduciaries] private market valuation index goes up. The disconnect between the public and private markets continues to be maintained. Linneman says he prefers the public market pricing benchmark "because I can trade it." He predicts the public markets for commercial real estate will continue to grow. According to Linneman, one reason why public market pricing for real estate is more volatile is that debt ratios for REITs are up by 25 percent. This substantially increased leverage produces a higher-risk premium in public market pricing, making it more difficult for REITs to raise new equity and thus to grow.

In the real estate debt markets, Linneman predicts that CMBS issuances will remain flat because of the "lost generation" of debt in the early 1990s. There is little debt from that period to be refinanced. He advises caution on delinquency rates on real estate loans, noting that bank losses are higher than those of insurance companies. At an annual default rate of 2.5 percent (or 25 percent over a ten-year period), and with a possible 70 percent recovery rate on defaults, the commercial loan portfolio losses of banks could be as high as 18 percent a decade. Linneman cautions that pricing loans at a 100 basis point spread does not compensate for this inherent risk profile.

A discussion of commercial real estate equity capital markets was moderated by symposium chair Mason Ross, chief investment officer of Milwaukee-based Northwestern Mutual. There has been little bad news about real estate for the last three to five years. Accordingly, pension funds are moving back into core real estate and single-asset transactions. Apartments and industrial properties are among the most sought-after sectors, producing lower returns as a result. Trophy real estate is making a comeback, with properties such as Rockefeller Center and the World Trade Center in New York City and the Bank of America headquarters in San Francisco drawing considerable attention; but there is little depth to these markets. Solid core real estate is being marketed at a 10 percent internal rate of return (IRR), with typical office buildings higher, at around a 12 to 13 percent IRR. Markets have become bifurcated, with New York City, Washington, D.C., San Francisco, and west Los Angeles drawing heavy attention. As a result of weaker tenancies, underwriting can be as low as 65 percent of current rolls. Replacement costs can be as high as New York City's $550 a square foot, with improvements, taxes, and expenses adding another $100 a foot.

Private equity markets have little depth and little liquidity, as real estate venture money has all been drawn off by venture capital funds. Institutional investors remain confused about whether a REIT is real estate or security, and most allocations are going to specific properties rather than to REITs. There continues to be demand for assets that are not marked to market every day.

As huge capital flows in the public stock market move from growth to value orientation, value buyers could possibly drive REIT prices, as well as underlying real estate prices, higher than would be prudent. In that case, much more real estate will become publicly held. A huge amount of capital could move from private equity investment to the public markets, leading to another wave of real estate mispricing, and, ultimately, to another crash. It is difficult to correlate REIT valuations to underlying real estate valuations, because there still is no real transparency or general knowledge of what real estate values are, especially in periods of illiquidity, such as that of today.

Real estate opportunity funds continue to have plenty of inventory for sale. It is more difficult to liquidate investments because of the general lack of liquidity in the real estate capital markets. On the buy side, these funds are heavily involved in international markets, especially in Europe. Returns are being maintained through heavy leverage, making them more like those of leveraged buyout firms.

Stephen Blank, ULI's senior resident fellow of finance, moderated the discussion of debt capital markets for commercial real estate. Insurance companies see a four-year secular low in mortgage refinancing (resulting from the "lost generation of debt"), making it difficult to maintain allocations. As a result, there may be more funds available for joint ventures, mezzanine finance, and participating mortgages. Although there are fewer major players in the life insurance company commercial real estate mortgage business, there appears to be plenty of competition for mortgage originations. While some major institutions conduct an annual investment allocation process, others have totally linked the capital markets and compete internally for funds to invest on the basis of relative value. A positive development for real estate debt markets is the deteriorating quality of corporate debt.

Commercial banks are feeling pressure from rising delinquencies on corporate loans, which affect a bank's stock price negatively and thus weaken the bank's ability to raise capital. In real estate, as markets soften, underwriting standards tighten. The conduit market remains at the mercy of the bottom "B piece" buyers. The recent Federal Deposit Insurance Corporation (FDIC) report, although somewhat controversial, was a warning to the banks to slow down commercial lending. There is much greater transparency in this area. Bank delinquency statistics are publicly available at the Web sites of the Office of the Comptroller of the Currency and the Federal Reserve System. (In 1991, however, no such data were available.)

Overall, CMBS originations in 2000 were down some 40 percent from their high in 1998. Although only five major commercial bank players remain in the traditional construction lending business, it was predicted that lending spreads on REITs will widen. In conclusion, symposium participants felt that credit remains attractively priced, but it is more difficult to access because lending capacity is sharply diminished from a decade ago. Borrowers can anticipate higher due-diligence standards and widened spreads.

Joseph F. Azrack, president and CEO of AEW Capital Management in Boston, moderated a discussion on changes that e-commerce will effect in real estate finance and investment. Discussion focused on the ability of the screen to supplant personal relationships, especially on larger transactions. An intriguing possibility is the potential to aggregate pools of equity capital from small investors.

Stan Ross, chairman of the Lusk Center for Real Estate at the University of Southern California in Los Angeles, facilitated a discussion of significant policy issues facing the commercial real estate industry. A major factor enabling e-commerce in real estate was the passage by Congress of the e-signature bill on mortgages (see "Digital Signatures," *Urban Land*, January 2000). Also significant is the fact that the Department of Labor now allows pension funds to purchase the subordinate pieces of CMBS issuances as long as they are investment grade. The REIT Modernization Act decreases the required shareholder distributions from 95 percent to 90 percent, thus allowing a modest increment in capital retention. It also now is possible to have a taxable REIT subsidiary to provide services to tenants.

In the area of accounting, more liberal provisions now allow for the pooling of interests, joint venture partnerships, and consolidations to be reported. The so-called "Starker" provisions for tax-free exchanges have been liberalized to allow one to purchase a swap asset 45 days prior to selling an asset.

The mandate of the ULI Credit Task Force, to which the McCoy Finance Symposium is a successor, was to provide an early warning to the industry of negative trends in the real estate industry. The posting of commercial bank real estate delinquency statistics on major public Web sites is a major step in that direction. Such early reporting and public disclosure should mitigate the overbuilding boom-bust that has been so common in the real estate cycle.

The public real estate equity market has been sharply curtailed by the flow of funds into dot.coms and technology. Although that trend has ceased, funds have not yet begun to flow into value investments, such as REITs. Vigilance is needed, especially if it appears that the real estate public and private equity markets are becoming too liquid.

At present, however, a liquidity squeeze in both the real estate debt and equity capital markets is providing excellent market discipline. Even so, underwriting standards in real estate should not be relaxed in the event that the country moves into a growth recession, or a pure recession, and lending opportunities to corporate borrowers shrink.

ULI's long-term goal to assist in bringing transparency to the real estate public and private equity markets is a long way from being met. If anything, the reversion of institutions to the single-asset, core real estate, private market is a reversal of that trend. E-commerce suffers from too many new and unproven market entrants and too few data on larger, institutional transactions. Ultimately, the Internet will enable true price discovery in the market, but the realization of this dream is probably further away than imagined a year ago.

Like it or not, real estate capital now is inexorably linked to public markets and to global markets. Lack of price disclosure should serve to shrink the amount of capital available to real estate. While there may be a few more years during which assets are not marked to public market values, the ultimate reward for such transparency should be a cheaper cost of capital for the real estate industry.

Source: *Urban Land* (Capital Markets column), February 2001.

26 Capital Markets Equilibrium?

A major concern is whether or not there will be a move from equilibrium to speculation and excess in the capital markets.

The tenth annual McCoy Real Estate Finance Symposium focused on what was presumed to be the "disconnect" between the pricing of real estate capital and the returns from operating real estate. The half-day meeting, held in New York City this past December [2003], concluded that real estate capital markets may be closer to equilibrium than had been thought.

The introductory session was moderated by Peter Linneman, professor of real estate finance at the Wharton School at the University of Pennsylvania, who is fundamentally bullish on the outlook for the economy. He urged participants not to use the recent sale of the General Motors Building in Manhattan at $800 a square foot as a proxy for the investment market. His comment led to general discussion about whether or not the sale was below or above replacement cost, and the answer, it was clear, depends on the land valuation. Participants all agreed that the building could not be replaced in its current location. Despite seeming anomalies in the prices paid by investors, the consensus was that most sales are still occurring at prices below replacement cost. As the economy improves and vacancies decline, allowing for new construction, especially in the office sector, purchases that seem unreasonable today will become more attractive.

Capitalization rates have declined 100 to 125 basis points, in line with decreases in interest rates, in both the public and private markets. There is a two-tiered market for property, with property with stabilized cash flow commanding high premiums. The low capitalization rates apply only to stabilized cash flows. Depending on property type and location, stabilized cash flow properties are selling at unleveraged capitalization rates ranging from 6.5 to 8 percent. There is intense competition for what is seen to be safe cash flow properties, with buyers outnumbering sellers. The new real estate syndicators have added substantially to the capital flows. Until recently, money was coming into real estate out of the stock market, where returns were seen to be lower. Raw real estate—untenanted buildings and the like—is an entirely different investment market. The option value has been priced higher, and the return demands are far higher than for stabilized properties. Capitalization rates on such properties might be as high as 14 to 15 percent. For those managing properties, expenses such as insurance and taxes are increasing while rental rates may be decreasing.

Private market operators can carry heavier debt loads than public companies, which must maintain bond ratings. Many individuals have borrowed heavily to take advantage of the low cost of borrowing. But there is a possible liquidity trap. Interest rates are likely to rise rapidly in a recovery as the Federal Reserve system heads off anticipated inflation. Interest rates will most likely rise faster than rents. Those who overborrow at short-term and with floating interest rates could find themselves in a delinquent or defaulted position on their borrowings. Short-term floating-rate loans carry no amortization factor, making them even riskier.

It was believed that the Federal Reserve system would maintain an inflation target of 2 percent. Real growth is projected at 3 to 4 percent, causing nominal growth of 5 to 6 percent. Inflation and deflation seem to be in equilibrium as well. Most participants felt that short-term interest rates are not likely to rise more than 300 basis points over the intermediate term.

The introductory session concluded that the capital markets for real estate have moved into equilibrium only in the past six months. The issue now is: Will we overshoot? Will prices begin to exceed replacement cost based on aggressive income assumptions and leveraging, moving the markets to excessive risk? The river of investment funds along with past performance of the real estate cycle would indicate that this risk is very real.

Discussion of the equity capital markets for real estate commenced with a review of the ramifications of the new corporate governance requirements for publicly held real estate companies. It was noted that the minimum annual cost of complying is

$500,000 a year. One real estate investment trust reported that such costs are the equivalent of ten cents a share in earnings. This, along with the stringent compensation issues, provide an advantage to privately held companies.

The concept of real estate investment trusts has spread to Japan, France, and England. This trend will lead ultimately to more liquid global property markets and greater transparency. Certain Japanese mutual funds are investing in U.S. real estate investment trusts.

There is capital availability for almost any type of real estate investment. Returns on domestic investment for opportunity funds have declined to around 15 percent, forcing investment overseas. There is no market for 15 percent return opportunity funds with a 20 percent carried interest. To attain higher returns domestically, one must invest in untenanted structures with leverage—a risk profile not acceptable to institutional funds.

Certain pension fund advisers are preparing detailed analyses of the returns from earlier opportunity fund portfolios, which should provide a much-needed ability to transparently benchmark relative returns from these funds.

Participants felt, somewhat optimistically, that institutional equity funds will probably come through this cycle without problems. Interest rates will probably ramp up after the 2004 election, but vacancies may decrease enough in the interim to allow properties to squeak through. Appraisals always lag, and by the time they catch up to the real property conditions, the economy will have caught up. Even though portfolios are not marked to current capitalization rates, they may grow their way out of any potential problems.

There was concern regarding the new generation of retail stock brokerage real estate syndicators. It was estimated that $15 billion to $20 billion of such funds have been raised. The compensation to the promoters is 15 percent, which is well above industry standards. It was felt that returns were likely to be mediocre, thus potentially giving real estate investment a bad name in the marketplace once again.

Discussion of the real estate debt markets focused initially on the new Basel (Switzerland) Capital Accords regarding risk-based capital standards for large money center commercial banks. Such rules will cause banks to focus on less risky loans, favoring corporate borrowers over real estate and reducing the overall banking capacity to make construction loans. Bankers at the symposium felt that large commercial banks had become much more sophisticated in credit analysis since the early 1990s and would not find the new accords all that restrictive.

Bank underwriting standards are bending, but not breaking. Loan-to-value ratios may reach as high as 80 percent on attractive deals. Lending is aggressive on solid cash flows, but not on pro forma projections. Concentration is avoided, with a maximum of $35 million retention in any single loan. Real estate loans are no more than 6 to 7 percent of total bank assets.

In the public debt markets, commercial mortgage–backed securities set the underwriting standards. Spreads have tightened as interest rates have declined. Next year should see a refinancing boom as a large volume of ten-year maturities come due. For publicly held real estate companies, liquidity management has become increasingly important. There is a significant volume of advance refunding as rates are perceived to be trending higher.

In conclusion, participants were more optimistic about the current state of real estate capital markets than was expected. This change to equilibrium has occurred only in recent months. The major concerns focus on whether or not we will move from equilibrium to speculation and excess in the capital markets and to what extent borrowers will rely too heavily on floating short-term funds to purchase long-term assets and find themselves caught in a liquidity trap.

Source: *Urban Land* (Capital Markets column), February 2004.

27 Managing for the Crisis

In uncertain times like these, effort above and beyond the usual must be devoted to strategic thinking.

A consensus among participants in the 11th annual McCoy Real Estate Finance Symposium, held in New York City in November [2004], is that there is a 60 percent chance that things will remain about the same, with a benign interest rate structure; a 10 percent chance that things will get better; and a 30 percent chance that the country will experience a major shock in the economy that will disrupt real estate markets.

The benign consensus called for interest rates on the ten-year Treasury bond to rise about 150 basis points, to around 5.5 percent. Such a move would not be harmful to the economy. To support a normal growth rate of 3 percent, an average of 250,000 jobs a month need to be created. In the beginning of the current recovery cycle, jobs were actually lost.

Factors contributing to slower job growth would include secular education problems, outsourcing overseas, and caution in corporate capital spending and hiring triggered by concerns over the trade deficit, the weak dollar, and government deficit spending. Hiring plans also continue to be conservative, due to the rising costs of health care and pensions. Ken Rosen, chairman of the Fisher Center of Real Estate and

Urban Economics at the Haas School of Business, at the University of California at Berkeley, who led the economic discussion, predicted a mild recession in 2005–2006 led by lagging consumer spending on housing and automobiles. Such a slowdown would also put a damper on interest rate increases.

In the commercial real estate sector, there is a race among rental rates, capitalization rates, and interest rates. Excess funds for investment in real estate along with declining returns on alternative investments are driving capitalization rates down. At the same time, rising expenses and declining rents are driving down net operating returns from properties. In theory, higher interest rates will both further reduce operating income from property and cause capitalization rates to rise—a double hit on valuations. A more benign interest rate forecast will mitigate the latter effect. For real estate owners, the real race will be between property returns and interest rates. If rentals go up earlier and faster than interest rates, all will be well; if not, owners can become caught in a liquidity trap as they refinance low- or floating-rate deals in a significantly higher interest rate environment.

There was some controversy as to whether there is a bubble in housing prices. If so, it is regional in nature. Further growth in housing prices will be offset by rising interest rates and the unseasoned credit experience of those purchasing new homes. Some buyers have created financing with negative amortization even at the current low rates.

Concerns about inflation were expressed. China's construction boom is causing prices to escalate, especially on oil and construction materials. Others felt that the entrance of cheap labor from south Asia and China into the world markets will mitigate inflationary trends. It was pointed out that 75 percent of all goods sold by Wal-Mart are made in China.

Investment capitalization rates of 7.5 percent and even lower for real estate appeared more normal to participants this year than in the past. They see evidence of a declining risk premium for real estate, caused by greater transparency and price disclosure in the public markets, the benefits of securitization, and banking consolidation, among other factors. When institutional investors make their asset allocations, they find they are looking at possible stock market returns of 7 to 8 percent and fixed-income returns of under 5 percent, so that real estate at 7.5 percent, with higher current cash returns, appears attractive on a relative basis. There is a huge amount of money waiting to come into the real estate investment market. Some is coming out of fixed-income investment. Opportunity funds are highly liquid. New market vehicles include private funds for individual investors and tenant-in-common (TIC) tax-deferral property exchange funds.

Commercial bankers reported that real estate loan portfolios are today's best-performing asset class, with record-low nonperforming assets. Syndicated bank loans are priced as capital market equivalents. They are managing risk through heavy reliance on the character of individual borrowers and on diversification. The major risk factor is in rising interest rates and refinancing problems. Insurance companies reported deteriorating appraisal standards in an attempt to boost loan proceeds. Credit-rating agencies also reported deteriorating underwriting standards with aggressive loan-to-value ratios, interest-only loans, and inadequate reserves for tenant rollovers, tenant improvements, and the like. "B piece" and mezzanine buyers will be limited by the new Basel II banking accords, which increase reserve requirements against such assets. Hedge funds are participating in this market, taking the bottom piece in heavily leveraged transactions.

Trends in the regulatory environment were also discussed. It was felt that the new TIC vehicles will become regulated. Terrorism insurance backed by the federal government has only a year of remaining life. International accounting standards will require "fair value" accounting for real estate holdings. Sarbanes-Oxley compliance requires disclosure of joint venture debt and floating-rate debt. The Basel banking accords will inject further conservatism into the system. As a result of new regulations, Japanese investors have purchased $4 billion of U.S. real estate funds. Real estate investment trust (REIT) legislation is moving ahead rapidly in places like the United Kingdom, Germany, France, and Hong Kong. Australia already has a REIT product similar to that of the United States.

The 10 percent chance of things getting better is something the country does not need to worry about. What about the 30 percent chance of a crisis? What form would the crisis take? It probably would be a combination of events of varying severity to cause the party to stop. The long-range outlook, particularly from a demographic point of view, remains positive, but there will be interruptions along the way. It is the imbalances that make the country vulnerable. The government deficit reduces the effectiveness of fiscal policy to mitigate recessions. Current budgets do not account for the full costs of either homeland security or the war in Iraq. If the alternative minimum tax is eliminated, the deficit will go up by $50 billion to $90 billion. In recent months, the real interest rate has been negative (current rate minus inflation), allowing for very little flexibility to use monetary policy to expand the economy. As a result of the trade deficit, foreigners now hold 42 percent of the nation's federal debt. That is good news for the present, but if confidence erodes in the dollar and they become net sellers of the nation's debt, interest rates will rise rapidly as the country is forced to reprice its bonds. Added to this are the possibilities of domestic terrorism, energy shortages, slow job growth, troubles with the economy in China, and problems with

Iran, North Korea, Taiwan, or elsewhere. The impact of such events ranges from loss of confidence and severe recession to hyperinflation and high interest rates.

With a one-in-three chance of such events occurring, what should a real estate owner/investor do to prepare? Some individuals are upside-oriented and will choose to take advantage of this "once in a lifetime" opportunity to lock in as much debt as possible at floating rates, with caps or swapped into fixed rate, and make opportunistic buys as they become available, taking on the refinancing risk. Those who are downside-oriented will fix all floating-rate debt and extend maturities as long as possible, no matter the give-up in pricing. Loan-to-"true value" ratios will be between 60 and 75 percent. Prudent operators who have lived through cycles in the past will do a bit of both, keeping some liquidity for the buying opportunities ahead, managing their debt structure and pricing, avoiding overleveraging, and having a well-conceived exit/refinancing strategy. In uncertain times like these, effort above and beyond the usual must be devoted to tenant satisfaction and retention, property maintenance, and strategic thinking about tenant mixes and opportunities for upgrading existing property. As Sam Zell, a leading real estate opportunist, and others have said, one person's crisis is another's opportunity.

Source: *Urban Land* (Capital Markets column), January 2005.

28 Is the End Near for Unrestrained Capital Flows?

It appears we are in for another cycle—it is time to manage debt structures prudently.

At last year's 11th annual McCoy Real Estate Finance Symposium, there was a surprising consensus that we were in a "perfect calm" of benign rental rates, capitalization rates, and interest rates. This year, at the 12th annual symposium, held in New York City in early December [2005], there was another surprising consensus. This time, the predominant view was that, despite the river of capital available for investment in commercial real estate, rates are likely to get higher and exacerbate the risks built into the system.

Since the last downturn in the early 1990s, real estate finance has been transformed through opportunity funds, commercial mortgage–backed securities (CMBSs), and the second wave of real estate investment trusts (REITs). While bringing much-needed transparency to the industry, these vehicles have not yet been severely tested in a down market. Within the next two years, there is likely to be a big problem brought about by a combination of higher interest rates and a slowdown in the economy. There is untested risk in the system caused by the twin deficits of government spending and trade, as well as speculation in various forms of real estate, hedge funds, credit derivatives, and the like.

Housing is likely to become a drag on the economy. Normalized housing starts run about 1.2 million a year. But some 1.7 million new homes are being built a year nowadays, thus borrowing from the future. It is estimated that 15 percent of single-family home sales are to speculators, up from a normalized 3 percent. Some of these individual speculators own as many as five to seven homes on which they have overborrowed at historically low rates, counting on a quick "flip" of the property to bail them out. Another risk in single-family homes is the increasing detection of fraud in the home mortgage business.

Short-term interest rates could easily go from 4 percent to 4.5 or 5 percent, and the ten-year Treasury could easily go from current levels of about 4.5 percent to 6 percent by the year's end. Pricing of commercial real estate has been based on a normalized 4 percent interest rate. The question is: What happens when interest rates go to 6 percent? Obviously, loan-to-value ratios will spike, and many investors and speculators will find themselves in an overborrowed position, and possibly in a real estate equity market not as favorable as at present.

It is estimated that 75 percent of the increase in value in core real estate over the past five years can be attributed to capitalization rate compression, as contrasted to operating income. As capitalization rates rise, in response to rising interest rates, returns on commercial real estate could turn negative, despite mostly healthy rental markets.

Real estate fundamentals appear generally good, with the exception of single-family homes in about a third of the markets and condominiums, which are generally overbuilt. Much commercial property is still trading at or below replacement cost, which is a healthy factor. Replacement cost is being driven up by shortages in raw materials and by labor shortages in the building trades. Lending standards are seen as generally deteriorating from a year ago, producing a latent fear of overbuilding.

Some participants at the symposium predicted increasing income returns from real estate operating properties, along with declining vacancies and little new development. Others saw a need for augmented downside planning. Real estate equity investors favored Asia for overseas investment, despite local problems of law, entitlement, capital repatriation, and the like. The more pessimistic cited slow rental growth and the jobless recovery.

The discussion focused on whether a rise in interest rates would produce a hard or soft landing for real estate. Some participants felt that up to a 200 basis point increase in interest rates would produce a soft landing. Others believed that an increase to 6 percent in the cost of borrowing would produce a very hard landing, because of an increasing lack of discipline in the system. A truly hard landing could be caused by a shock to the system, such as the condominium bubble bursting or a major CMBS default.

In these cases, risk capital for real estate would evaporate. There would be a complete pullback of debt markets, with resulting foreclosures and defaults such as have been seen previously. A booming stock market in 2006 also could cause a pullback of the river of investment funds currently available to commercial real estate. Increasing participation in tenant-in-common interests is a further factor in inflating prices.

In the discussion of debt markets, it was agreed that over the past year underwriting standards have deteriorated and spreads have narrowed. Refinancing current debt in a 6 percent market would not work unless there was significant growth in operating income. Some loans are being done with negative amortization, relying entirely on rental growth to pay off the loan. Structured debt has moved loan-to-value percentages up into the 90s. In many cases, there are no covenants, no lead investor, no controls, and no defined way to deal with past-due loans and workouts. Commercial bank lending standards have deteriorated as well.

It would be ironic if the financial instruments that alleviated the credit crisis of the early 1990s became contributors to a credit squeeze in real estate in the next few years. As equity REITs mature, there is a growing tension between capital expenditures and property improvements, and sustained dividend growth. This tension also puts more pressure on REITs to leverage up their assets. Mortgage REITs are beginning to speculate in credit derivatives, a highly risky form of investment. Awash in capital, real estate opportunity funds face liquidity issues with respect to maturing investment portfolios, as well as the continued "moral hazard" of investing their funds even when markets appear to be overpriced. One is reminded of chairman of Chicago's Equity Group Investments Sam Zell's eating sardines and trading sardines. The odor from some of the sardines may be getting a bit strong. Finally, CMBS and structured real estate debt remove the property too far from the hands of accomplished real estate operators. A credit crisis in this area will be worse than usual because of the lack of covenants, controls, and the ability to make quick operating decisions.

The strong advice coming out of this symposium over recent years has been to lock up as much cheap money as you can for as long as you can. This year, the tone was different. There are clouds on the horizon. We are coming out of about five years of the most benign real estate environment most of us have ever seen. That positive environment was a result of the financial discipline we all learned during the 1990s. It appears we are in for another cycle. Those who have lived through more than one of these cycles will know it is time to trim the sails, batten down the hatches, prudently manage debt structures, and put in place the downside plans. Smooth sailing!

Source: *Urban Land*, February 2006.

PART 5

Values-Based Leadership

Character and Personal Responsibility

Globalization of Business Ethics

Ethics and Real Estate

Note to readers: In part 1 of this book, the author summarizes the key issues and points covered in the individual articles, and offers additional commentary to provide context and a longer-term perspective. Commentaries on articles 29 to 36 may be found on pages 26 to 30.

29 The Parable of the Sadhu

After encountering a dying pilgrim on a climbing trip in the Himalayas, a businessman ponders the differences between individual and corporate ethics.

It was early in the morning before the sun rose, which gave the climbers time to climb the treacherous slope to the pass at 18,000 feet before the ice steps melted. They were also concerned about their stamina and altitude sickness, and felt the need to press on. Into this chance collection of climbers on that Himalayan slope an ethical dilemma arose in the guise of an unconscious, almost naked sadhu, an Indian holy man. Each climber gave the sadhu help but none made sure he would be safe. Should somebody have stopped to help the sadhu to safety? Would it have done any good? Was the group responsible? Since leaving the sadhu on the mountain slope, the author, who was one of the climbers, has pondered these issues. He sees many parallels for business people as they face ethical decisions at work.

Last year [1982], as the first participant in the new six-month sabbatical program that Morgan Stanley has adopted, I enjoyed a rare opportunity to collect my thoughts as well as do some traveling. I spent the first three months in Nepal, walking 600 miles through 200 villages in the Himalayas and climbing some 120,000 vertical feet. On the trip my sole Western companion was an anthropologist who shed light on the cultural patterns of the villages we passed through.

During the Nepal hike, something occurred that has had a powerful impact on my thinking about corporate ethics. Although some might argue that the experience has no relevance to business, it was a situation in which a basic ethical dilemma suddenly intruded into the lives of a group of individuals. How the group responded I think holds a lesson for all organizations no matter how defined.

The Sadhu

The Nepal experience was more rugged and adventuresome than I had anticipated. Most commercial treks last two or three weeks and cover a quarter of the distance we traveled.

My friend Stephen, the anthropologist, and I were halfway through the 60-day Himalayan part of the trip when we reached the high point, an 18,000-foot pass over a crest that we'd have to traverse to reach the village of Muklinath, an ancient holy place for pilgrims.

Six years earlier, I had suffered pulmonary edema, an acute form of altitude sickness, at 16,500 feet in the vicinity of Everest base camp, so we were understandably concerned about what would happen at 18,000 feet. Moreover, the Himalayas were having their wettest spring in 20 years; hip-deep powder and ice had already driven us off one ridge. If we failed to cross the pass, I feared that the last half of our "once in a lifetime" trip would be ruined.

The night before we would try the pass, we camped at a hut at 14,500 feet. In the photos taken at that camp, my face appears wan. The last village we'd passed through was a sturdy two-day walk below us, and I was tired.

During the late afternoon, four backpackers from New Zealand joined us, and we spent most of the night awake, anticipating the climb. Below we could see the fires of two other parties, which turned out to be two Swiss couples and a Japanese hiking club.

To get over the steep part of the climb before the sun melted the steps cut in the ice, we departed at 3:30 a.m. The New Zealanders left first, followed by Stephen and myself, our porters and Sherpas, and then the Swiss. The Japanese lingered in their camp. The sky was clear, and we were confident that no spring storm would erupt that day to close the pass.

At 15,500 feet, it looked to me as if Stephen were shuffling and staggering a bit, which are symptoms of altitude sickness. (The initial stage of altitude sickness brings a headache and nausea. As the condition worsens, a climber may encounter difficult breathing, disorientation, aphasia, and paralysis.) I felt strong, my adrenaline was flowing, but I was very concerned about my ultimate ability to get across. A couple of our porters were also suffering from the height, and Pasang, our Sherpa sirdar (leader), was worried.

Just after daybreak, while we rested at 15,500 feet, one of the New Zealanders, who had gone ahead, came staggering down toward us with a body slung across his shoulders. He dumped the almost naked, barefoot body of an Indian holy man—a sadhu—at my feet. He had found the pilgrim lying on the ice, shivering and suffering from hypothermia. I cradled the sadhu's head and laid him out on the rocks. The New Zealander was angry. He wanted to get across the pass before the bright sun melted the snow. He said, "Look, I've done what I can. You have porters and Sherpa guides. You care for him. We're going on!" He turned and went back up the mountain to join his friends.

I took a carotid pulse and found that the sadhu was still alive. We figured he had probably visited the holy shrines at Muklinath and was on his way home. It was fruitless to question why he had chosen this desperately high route instead of the safe, heavily traveled caravan route through the Kali Gandaki gorge. Or why he was almost naked and with no shoes, or how long he had been lying in the pass. The answers weren't going to solve our problem.

Stephen and the four Swiss began stripping off outer clothing and opening their packs. The sadhu was soon clothed from head to foot. He was not able to walk, but he was very much alive. I looked down the mountain and spotted below the Japanese climbers marching up with a horse.

Without a great deal of thought, I told Stephen and Pasang that I was concerned about withstanding the heights to come and wanted to get over the pass. I took off after several of our porters who had gone ahead.

On the steep part of the ascent where, if the ice steps had given way, I would have slid down about 3,000 feet, I felt vertigo. I stopped for a breather, allowing the Swiss to catch up with me. I inquired about the sadhu and Stephen. They said that the sadhu was fine and that Stephen was just behind. I set off again for the summit

Stephen arrived at the summit an hour after I did. Still exhilarated by victory, I ran down the snow slope to congratulate him. He was suffering from altitude sickness, walking 15 steps, then stopping, walking 15 steps, then stopping. Pasang accompanied him all the way up. When I reached them, Stephen glared at me and said: "How do you feel about contributing to the death of a fellow man?"

I did not fully comprehend what he meant.

"Is the sadhu dead?" I inquired.

"No," replied Stephen, "but he surely will be!"

After I had gone, and the Swiss had departed not long after, Stephen had remained with the sadhu. When the Japanese had arrived, Stephen had asked to use their horse to transport the sadhu down to the hut. They had refused. He had then asked Pasang to have a group of our porters carry the sadhu. Pasang had resisted the idea, saying that the porters would have to exert all their energy to get themselves over the pass. He had thought they could not carry a man down 1,000 feet to the hut, reclimb the slope, and get across safely before the snow melted. Pasang had pressed Stephen not to delay any longer.

The Sherpas had carried the sadhu down to a rock in the sun at about 15,000 feet and had pointed out the hut another 500 feet below. The Japanese had given him food and drink. When they had last seen him he was listlessly throwing rocks at the Japanese party's dog, which had frightened him.

We do not know if the sadhu lived or died.

For many of the following days and evenings Stephen and I discussed and debated our behavior toward the sadhu. Stephen is a committed Quaker with deep moral vision. He said, "I feel that what happened with the sadhu is a good example of the breakdown between the individual ethic and the corporate ethic. No one person was willing to assume ultimate responsibility for the sadhu. Each was willing to do his bit just so long as it was not too inconvenient. When it got to be a bother, everyone just passed the buck to someone else and took off. Jesus was relevant to a more individualistic stage of society, but how do we interpret his teaching today in a world filled with large, impersonal organizations and groups?"

I defended the larger group, saying, "Look, we all cared. We all stopped and gave aid and comfort. Everyone did his bit. The New Zealander carried him down below the snow line. I took his pulse and suggested we treat him for hypothermia. You and the Swiss gave him clothing and got him warmed up. The Japanese gave him food and water. The Sherpas carried him down to the sun and pointed out the easy trail toward the hut. He was well enough to throw rocks at a dog. What more could we do?"

"You have just described the typical affluent Westerner's response to a problem. Throwing money—in this case food and sweaters—at it, but not solving the fundamentals!" Stephen retorted.

"What would satisfy you?" I said. "Here we are, a group of New Zealanders, Swiss, Americans, and Japanese who have never met before and who are at the apex of one of the most powerful experiences of our lives. Some years the pass is so bad no one gets over it. What right does an almost naked pilgrim who chooses the wrong trail have to disrupt our lives? Even the Sherpas had no interest in risking the trip to help him beyond a certain point."

Stephen calmly rebutted, "I wonder what the Sherpas would have done if the sadhu had been a well-dressed Nepali, or what the Japanese would have done if the sadhu had been a well-dressed Asian, or what you would have done, Buzz, if the sadhu had been a well-dressed Western woman?"

"Where, in your opinion," I asked instead, "is the limit of our responsibility in a situation like this? We had our own well-being to worry about. Our Sherpa guides were unwilling to jeopardize us or the porters for the sadhu. No one else on the mountain was willing to commit himself beyond certain self-imposed limits."

Stephen said, "As individual Christians or people with a Western ethical tradition, we can fulfill our obligations in such a situation only if 1) the sadhu dies in our care, 2) the sadhu demonstrates to us that he could undertake the two-day walk down to the village, or 3) we carry the sadhu for two days down to the village and convince someone there to care for him."

"Leaving the sadhu in the sun with food and clothing, while he demonstrated hand-eye coordination by throwing a rock at a dog, comes close to fulfilling items one and two," I answered. "And it wouldn't have made sense to take him to the village where the people appeared to be far less caring than the Sherpas, so the third condition is impractical. Are you really saying that, no matter what the implications, we should, at the drop of a hat, have changed our entire plan?"

The Individual versus the Group Ethic

Despite my arguments, I felt and continue to feel guilt about the sadhu. I had literally walked through a classic moral dilemma without fully thinking through the consequences. My excuses for my actions include a high adrenaline flow, a superordinate goal, and a once-in-a-lifetime opportunity—factors in the usual corporate situation, especially when one is under stress.

Real moral dilemmas are ambiguous, and many of us hike right through them, unaware that they exist. When, usually after the fact, someone makes an issue of them, we tend to resent his or her bringing it up. Often, when the full import of what we have done (or not done) falls on us, we dig into a defensive position from which it is very difficult to emerge. In rare circumstances we may contemplate what we have done from inside a prison.

Had we mountaineers been free of physical and mental stress caused by the effort and the high altitude, we might have treated the sadhu differently. Yet isn't stress the real test of personal and corporate values? The instant decisions executives make under pressure reveal the most about personal and corporate character.

Among the many questions that occur to me when pondering my experience are: What are the practical limits of moral imagination and vision? Is there a collective or institutional ethic beyond the ethics of the individual? At what level of effort or commitment can one discharge one's ethical responsibilities?

Not every ethical dilemma has a right solution. Reasonable people often disagree; otherwise there would be no dilemma. In a business context, however, it is essential that managers agree on a process for dealing with dilemmas.

The sadhu experience offers an interesting parallel to business situations. An immediate response was mandatory. Failure to act was a decision in itself. Up on the mountain we could not resign and submit our resumes to a headhunter. In contrast to philosophy, business involves action and implementation—getting things done. Managers must come up with answers to problems based on what they see and what they allow to influence their decision-making processes. On the mountain, none of us but Stephen realized the true dimensions of the situation we were facing.

One of our problems was that as a group we had no process for developing a consensus. We had no sense of purpose or plan. The difficulties of dealing with the sadhu were so complex that no one person could handle it. Because it did not have a set of preconditions that could guide its action to an acceptable resolution, the group reacted instinctively as individuals. The cross-cultural nature of the group added a further layer of complexity. We had no leader with whom we could all identify and in whose purpose we believed. Only Stephen was willing to take charge, but he could not gain adequate support to care for the sadhu.

Some organizations do have a value system that transcends the personal values of the managers. Such values, which go beyond profitability, are usually revealed when the organization is under stress. People throughout the organization generally accept its values, which, because they are not presented as a rigid list of commandments, may be somewhat ambiguous. The stories people tell, rather than printed materials, transmit these conceptions of what is proper behavior.

For 20 years I have been exposed at senior levels to a variety of corporations and organizations. It is amazing how quickly an outsider can sense the tone and style of an organization and the degree of tolerated openness and freedom to challenge management.

Organizations that do not have a heritage of mutually accepted, shared values tend to become unhinged during stress, with each individual bailing out for himself. In the great takeover battles we have witnessed during past years, companies that had strong cultures drew the wagons around them and fought it out, while other companies saw executives supported by their golden parachutes, bail out of the struggles.

Because corporations and their members are interdependent, for the corporation to be strong the members need to share a preconceived notion of what is correct behavior, a "business ethic," and think of it as a positive force, not a constraint.

As an investment banker I am continually warned by well-meaning lawyers, clients, and associates to be wary of conflicts of interest. Yet if I were to run away from every difficult situation, I wouldn't be an effective investment banker. I have to feel my way through conflicts. An effective manager can't run from risk either; he or she has to confront and deal with risk. To feel "safe" in doing this, managers need the guidelines of an agreed-on process and set of values within the organization.

After my three months in Nepal, I spent three months as an executive-in-residence at both Stanford Business School and the Center for Ethics and Social Policy at the Graduate Theological Union at Berkeley. These six months away from my job gave me time to assimilate 20 years of business experience. My thoughts turned often to the meaning of the leadership role in any large organization. Students at the seminary thought of themselves as antibusiness. But when I questioned them they agreed that they distrusted all large organizations, including the church. They perceived all large organizations as impersonal and opposed to individual values and needs. Yet we all know of organizations where peoples' values and beliefs are respected and their expressions encouraged. What makes the difference? Can we identify the difference and, as a result, manage more effectively?

The word "ethics" turns off many and confuses more. Yet the notions of shared values and an agreed-on process for dealing with adversity and change—what many people mean when they talk about corporate culture—seem to be at the heart of the ethical issue. People who are in touch with their own core beliefs and the beliefs of others and are sustained by them can be more comfortable living on the cutting edge. At times, taking a tough line or a decisive stand in a muddle of ambiguity is the only ethical thing to do. If a manager is indecisive and spends time trying to figure out the "good" thing to do, the enterprise may be lost.

Business ethics, then, have to do with the authenticity and integrity of the enterprise. To be ethical is to follow the business as well as the cultural goals of the corporation, its owners, its employees, and its customers. Those who cannot serve the corporate vision are not authentic business people and, therefore, are not ethical in the business sense.

At this stage of my own business experience I have a strong interest in organizational behavior. Sociologists are keenly studying what they call corporate stories, legends, and heroes as a way organizations have of transmitting the value system. Corporations such as Arco have even hired consultants to perform an audit of their corporate culture. In a company, the leader is the person who understands, interprets, and manages the corporate value system. Effective managers are then action-oriented people who resolve conflict, are tolerant of ambiguity, stress, and change, and have a strong sense of purpose for themselves and their organizations.

If all this is true, I wonder about the role of the professional manager who moves from company to company. How can he or she quickly absorb the values and culture of different organizations? Or is there, indeed, an art of management that is totally transportable? Assuming such fungible managers do exist, is it proper for them to manipulate the values of others?

What would have happened had Stephen and I carried the sadhu for two days back to the village and become involved with the villagers in his care? In four trips to Nepal my most interesting experiences occurred in 1975 when I lived in a Sherpa home in the Khumbu for five days recovering from altitude sickness. The high point of Stephen's trip was an invitation to participate in a family funeral ceremony in Manang. Neither experience had to do with climbing the high passes of the Himalayas. Why were we so reluctant to try the lower path, the ambiguous trail? Perhaps because we did not have a leader who could reveal the greater purpose of the trip to us.

Why didn't Stephen with his moral vision opt to take the sadhu under his personal care? The answer is because, in part, Stephen was hard-stressed physically himself, and because, in part, without some support system that involved our involuntary and episodic community on the mountain, it was beyond his individual capacity to do so.

I see the current interest in corporate culture and corporate value systems as a positive response to Stephen's pessimism about the decline of the role of the individual in large organizations. Individuals who operate from a thoughtful set of personal values provide the foundation for a corporate culture. A corporate tradition that encourages freedom of inquiry, supports personal values, and reinforces a focused sense of direction can fulfill the need for individuality along with the prosperity and success of the group. Without such corporate support, the individual is lost.

That is the lesson of the sadhu. In a complex corporate situation, the individual requires and deserves the support of the group. If people cannot find such support from their organization, they don't know how to act. If such support is forthcoming, a person has a stake in the success of the group, and can add much to the process of establishing and maintaining a corporate culture. It is management's challenge to be sensitive to individual needs, to shape them, and to direct and focus them for the benefit of the group as a whole.

For each of us the sadhu lives. Should we stop what we are doing and comfort him; or should we keep trudging up toward the high pass? Should I pause to help the derelict I pass on the street each night as I walk by the Yale Club en route to Grand Central Station? Am I his brother? What is the nature of our responsibility if we consider ourselves to be ethical persons? Perhaps it is to change the values of the group so that it can, with all its resources, take the other road.

Source: *Harvard Business Review*, September/October 1983.

30

On Business Ethics

The Counselors of Real Estate is presenting its 1995 High Level Conference on "The Ethics of Organizations—An Exploration of the Shared Responsibility of Individuals and Their Institutions." Buzz McCoy, CRE, is serving as chairman. The conference, August 4-6, 1995, at the Resort at Squaw Creek in Olympic Valley (Lake Tahoe), California, will explore the question: What individual responsibility do we have for our political, social, and corporate institutions?

I have been concerned with business ethics ever since I was initially entrusted with the responsibility of managing the careers of others some 20 years ago. The desire to become more aware of the ethical underpinnings of business behavior has led me on a lengthy tour of business literature and the social sciences of organizational behavior as well as moral philosophy and theology. As a result, I have found myself a teacher of ethics in graduate business schools, in churches, and even in a seminary. The anecdotal behavior patterns over the past years in my chosen profession, investment banking, have added to the drama of my personal quest.

Many argue that ethics cannot be taught, especially to young adults whose values already have been formed. I shall discuss this issue in some detail below, but one might even cede this premise and still find a valuable purpose in teaching ethics. I attempt to blunt the issue by stating that my purpose in an ethics class is to take a very brief tour through ethical decision making. What are the issues? Who are the stake-holders? If one can merely raise the group's ethical awareness and imagination, a great deal has been accomplished.

When I teach a 90-minute ethics orientation class to incoming MBA candidates at a major graduate school of business, I suggest they spend an extra five minutes on each case they are assigned and jot down any ethical issues they can see. After two years and hundreds of cases, their ethical imagination can be sharpened immeasurably by this process.

I caution the students not to raise all these issues in the classroom. No one wishes to be thought of as an obstructionist, always wearing one's heart on one's sleeve. As we shall discuss in this article, the truly great ethical clashes in our lives, where we must make a stand or lose our sense of humanity, are quite rare. We often magnify into great ethical issues, those issues where we lose out to others, where we are right and everyone else is wrong. If we can allow ourselves to broaden the list of potential stake-holders from a small party of one, we may come to see the issue in a new light. Warren Buffet has stated that a full business career involves possibly as few as 20 truly career-making decisions.

I urge students to develop their own awareness of ethics and to begin feeling more comfortable with the paradox and ambiguity of professional life. I urge them to develop a community in which they can comfortably discuss and share ethical concerns that trouble them without having to "go public" every time they are uncom-fortable. Above all, I urge them to begin to know what are their real limits, where they will take their stand. The worst thing that can happen is to walk through a major ethical dilemma unconsciously carried along by the crowd, only to become blindsided into doing something that would be inconceivable to you in the full light of day.

When I talk about professional ethics, I speak in the context of one who has spent 30 years as an investment banker, where the rewards and recognition are meted out primarily on the basis of one's prowess in doing deals. Accordingly, I became an expert in serving client needs, thwarting competition, dealing, negotiating, compro-mising, prevailing, pushing the limits, living on the edge, and living with ambiguity and paradox. Later, as a manager, I became adept at influencing others to do the same.

At the same time, a core of us built the business in our firm from an employee base of 140—30 years ago—to 7,500 today. Such dramatic growth required focus and prioritization, coherence and clarity of purpose, rewards and punishments, trading off empowerment and control. We could not be so rigid that we could not push our-selves to the edge of the envelope in creating new businesses and markets. Nor could we be so devious and amoral that we could not command the respect of our colleagues and clients. Above all, we had to build systems and procedures that supported our risk takers.

We learned that the seemingly small, informal actions of the senior managers could have far greater impact than the formal management systems. Donald Siebert, former CEO of JCPenney, liked to tell little vignettes of improper senior management behavior.

"Keep it out of the board report!"

"Get my niece a job!"

"I don't care what you call it—call it corporate expense!"

Thus, over time, is the culture established.

Bad practices grow incrementally. Each small twist of the wheel goes unnoticed. People are rewarded for behavior that reinforces bad practices instead of good practices. We are told from natural science that a frog will sit in a pan of tepid water as the heat is slowly turned up until it dies. While, if the frog is thrown into overheated water, it will jump out. Entitlement replaces responsibility. We each have our own vision of organizations gone awry; and as we wonder how senior management could have condoned such bad practices, perhaps the only answer is the incremental gradualism of evil where there is a lack of moral awareness or imagination.

Organizations where bad practices are condoned and even rewarded develop a pluralistic ignorance. Individual ethics and good practices are drowned out by the cultural norm of the group in ignoring them. We have seen examples of this in the 39 New Yorkers refusing to hear the screams of Kitty Genovese; in the Jim Jones mass suicides; in the reformed church in Nazi Germany; and in many of our large organizations.

Sometimes a single individual can change the course of an organization, though he takes great risk in so doing. Vaclav Havel terms politics "the art of the impossible." I am reminded of Hannah Arendt's amazing tribute to William Shawn, the great editor of the New Yorker: "He had perfect moral pitch." It is too bad we cannot all work for such a master.

We are each individual moral agents with great potential to do good as well as evil. The problem is that we rarely live up to our potential and that we too readily give up our moral authority to others, including the organizations where we make our living. Let me give you a couple of simple illustrations.

There was a sociological experiment where a so-called teacher and a so-called pupil were in cahoots. The unsuspecting target was told that the student was a poor learner and required motivation. The teacher had invented an electric shock device to motivate the student. The target was told to shock the student each time she gave a wrong answer, in order to test the new device. This test was administered on a college campus under the rubric of research.

Of course, the putative student always gave the wrong answer, and by and large the target kept turning up the juice, even into a danger zone marked on the device. The student appeared to be in pain. Afterward, when the target was debriefed, he claimed he was only following instructions.

Likewise, many years ago, at the Union Theological Seminary, Columbia University, an authority figure ordered a series of seminarians to drop everything and fetch a paper off his desk located in another office, and return it to him immediately. In order to fetch the paper, the seminarians had to step twice, going and coming, over the body of a prostrate student lying on a rug in the outer office. In most cases they performed the mission without providing assistance to their prostrate peer. Once again, afterward, they said they were just obeying orders.

Sound familiar? This is what Hannah Arendt described as "the banality of evil."

Types of Ethics

A problem in discussing ethics is deciding which language to use. Few of us are accustomed to expose our individual ethics before a group. We tend to become defensive. In today's norm of cultural relativism—"I'm OK, you're OK"—we are reluctant to publicly criticize the value systems of others. In a graduate business school, learning is compartmentalized into marketing, production, control, finance, human behavior, and the like. Ethics intrudes into all those areas but without a common language. I have found it useful in discussing ethics to attempt to frame a definitional language by discussing types of ethics. The following list is by no means inclusive. It is meant only to gain a primitive hold on a possible common language.

Normative Ethics

In simple terms, normative ethics is that behavior that society at large condones as proper over time. Normative ethics may be codified as the law, but it embraces large areas of behavior not codified by the law. It encompasses our behavior in groups (do not yell "fire!" in a crowded theater); expressions of our sexuality; our dress; and the like. Cultural relativism is a current norm, as is situational ethics. There are those who would say that today's norm is that there are no rules, no easily identifiable broad set of values in which we can all agree. It is easy to go along with the norm; but the norm can easily lead to the incremental gradualism of bad practice as well as pluralistic ignorance.

A very important aspect of normative ethics is that it changes over time as people's attitudes change. Sociologists have even described long-wave rhythms of societal norms swinging back and forth between conservatism and liberality. Thus, if we base our behavior purely on societal norms, we must be prepared to have the rug pulled out from beneath us. Somewhat arcane but valid illustrations would include price-fixing, antitrust, insider trading, or the nonpayment of social security taxes for part-time domestic employees. If we base our behavior on current norms, we might find ourselves a criminal 20 years in the future.

Kantian Ethics

Named after the famous 19th-century moral philosopher, Kantian ethics has come to mean rigid ethical rules or duties. Attributed to Kant is the categorical imperative, which is to say, there are certain things we simply must do in order to maintain our basic humanity. As much as certain elements of our normative society are crying out for at least some rules to live by, others would say that Kant's approach is too rigid for contemporary society.

An apocryphal extension of Kantian ethics would be to recount a story of World War II Amsterdam when Anne Frank knocks on your door and you hide her in your attic to save her from the Gestapo. When the Gestapo knocks on your door and inquires as to Anne's whereabouts, you tell them she is hiding in your attic. According to Kant, there is never a good excuse for a lie.

I tell this story to my students; then I tell them they are each Kantians. They object to this. As living practitioners of normative ethics, they could never be so rigid. Yet, I repeat my charge. We are all Kantians. The trouble is, we are each Kantian about different things. For each of us there are certain things we could never cause ourselves to do. In doing them we would lose our humanity Yet for each of us the limits are somewhat different. This is what makes governance so difficult for any type of social structure; and this is why, in an age of cultural relativism, we often come together at the lowest common denominator or at the worst bad practice.

Utilitarian Ethics

Stemming from Jeremy Bentham and John Stuart Mill, utilitarianism (the greatest good for the greatest number) is a powerful shaper of our normative ethic. Utilitarian ethics drive government policy making, economic input/output modeling, and cost-benefit analysis and basically determines how our world works. Health care reform is based on utilitarian ethics. As a society we will not condone paying $500 for a pint of blood when it is commonly available at $100 a pint. The odds of contaminated blood may be 1:100,000 at $100 a unit, and 1:1,000,000 at $500 a unit. We as a society do not think that is a good trade. But if our loved one is infected through contaminated blood, we will sue the hospital for millions of dollars for not using the more expensive blood.

We can calculate the value of a human life and enter the sum into our input/output models to determine how many kidney dialysis machines we can afford economically. We can calculate your future earning power. We can also calculate how much you would be willing to pay to save your own life. A result is that people's lives are worth more in wealthy countries than in poorer countries. The *Economist*, for example, reports that a human life is calculated to be worth $2.6 million in America and $20,000 in Portugal. Robert McNamara ran the Vietnam War on an acceptable kill ratio of 20:1. They killed 56,000 of ours, and we killed over a million of them. The Gulf War will be a prized case of a successful kill ratio (unless, of course, someone you loved was killed).

Utilitarian ethics are pervasive in our society. The majority vote wins. The only real losers are the minority.

Social Justice Ethics

Social justice ethics are an antidote to the excesses of majority rule utilitarianism. It takes care of those who lose out to the mainstream of society. The social safety net is a good example of social justice. Critics of social justice politics brand it as single-issue politics, or the tyranny of the minority.

Religious Ethics

As we shall discuss in this article, moral philosophy and theology play a major role even in normative ethics. Will Durant writes in *The Story of Civilization*: "Conduct, deprived of its religious supports, deteriorates into epicurean chaos; and life itself, shorn of consoling faith, becomes a burden alike to conscious poverty and to weary wealth." The issue for society of course is which religion do we choose? Even in a country like Nepal, with an announced state religion, religious diversity is present. The problem, of course, is that nothing has divided mankind more throughout history than religious differences. In the United States, where religion is pervasive in our normative culture, we continue to attempt to preserve the notion of the secular state. In his recent book, *The Culture of Disbelief*, Stephen L. Carter writes of the ubiquity of religious language in our public debates as a form of trivialization of religion, as our politicians repeat largely meaningless religious incantations.

Communitarian Ethics

A more secular and perhaps less controversial approach to moral theology, but based purely on the social sciences, is communitarianism. Most recently espoused by Amitai Etzioni in his book *The Moral Dimension* and reported by *Time* magazine, communitarianism relies on: 1) the individual, 2) society, and 3) transcendent values. Transcendent values can be any of the world's religions, or even a deeply rooted humanism.

The great Protestant theologian Paul Tillich discussed evil in terms of isolation, loneliness, and alienation. We must be in community with ourselves, our community, and our God. Such a theology is validated by the great depth psychologists.

To many of us, communitarianism resonates from the one great commandment of the New Testament: We must love our neighbors as we love ourselves (which means implicitly, by the way, that we must first love ourselves), and we must love the Lord our God with all our heart and all our mind and all our strength. This commandment may be found in the Jewish and Islamic religions as well. The universality of these ideas may not be completely accidental.

One Ethics Model

This brief review of a few ethical systems is meant only to begin bringing clarity to our thinking. So often we bring all these systems to bear in a single conversation, confusing the listener as well as ourselves. I enjoy listening to a presidential debate and saying to myself, "Aha, that's utilitarian. Now he's a Kantian. No, that's normative." It is helpful to begin developing a language of ethics if we are ever to reason together.

Ethics babble persists because ethics crosses so many lines. The following illustration makes the point. Moral philosophy and theology provide the ethics underpin-

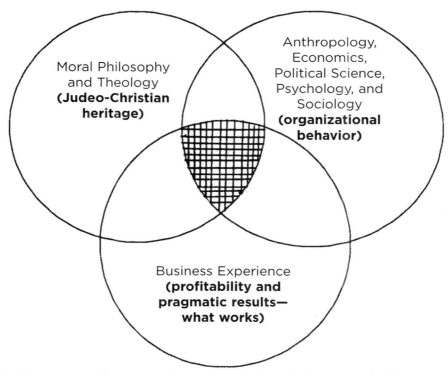

One Way of Thinking about a Viable Approach to Business Ethics

Work to maximize the potential for constructive agreement.

nings. The social scientists, including also economists and political scientists, intellec-tualize about how ethics actually works. Practitioners, managers, and leaders have pragmatic experience that is invaluable in determining how to foster and stimulate an ethical corporate culture.

The schematic diagram indicates that all inputs are essential and that the area of overlap is small. Very few academics or practitioners are confident when expressing themselves in all three areas. Universities are not organized to foster such cross-discipline specialties. Too often we are left with business people knocking the doors down in a church, church people knocking down the doors in a business, and aca-demics lecturing to a nonaudience.

Business schools and universities do not deem it appropriate to teach theology, moral philosophy, or values. These must be taught at home. Such edicts ignore the fact that the majority of students were not reared in a nuclear family and that, according to the findings of social scientists, in the aging of mankind the search for meaning and values becomes even more pronounced in late middle age. The younger upwardly mobile are not too old to learn values; they are too young and overwhelmed by career and family choices. I differ from the majority view in my feeling that moral philoso-phy is entirely appropriate to include in a business school ethics class. Students are hungering for values and for ideas upon which they can build in later stages of their continuing growth.

The other two circles—social sciences, including organizational behavior, and pragmatic business experience—are entirely appropriate curricula for a business school. A solid case can be made for a course in ethical awareness, imagination, and decision making utilizing just two of these spheres of knowledge; but, in my experi-ence, students need and appreciate the third as well.

Finally, business school administrators assert that values certainly cannot be taught or graded. How, in an age of cultural relativism, can we grade someone's values? My own experience indicates that almost any case study has more than a single answer. We are not grading answers, we are grading the ability to ingest large amounts of data offered in a jumbled state; to provide clarity, prioritization, and focus; and, by way of an intelligent and ordered reasoning process, to discern a viable plan of action. At least that's what I thought the top business schools did.

Ethical Decision Making

I am indebted to my friend, Michael Josephson of the Josephson Institute of Ethics, for much of the structure that follows. Michael proposes a five-step ethical decision-mak-ing process, which I shall discuss in some detail.

- *Identify the stakeholders.* Paul Tillich writes that if we become isolated moral agents we are almost certain to commit immoral acts. We find our morality in community, removing our ego and letting in the world. Many social scientists echo Tillich's theology. Teachers of ethical reasoning urge us to include as many stakeholders as imaginable in our decision-making process. The more creatively and imaginatively one begins to think about broadening the list of stakeholders, the more ethically aware one becomes. What about Michael Millken's children? What about the children of laid-off workers in a takeover? Moreover, the broader the community of decision makers, the broader the list of stakeholders. I urge my students to avoid isolation. A peer group on the job to discuss issues is always best. Since we do not always work in an open environment, a professional peer group of former classmates, a church professional group, or trusted close friends become essential.

- *Identify the ethical principle.* We often confuse our hurt feelings or disappointments for ethical issues. Through discussion, be certain a real ethical issue exists. My father always told me: "You get your loving at home!" If there are only 20 or so key issues in a career, be certain you are not using yours up too rapidly. Ethics is tough-minded business. If utilitarianism is the norm, begin to discern the difference between the issues of being in the minority and basic unfairness or lack of integrity. Strip out the emotion. Ethics trump expediency.

- *Choose one ethical principle.* The true spirit-crushing ethical dilemmas are when one is caught between two opposing powerful ethical issues. These are among the 20 big-time life decisions. If you are to be human and act out your own life, you must make a choice. To refuse to choose is to lack integrity. This is the stuff of great drama and great literature.

Paul Tillich in his *My Search for Absolutes* wrote: "no moral code can spare us from a decision and thus save us from moral risk. . . .Moral commandments are the wisdom of the past as it has been embodied in laws and traditions, and anyone who does not follow them risks tragedy. . . .Moral decisions involve moral risk. Even though a decision may be wrong and bring suffering, the creative element in every serious choice can give the courage to decide. . . .The mixture of the absolute and the relative in moral decisions is what constitutes their danger and their greatness. It gives dignity and tragedy to man, creative joy, and pain of failure. Therefore he should not try to escape into a willfulness without norms or into a security without freedom."

Likewise in his autobiography, *Memories, Dreams, Reflections*, Carl Jung writes of the existential anxiety of moral decision making: "We must have the freedom in some circumstances to avoid the known moral good and do what is considered to be evil, if an ethical decision so requires. As a rule, however, the individual is so unconscious that he altogether fails to see his own potential for decision. Instead he is consistently looking around for external rules and regulation which can guide him in his perplexity."

In resolving true ethical choices, be certain to understand why you chose the path you chose and why you rejected the path you rejected. Loyalty is perhaps the weakest ethical standard, and the preservation of human life may be the strongest. You must be tough enough to make a decision when you have sought out divergent points of view and all that needs to be known cannot be known. You must at times answer questions that have no established solutions.

- *Creatively examine options.* We so often lock ourselves into a binary decision path. The answer must be either/or. Yet so many issues come at us all jumbled amidst ambiguity and paradox. We often sail right through without even discerning the ethical issues, or else we make a snap either/or judgment. The ambiguity of many dilemmas cries out for a polyphonous response. Stop, gather your community of peers, and come up with as many options as possible for consideration. Perhaps, for example, in a downsizing strategy, instead of firing everybody, you can afford to keep their health benefits going for an additional six or 12 months.

- *Maximize long-term benefits.* We are back to the utilitarian model once again. Note the key words "long term." A broad list of stakeholders will help move from my short-term needs to the long-term needs of others. At an earlier step, we suggested stripping out emotion. Perhaps at this final step we may reintegrate emotion and compassion. The utilitarian greater good must be balanced with the need of the minority. Solutions may appear ambiguous. We may both rely on virtue and impose sanctions. We may empower others with our solutions, but we will also insist on accountability. The best solutions may follow the tight/loose Peters and Waterman model described in *In Search of Excellence*—a model of freedom with control.

Ethics of Organizations

We have been speaking, thus far, of individual ethics; but what of institutional ethics? How do we inculcate an ethic within an organization or an institution or a society? There are those who say that in an age of normative ethics and utilitarian ethics, our institutions no longer work for us.

In his recent book on professional compensation, Derek Bok quotes T.S. Eliot: "As a society we much prefer to leave our values undisturbed while going to great lengths to create in T.S. Eliot's words, 'a system that is so perfect that no one needs to be good.'"

In many ways each of us is as much a social justice or single-issue politician as we are a Kantian. We take umbrage when we find ourselves in the minority within the context of an organization, institution, or society at large; and we wrap ourselves in the cloak of moral self-righteousness and attack the "evil" organization that has done us in. Yet we know in our hearts that good leaders require good servants. In fact, as the late

Robert Greenleaf noted, good leaders need to be good servants. We must each learn to be loyal members of institutions while retaining our individual ethical vigilance.

Perhaps John Gardner came closest to describing the covenantal relationship required between individuals and organizations in his fairly recent Stanford commencement address. Gardner stated that we must find a wholeness incorporating diversity. We must neither suppress it nor make it a tyrant. We must respect diversity. Each of us must ask what we can contribute to the whole. Gardner concludes that wholeness incorporating diversity defines the transcendent task of our generation.

Conclusion

Ethics is not easy or loose. Ethics is tough and hard. We must learn and decide who we are. Where do we draw the line? What are we willing to lose for? Ethics isn't always winning. Cheaters do prosper. Ethics is losing in the short term for a longer-term sense of self-worth and transcendent values. Learning to live ethically is learning to live with oneself, learning to live in community, and learning to live in that great stream of humanism, including theology and religion, that forms our Western culture. It is not a process that is completed at our mother's knee or in graduate school. For the truly conscious person, it is a lifelong process of growth and maturation that, by its very nature, can never be perfect or complete.

Source: *Real Estate Issues*, December 1994.

31 Emotional Intelligence Provides Key to Life Success

Recently I read a book, *Emotional Intelligence* by Daniel Goleman, which was published in hardcover by Bantam Books in 1995. This book convinced me that what we were really looking for during my tenure at Morgan Stanley was emotional intelligence.

The author states that there are widespread exceptions to the rule that IQ predicts success. At best, IQ contributes about 20 percent to the factors that determine life success, which leaves 80 percent to other forces, ranging from social class to luck.

Goleman defines emotional intelligence as the ability to motivate oneself and persist in the face of frustrations; to control impulse and delay gratification; to regulate one's moods and keep distress from swamping the ability to think; to empathize; and to hope. He goes on to say that while IQ cannot be changed much by experience, these other factors can be. People who are emotionally adept—who know and manage their own feelings well, and who read and deal effectively with other people's feelings— are at an advantage in any domain of life, whether romance and intimate relationships or picking up the unspoken rules that govern success in organizational politics. Such people are also more likely to be content and effective in their lives. People who cannot marshal some control over their emotional life fight inner battles that sabotage their ability for focused work and clear thought.

People who cannot control their emotions are more likely to become tipped over the edge—enraged by something seemingly trivial—a trait that the author terms "emotional hijacking." Such a hijacking causes "toxic emotion" to break out, which is stress and anxiety that is out of proportion and out of place. I'm certain each of us has experienced such behavior in others—as well as in ourselves.

As I look back on my career, those who were most successful over time had a high skill level of emotional intelligence. I am reminded of General Bagration in Tolstoy's *War and Peace*. He was caught up in the din and confusion of the great battlefield. He had no idea what was going on around him. His generals, intensely anguished, came galloping up to him for instructions. Bagration remained a sea of calm and counseled them to return to their positions and do what they thought best under the circumstances. His subordinate generals returned to the fray, instructionless, but filled with confidence and hope from Bagration's high level of emotional maturity. As a result, they went on to defeat Napoleon.

In his most recent book on leadership for the future, Peter Drucker says our leaders must have the emotional maturity to deal with the high rate of change and stress encountered in every business situation. One reason I have been drawn to the Counselors of Real Estate (CRE) is because of the high level of emotional maturity exhibited by so many members. Within this association, we see the masters of their profession at work, without the din and confusion of the investment banking or brokerage communities.

I'm certain many of us would benefit greatly from this book. Likewise, there are many Counselors of Real Estate who need not take the time. They are already there.

Source: *The Counselor* (Counselors of Real Estate), 1997.

32

Toward a Global Ethic?

A move toward a global ethic requires discovery of those aspects of universal humanity that transcend barriers.

For some time, Americans have witnessed how worldwide information and communication have made national boundaries and cultures increasingly permeable. Especially since the tragic events of September 11, it is no longer is possible to live under the illusion of impenetrable boundaries.

Ironically, the integration of worldwide money and capital markets makes it harder for a sovereign state to control its monetary base and easier for supranational terrorist groups to hide their wealth. Now, global communication networks, such as CNN, make it easy for small terrorist groups to have an effect on the entire world overnight, while making it more difficult for a nation to fight a sustained, bloody conflict when pictures of the maimed and dying are transmitted hourly into the living rooms of the homeland.

At a time when fundamentalist groups are waging a separatist war on nation-states, researchers into the human brain are concluding that all mankind shares an innate longing for transcendent truths. There is further irony in the mission of terrorist groups to fragment and separate a world that is just beginning to recognize its environmental interdependence. Many shared a vision that the end of the Cold War, together with increasing care for the future of humanity and Earth, made this a historic opportunity for cooperation and integration. Yet deep cultural issues, often flowing from religious antecedents, are divisive. Religion has the potential to separate people into tribes and to shut down reason; institutionalized religion often puts itself beyond criticism and closes down dialogue.

In recent years, a number of transnational social, political, religious, and business organizations have attempted to formulate a global ethic. The United Nations Educational, Scientific, and Cultural Organization (UNESCO) focuses on respect for human rights, fundamental freedoms, and the rule of law. It states that a multicultural consensus of people, religions, and traditions calls for a meeting of basic human needs through sustainable development, protection of the environment, and achievement of social equity. It also calls for collective security arrangements and disarmament.

Hans Kung, the noted Catholic theologian, would base a global ethic on nonviolence; respect for life, justice, and solidarity; truthfulness and tolerance; and a mutual respect and partnership. The Parliament of the World's Religions stresses solidarity and relatedness, along with respect for life, dignity, individuality, and diversity. A move toward a global ethic would require discovery of those aspects of universal humanity that transcend religious barriers.

The Minnesota Center for Business Ethics emphasizes global corporate responsibility, friendship, understanding and cooperation, common respect for the highest moral values, and responsible actions by individuals in their own sphere of influence. Until intellect is globalized, says Jack Welch, retired CEO of General Electric, global enterprises really cannot be created. He sees social stability as being as important as financial stability.

According to a recent paper by Harvard University professor Lawrence E. Harrison, there are ten values that distinguish cultures fostering economic growth. They include:

- an orientation toward the future, instead of a focus on the present or past;
- a positive attitude toward work, instead of work looked on as a burden;
- a propensity to save and invest, instead of a focus on seeking income equality;
- mass availability of education, instead of education for the elite;
- fairness in advancement, instead of reliance on cronyism and connections;
- trust in a broad range of extended communities, instead of trust primarily in the family;
- a strong ethical code and a relative absence of corruption, instead of resorting to legal sanctions;
- justice and fair play, instead of a focus on "who you know and how much you pay off";

- dispersed authority and broad empowerment, instead of hierarchy and command and control systems; and
- religion as essentially a private matter allowing for plurality and dissent, instead of orthodoxy and conformity.

While the Western model for business exports its values of transparency, opportunity, accountability, and citizenship, global business values have been in transition. Individuals worldwide are reprioritizing their values in order to participate in the global marketplace; however, that marketplace is becoming an area of conflicting world views where many see capitalism as inhumane.

The global entertainment, finance, and communications markets, among others, are based on the Judeo-Christian ethical system. This is not to suppose that all the actors are Jewish or Christian, or even religious; it is merely to affirm that the cultural norms underlying these markets come from the Judeo-Christian belief system. God is as much a part of Western historical culture as is the cosmic dust that emanates from the initial big bang. Western cultures have a system in place that supports their business communities: There is a rule of law, competition, efficiency, opportunity, transparency, an open search for talent, a reward system for achievement, and a common understanding of the importance of time. In such systems, one need not be anxious about leaving one's family or village to seek one's fortune, because the preconditions for success are in place.

But in certain parts of the world, the social support systems focus on the family, the village, and the tribe. Connections are vital. One is loyal to one's affiliations; indeed, one has an obligation to engage in reciprocity among one's close relationships. Personal ties remain important in such cultures, and one leaves the benevolence of one's family and affiliations at considerable risk. The society, often informed by such religious cultures as Hinduism, Buddhism, and Islam, often supports family, village, and tribal relationships rather than the impersonal institutions designed by the West, such as the International Monetary Fund (IMF), whose policies are not always enthusiastically supported by countries like Malaysia and Indonesia. The West often accuses the business establishments in such societies of engaging in cronyism and lacking transparency, when they, in fact, are just following deeply imbedded cultural norms.

Why do extreme fundamentalists and zealots hate Americans? An easy answer is U.S. support of Israel, and the more than 50 years of hopelessness and anger of Palestinian refugees. Yet, Thomas Friedman, in a post–September 11 editorial in the *New York Times*, and a number of others argue that this deep antipathy toward Americans would persist even without Israel. Osama bin Laden is a wealthy Saudi, not a homeless refugee.

Many suggestions have been offered. One is that certain nations that are formed around religious orthodoxy, and conformity cannot bear to see or understand the contradiction represented by the economic success of nations that are deeply opposed to their lack of religious tolerance and freedom. Some are truly offended by the global reach of U.S. communications and entertainment networks that frequently display violence, sexuality, vulgar language, and women's rights that their doctrines fundamentally oppose. They cannot fathom how such a culture can be so successful economically, and they perceive this as an injustice that needs to be righted. When misguided souls of the West attempt religious evangelism inside these nations, the issue becomes even worse. The social injustice of the fact that the United States has 5 percent of the world population but consumes 25 percent of the world's gross national product (GNP) has moved a much greater proportion of the world's people to action than just the fringe loonies, as is witnessed by demonstrations worldwide against the IMF, the World Bank, and other global organizations.

How can capitalism be humanized and adapted to local cultures? One way is through analysis of how to integrate friendship, reciprocity, and community into a global market. How can there be impartial justice for all, without personal relationships being destroyed? The question then becomes how to humanize capitalism and resolve competing rights in a utilitarian model. The utilitarian model that drives many business decisions attempts to quantify costs and benefits and provide solutions that result in the greatest good for the greatest number. The system works well, as long as one is a winner. Losers must seek recourse another way, often under the rubric of social justice or single-issue politics. The majority resents the now-reenfranchised minority for attempting to sway public opinion through often unorthodox methods. Yet social justice movements provide a peaceful method for resolving important minority issues, such as civil rights. Repression of such minorities leads only to bigger problems later, as unfortunately has been witnessed.

As Americans react to the events of September 11, there suddenly is recognition of who the true heroes are: First to be honored are the fire and police professionals who dutifully head into harm's way. American flags are flown. There are tears while people sing patriotic songs whose words are half forgotten. Churches and synagogues are filled. Crime rates plummet. People suddenly feel as though they are in touch with some deeper, more fundamental aspect of themselves and with their neighbors. They even find that the value of their 401(k) investments seems less important than before the attacks. It is this kind of core of national character that people turn to in times of stress. It takes an event of unthinkable proportions to shock people back into caring for one another.

There now is a job to do—a national purpose: to destroy terrorism throughout the world. This may become an impracticable vision, but there is a need first to see what can be accomplished. In the course of protecting the homeland, some personal freedoms will be sacrificed. There is the power and the will to inflict great harm on the country's enemies, but anger must be tempered with justice. Above all, the country's response must be measured so as not to generate an ongoing cycle of terror. In the long term, the issues are even more complex.

In his nationally broadcast sermon at the National Cathedral on September 14 [2001], the Reverend Billy Graham discussed the mystery of evil, the need for community, and the power of hope. How does one find the good in all this? To do so, a number of issues must be explored seriously, including: How do Americans become more responsible stewards of the world's economic resources? Is there a positive manner in which the United States can participate in the global warming discussions? Can this country continue its level of economic growth and disproportionate share of world GNP without being considered evil by a strong minority throughout the world? It is one thing to be the envy of the world; it is an entirely different matter to be hated. How is the country's economic prowess to be maintained while the hate and anger are mitigated? What responsibility does the United States have as the world's leader to elevate world culture instead of diminishing or trivializing it? How can the country export its basic values of goodness and caring without seeming to want to convert the world to a particular religious faith? Is it possible to globalize world cultures, economies, and religions, or is life essentially local?

As the world tries to move toward a global ethic, it must be realized that the world is not likely to be moving toward complete universality. It is doubtful that there ever will be one worldwide religion, for example. The saying "think globally, act locally" no doubt will prevail. Global institutions, including multinational business enterprises, will think globally and reflect the currently dominant Judeo-Christian value system. But they will operate locally throughout the world, where they must adapt to local cultures, including those cultures' reliance on family and relationships over larger Western social structures. There always will be differences, and the diversity must be celebrated, while we all work together to help build and sustain organizations that can bring everyone together.

Source: *Urban Land* (Point of View column), November/December 2001.

33

Breaking
Public Trust

The best outcome of Enron's collapse would be confirmation of ethics as crucial to business decision making.

The bad practices at Enron did not emerge all at once, but developed incrementally. Innovation and success can generate a hubris that can distort reality. Only people of exceptionally strong ethical discernment, courage, and character will blow the whistle when, at least superficially, everything appears to be going well. In finance, Gresham's law states that bad currency drives out good currency. Likewise, without ethical leadership, bad practices can drive out good ones.

Large public accounting firms, for example, have gradually changed their role from obstruction (telling clients what they cannot do) to facilitation (helping clients to "interpret" laws and regulations). There is increased pressure to conform to the wishes of aggressive clients because always there is the shadow of another accounting firm that will do what the client wants. At the same time, as is the case at law firms, billable hours become increasingly important to accounting firms, as do "value-added" and "success-fee" billings, which ignore hours and seek to obtain a percentage of additional revenues generated. With an eye toward the ongoing success of management consulting firms such as McKinsey & Company and Boston Consulting Group, public accounting firms have engaged in the higher-margin business of consulting, and the revenues generated have become more important than accounting fees. In theory, accounting and consulting can be maintained in the same firm, so long as the conflicts are identified and a culture is created to manage them. Investment banks are filled with conflicts, but the best firms actively manage them. However, the gradual deterioration of the independence of stock analysts within investment banks is another example of bad practices prevailing over good ones. Enron appears to have suffered a pandemic of bad practices engaged in by its senior management, public accountants, board of directors, and its independent law firm.

A great deal of the upcoming public discourse concerning Enron will focus on whether laws were broken and who broke them. During the insider trading scandals of the 1980s, individuals such as Drexel Burnham Lambert's Michael Milken were imprisoned on arcane and highly technical infractions of securities regulations. The issues were murky enough to allow some of those convicted to continue to protest their innocence after their release from prison.

The situation is similar with Enron: The rules and regulations have not been written definitively to cover all the technicalities of hedging and use of derivatives, and Enron appears to have created some de novo. Professionals can argue about the extreme limits of "thin capitalization"; many industrial corporations and financial institutions have failed to disclose fully their off-balance-sheet liabilities; and there are plenty of weak boards of directors. Like some Enron executives, movie stars and athletes are sometimes paid unconscionable sums in relation to their contributions to society. However, the main issue at Enron, as it was with the insider trading scandals, does not lie in technical aspects of laws and regulations; one can live within them and still commit fraud. Like insider trading, fraud is a state of mind, and a state of mind is beyond the scope of the legal system. The great crime at Enron is the breaking of public trust.

In the insider trading scandals, the public became incensed at the hubris, greed, and abuse of power, and insisted that something, anything be done to stop the excesses. As generations change, so do the types of behavior the public can condone, and the public has changed its attitude toward insider trading, monopolistic behavior, price fixing, payment of taxes for part-time help, and the like. Thirty years ago, the U.S. Supreme Court ruled that it was not a violation of insider trading rules for a chief investment officer of a financial institution to "front run" the news tape, giving him or her advance knowledge, and to purchase stock in a corporation for the institution's pension fund clients, because he or she had not personally gained from the transaction. In recent years, just overhearing a conversation about a stock and acting upon it could send one to prison. That is an immense swing in public attitude from what once was expressed by the nation's highest court. Those who live close to the edge can find themselves in deep trouble when society's attitudes change.

The insider trading issue was so important in the 1980s that a partner of Goldman Sachs and two employees of Kidder, Peabody were handcuffed on their respective trading floors, and their photos were plastered on the front pages of newspapers. The Goldman Sachs partner went to prison, though the firm continues to protest his conviction, but the two from Kidder were never indicted. Soon afterward, the chief agents of the U.S. Treasury, the Securities and Exchange Commission, and the Federal Reserve Bank of New York convinced the money center banks to pull in their overnight broker call loans to Drexel. Drexel was left short of funds and could no longer use overnight bank borrowing to fund long-duration positions of junk bonds. The withdrawal of bank support caused Drexel to declare bankruptcy, and 10,000 employees lost their jobs.

Why did society throw everything it had at the suspects in this scandal? The issue was the breaking of public trust. America has the deepest, most transparent capital market in the world, and that market is based on trust. Trillions of dollars trade by phone or computer, with paperwork following a few days later. When settlement occurs, one party is in the money, and the other party is out of the money. If the lost trust in the capital market system had not been restored, the country never would have experienced the economic growth of the 1990s, and individuals would not have returned to the market with their retirement plans.

The Enron situation has raised issues of public trust in respect to public accounting firms, law firms, management consulting firms, boards of directors, financial reporting, business leadership, and the stock market itself. In this age of globalization of money and capital markets, the U.S. capital markets are looked upon throughout the world as the model to be emulated. Enron thus broke trust with institutions throughout the world.

In his *Divine Comedy*, Dante reserved the lowest circles of hell for public leaders who committed fraud; the lesser crimes—lust, avarice, and the like—were punished less severely. Leaders of large, publicly held companies, and especially those who have the gall to claim they are "reinventing" American business, have a huge responsibility to the public that goes far beyond obeying the law. It is a privilege to operate in a position of leadership and power, and to reap vast rewards from this society and its market system. Those who set themselves above the will and the trust of the people to focus primarily on themselves are guilty of a sin that goes beyond the law, and society will punish them for it.

An essential quality of professionalism is an enduring ethic that causes the public in general to trust a person's work. A professional leader must have a set of core

values that transcend the drive for wealth or success and that allow him or her to have
both the ethical sensitivity and the imagination to perceive a problem and the courage
to speak out about it. Such leadership was lacking not only within Enron, but in its
board of directors and in the professionals who advised the firm. A leader, both explic-
itly and implicitly, creates a context for good or bad practices, and a leader's actions
carry far greater weight than written corporate policies. Certainly unwittingly,
Salomon Brothers CEO John Gutfreund, by encouraging macho, high-stakes "liar's
poker" in the 1990s, condoned and strengthened a reckless trading culture at the
investment firm that led to the bad practice of committing fraud against the U.S.
Treasury. This constituted a breach of public trust of the most serious magnitude, and
it cost Gutfreund his job and reputation and Salomon Brothers its independence,
almost putting the firm out of business. It appears Arthur Andersen may follow the
same course.

Although the jury is still out, the leaders at Enron appear to have encouraged a
reckless, no-holds-barred trading culture in many ways, not the least of which was
encouraging the establishment of a fake trading floor, staffed with clerical and support
help, to defraud visiting financial analysts and bond-rating agencies. One senses from
reports that the leaders at Enron winked at excesses such as bending the accounting
and reporting rules. The law was viewed not as a constraint, but as something to be
gotten around. One employee was quoted in the press as saying Enron "used the
accounting rules to make money."

It is the responsibility of leaders to set limits and establish controls. At its
highest level, the role of leadership is to establish a transcendent goal for the enterprise
that rises above annual bonuses and momentary success. If leaders encourage employees to take risks, they must back them up when the employees make mistakes, and they
must vigilantly help them establish limits, taking full responsibility for employees'
errors in judgment. The oft-quoted phrase of senior management, "I am not an
accountant," is an abrogation of a leader's responsibility. It is a huge mistake to base
annual bonus payouts—which appeared to drive the culture at Enron, just as they do
at investment banks—purely on production. Management must retain the discretion
to reward and punish professionals based on such criteria as skills in leadership, ethics,
training, recruiting, and mentoring. Otherwise, management abandons its role and the
inmates control the institution.

The best companies have an almost covenantal leadership structure in which
employees know where they stand and what their roles are through both articulated
and tacit agreements with management. Such covenantal expectations cannot be
forged when a crisis hits, but are built over time through consistent behavior.
Otherwise, when a crisis occurs, the firm splinters, with every employee operating for

himself or herself. A true leader has a deep sense of purpose, calm, and even detachment during a crisis; the aura of trust that has been built up sustains leadership among employees during a time of high anxiety and stress. At Enron, in contrast, the atmosphere seemed to have been one of chaos and confusion, leading to shredding, bailouts, last-minute bonuses, and hasty, false reassurances that all was well.

Recent studies have confirmed that what employees really want from a job is a sense of fulfillment, trust, and personal growth. Money and status are important, but less so. Through its lack of leadership, Enron's senior managers not only broke trust with the public, but also with their principal asset, the thousands of employees and stockholders who mistakenly placed their faith in them. It will be interesting to see how the various Enron stakeholders assert their claims for justice.

An entity is either trustworthy or it is not trustworthy. Trust is not easily created, but it is easily destroyed. It is not easily taught; it certainly cannot be legislated. The proper response to the Enron fiasco is not to pile on more laws and regulations; they can be twisted as easily as the old ones by those who wish to commit fraud. Instead, the country needs to rethink the role of the accounting profession and the transparency of financial reporting. More than that, the country needs to honor leadership and values in its business community and in its professions. The teaching of organizational ethics in graduate schools of law and business has been problematic at best; perhaps as a result of the recent round of scandals, it will become possible to elevate the teaching of ethical awareness and sensitivity at such institutions. The best outcome of the Enron mess would be to validate ethics as a crucial component in making business decisions.

Source: *Urban Land* (Point of View column), June 2002.

34 Real Estate Ethics

An experienced real estate professional discusses why it is important to teach ethics in business school.

Students in business schools should be expected to acquire the sense of moral awareness to make ethics an instinctive input in business decisions. They must learn the difference between a rules-based approach to ethics and an approach emphasizing consequences. The global economy has triggered a need for professionals to practice a global ethic that should incorporate Western practices as well as acknowledge the core beliefs of other world cultures and religions. Students should be exposed to ethical dilemmas that will prepare them to deal with the problems they will encounter in their careers. It is important to learn that an ethical leader must have the ability to discern issues where others may not; further, they must possess the self-confidence to seek out different points of view. Eventually, for such leaders, an ethical component of decision making should become intuitive.

In the early 1970s, I was given the responsibility for Morgan Stanley's real estate unit, which was pioneering real estate investment banking. At the time I was 35 years old, and was about to embark on what turned out to be an amazing learning experience.

As my colleagues and I struggled to build a new business, we looked forward to the time when we would all be successful. Many of the folks who worked with me became major players in the field of real estate finance. But in reviewing that period, almost 30 years ago, the real enjoyment and satisfaction came as much from the struggle as from the success.

Throughout that phase of my career I was concerned with the bottom line, efficiency, serving client needs, thwarting competition, dealing, negotiating, and pushing the limits. My staff had to have the same concerns. They needed the freedom to push themselves to the edge, but not be so devious that they could not command the respect of their colleagues and clients. During this period, Morgan Stanley evolved from a strictly client-relationship firm to a transactional firm, growing from 140 individuals when I joined in 1962 to 7,500 when I retired in 1990. A premium was placed on people who could perform for both relationship and transactional clients, as well as run a business unit. Upon reflection, it is clear that it is much easier to do deals than to build a business, and many employees could not make this transition. In fact, as financial institutions were deregulated in the 1970s, several hundred firms were acquired by others or went out of business, as they could not adjust to the rapidly changing environment.

I learned quickly that my decisions about bonuses and promotions, as well as terminations, had an immense impact on the organization in terms of both communicating and generating the type of behavior that is rewarded or punished. So did choices about which clients to accept or reject. It became obvious that if I expected my people to take risks, they must be supported by the organization, that is—me. I needed to be concerned with issues such as how to set the limits of behavior, how to engender successful but "good" behavior, and how to encourage risk taking without going "over the line." I realized that a leader creates a context, for good or ill.

Perhaps the most difficult decision a leader can take is to break and change the covenants that have woven together an organization. Such covenants are both explicit and implicit. A good leader learns what the covenants are and leads by resonating with them, not by manipulating them. There are times when the system of covenants must be changed in order for the enterprise to survive. An example is Hewlett Packard, which was once a purely scientific instrument company, with a policy of no layoffs and no debt. The transition to a computer company brought wrenching changes to the ingrained Hewlett Packard culture. At one point it was highly questionable whether such changes could even be made. The final solution was to spin off the scientific instrument company in a public offering.

I retired from Morgan Stanley about ten years ago, and now, among other activities, I teach business ethics at the graduate level in business schools. For the past nine years I have taught a six-hour business ethics module in the Master of Real Estate Development program at the University of Southern California. In my class I do not try to tell the students what to do, or give them the "right" answers. Rather I try to help them acquire the sense of moral awareness to make ethics an instinctive input when undertaking business decisions. An ethical leader must have the ability at an early stage to discern ethical issues when others may not, the self-confidence to seek out different points of view, and the tough-mindedness to make decisions in the seemingly chaotic mix of paradox and ambiguity.

Ethical Systems

I divide my class into three parts. First, we discuss ethical terminology in the context of a case on insider trading. Second, we consider an actual ethical dilemma (based on my own experience). Third, we discuss students' assignments that document their own ethical stories.

In order to discuss ethics it is necessary to have a common language that is neither arcane nor doctrinaire. In the context of a case on insider trading, for example, we discuss *normative ethics*. Society has firm views on what is appropriate behavior, including such matters as expressing our sexuality, dress, gender roles, and attitudes toward race, as well as business issues such as price fixing, insider trading and antitrust. The trouble is that society frequently changes its mind about such matters. As real estate is more often owned by public companies, real estate practitioners have become bound by different rules than 30 years ago. While competitive practices that would have been unthinkable, such as busting up deals or violating auction proceedings, are tolerated by public companies, there is much less tolerance for insider trading, blatant bribery, and bid rigging. Further, overt family favoritism plays differently in a public company than in a family-owned firm. As a result, the "easy" ethical calls of the past look seriously flawed today. This has serious ramifications. If one is exposed on the edge of the risk profile when society changes its mind about what may be appropriate behavior, one may find him- or herself in serious professional jeopardy and perhaps even jail.

The class discusses the difference between a rules-based approach to ethics and an approach emphasizing consequences. Enterprises based on trust require fewer rules and regulations, and fewer bureaucratic enforcers. Therefore, they are more efficient, attract a better class of coworker, and are more fun to work in. The problem is, being humans, we respond to both virtue and sanctions. Even the best trust-based environments need to make use of rewards and punishments.

We also examine ethical systems based on religious faith. Using Dante's *Divine Comedy*, we discuss: 1) the surface story line—where we each spend most of our lives;

2) the allegorical level—where we use our favorite stories and heroes to make meanings out of our experience; 3) the moral level—the mores of society, the limits of behavior that society conventionally allows from time to time; and 4) the ethical level—the deep, the spiritual, the religious, where we make our intuitive meanings. A system of law, or morality, that is not rooted in the deep ethical level is rudderless and cast adrift. The issue then becomes, in a multicultural, pluralistic, values-free global economy: Whose religion do we use?

For Christians, a good place to start is the great commandment to love God with all your heart and soul and mind and spirit; and the great corollary, to love your neighbor as yourself. This occurs five times in the New Testament. Interestingly, it also occurs twice in the Hebrew Bible and at least once in the Koran. So it is one of the great explicit societal organizing principles of three of the world's great religions. I would posit that it is implicit in each of the other great religions as well. All the major religions advise us to focus on others rather than on ourselves. This is the beginning of all ethical behavior.

Peter Drucker, the sage of business management, describes the leader of the future as someone who believes in himself, has a genuine love of people, and feels a transcendent passion for the mission of the enterprise. To me, this secular description resonates perfectly with the great commandment and its corollary. Drucker goes on to state that a leader for the future must have the emotional strength to manage anxiety and change. Each of the world's great religions likewise focuses on creating centeredness, a sense of inner calm and peace, a sense of knowing who you are.

The chief difference between a profession and a job is that a profession has ethical underpinnings. A profession denotes an unbiased service or value creation for the other, and not just personal aggrandizement. An occupation that has as its cultural norm the practice of self-dealing, for example, is not by this definition a profession. There are many individuals and organizations attempting to work out a global ethic as the underpinning of the emerging global economy. To the extent that the global economy is triggered at present primarily by Western practices, it implicitly passes on the Judeo-Christian preconceptions, which undergird Western cultural patterns. To be truly universal, however, such a global ethical system must incorporate also core beliefs from the Muslim, Buddhist, Confucian, Hindu, Sufi, and other religions of the world. One who chooses to do business in a Muslim or Hindu culture without attempting to understand the ethical belief system is unlikely to succeed.

An Ethical Dilemma

My own ethical story involves a serious situation that took a random group of individuals completely by surprise. It occurred during a 1981 sabbatical, trekking though the

Himalayas in Nepal. Our group was about 30 days out, about to traverse an 18,000-foot pass over the Annapurna range. We were thrown together with three other climbing groups of differing skills, cultural backgrounds, and ages. My sole Western companion and I were sleep-deprived.

I had also experienced a 30-pound weight loss, and I was concerned about altitude sickness, which I had suffered on a previous Himalayan journey. Nevertheless, we had to cross the pass if we wanted to finish our trek.

Suddenly we encountered a sadhu or pilgrim. He was carrying no belongings, wore only a thin cotton robe, and appeared to be dying. He may even have come to this pass to enjoy a perfect death. The climbers were taken by surprise. Since we were days from any settlement, rescuing him was far beyond our capacity. We agonized over the situation, its solution, and the problems of the group. Some did not see an ethical choice—the group of Japanese had the necessary resources to help the pilgrim but refused to get involved. The situation was too complex for one person, or even two or three, to resolve. Our own lives were at risk as well—how much were we willing to sacrifice for this stranger? To take effective action, we would have to act as a cohesive group, agreeing on common goals and values. The difficulty was that without an underlying core of previously agreed-upon values, it was impossible to coalesce the group around the emergency. I have always suspected that we would have reacted differently if it were our mother rather than a stranger we encountered, as we have a set of basic precepts on how to deal with family. Finally, we left the sadhu with clothing, food, and drink, and moved on. We never found out what happened to him. The story always provokes vigorous debate among my students. The point is that if a common sense of values has not been discussed and articulated before an ethical issue intrudes unexpectedly, it is too late. The situation also contains elements of multiculture, and issues of religion, gender, and race.

Issues

The students have generally had prior business experience in the real estate field, with brokers, developers, construction firms, architects, and bankers. I ask them to describe an ethical problem or situation that they have actually encountered in what was typically their first job situation in real estate. The issues that their stories have raised over the past nine years fit into a fairly consistent pattern:

Hard Bargaining versus Lying. When does one go over the line? When does self-promotion become overstating one's qualifications? At what point do we cease taking on new business if we are not adequately staffed or trained? When does "puffing" projections become an outright lie? Is it contextual? Does the level of sophistication of your counterparty make any difference? Are there circumstances where it is not okay to bluff?

Networking versus Spying. When is it okay to pose as a potential real estate buyer to gain competitive information, and when is it offensive, i.e., lying?

Cheating, Lying, Falsifying Data. It is disturbing how often obviously improper requests are made by superiors to entry-level professional employees in the real estate business. Students report being asked to falsify data, participate in kickback schemes, approve substandard work, and perform similar unethical activities.

Whistleblowing, Turning in a Friend. In my experience, this is a bigger issue for younger folks than for older folks, since it is easier for a new employee to develop a personal relationship than to acquire a deep-seated loyalty to the enterprise. A significant number of students report being uncomfortable with their peers' and superiors' unethical and even illegal business behavior. However, it is always easier not to rock the boat.

Confronting Issues. When should you go to the boss? If you go to the boss every week with a problem, you are in the wrong profession. If you never go, you are in the wrong company. Over time, we accept group norms that would have worried us when we were new to the job. Bad practices are invidious, since they can grow on us incrementally. Although many of us must compromise our value systems, from time to time, in order to get the job done, an ethical person is aware of doing this and does not become hardened. Such an individual retains a capacity for dealing with the really important issues when they arise.

Dealing with Improper Requests. When should you disobey "bad" rules? In whose judgment are the rules "bad"? It is best to have an open atmosphere where such issues can be brought into the open and, perhaps, properly explained.

Achieving Closure. Where does my responsibility as an ethical person end?

Periodically I am asked to address the advisory board of the Lusk Center for Real Estate at USC, each member of which is an experienced and successful real estate practitioner. I summarize the ethical stories of my students for them and then inform them that they are presenting such a face to first-time employees. In many cases, bad practices are buried deep, hidden in an organization—and the senior leaders are simply unaware of them. In other cases, bad practices permeate the day-to-day operations of the organization. In my experience, their reaction is generally one of denial: These abuses may occur in other companies, but not in their firm.

Conclusion

One is more likely to come up with the "correct" ethical answer if one broadly defines the group of affected parties. The deeper the list of stakeholders whose interests are a matter of concern, the better the chance of making the right decision. Back when Warren Buffet was the richest private citizen in the world, he was interviewed by Forbes. Buffet stated that in his 50-year business career there had been only about 20 key, strategic decisions. Now, if we apply this in ethical terms, it suggests that if you never encounter an ethical dilemma during your entire career, you are probably not calibrated properly from an ethical point of view. Conversely, if you face an ethical crisis more often than perhaps every two years, you are probably not properly calibrated ethically for that job either. We cannot quit our jobs every six months. So the issue is: When do we stop trading off? Where do we take our stand?

When we consider whether or not this is the time to take our stand, it is very important to have a peer group with whom we can discuss the issue. If such a person or group exists at your place of work, you are most fortunate. An open environment that tolerates questioning and ambiguity is a treasure. If not, your peer group must come from elsewhere: friends, family, a loved one, your church, and the like. It is very difficult and probably unwise to go this road alone. In a society that exalts winners, ethics can be what you are willing to lose for. Taking an ethical stand defines who you are. The more comfortable you are with who you are, the better chance you can match up with Drucker's requirements for the leaders of the future.

The determination of ethical behavior is a deeply centered and personal aspect of one's life. My attempt is to encourage students to become ethically fit, to obey the unenforceable, to grapple with the tough issues, to make ethics intuitive. In most cases the real impact of such considerations will not be known for many years. In my own experience, the way in which one almost unconsciously responds to a true ethical dilemma can make all the difference in a life, not just a career. Finally, just as in sports or business, practice and exposure make one better able to deal with the spontaneous circumstances that arise, so I too believe exposing students to ethical conflict prepares them to deal with the ethical problems that they will encounter early in their careers.

Source: *Wharton Real Estate Review,* fall 2000.

35

A Question of Ethics

A spirited discussion on the complex relationship between business and social responsibility.

Decades after Milton Friedman framed the debate over the social responsibility of business with an article in the *New York Times Magazine*, the discussion continues. Should businesses concentrate on achieving socially desirable outcomes? Can business be guided by the rule of law when governments are sometimes corrupt? How does operating globally affect a company's behavior? These and other issues were the focus of one of the sessions during the Stanford Business School's 75th anniversary celebration in May [2000]. The participants included business leader Bowen "Buzz" McCoy, Stanford Business School faculty members Kirk Hanson and David Brady, and Nobel economist Milton Friedman. The following text is an excerpt from that session.

The Overview

Buzz McCoy

I was a successful and pretty aggressive investment banker for about 30 years. I became general partner at Morgan Stanley in 1970, when it had 250 employees, 33 general partners, and $10 million in capital, and we were a leading firm on Wall Street. I became one of a group of people who helped Morgan Stanley transition from a narrowly based, private firm to the global powerhouse it is today. Through all this I maintained a very active connection to my church and to various philanthropic activities, including Stanford.

I was a boundary person, a Christian in business striving to be an aggressive investment banker and still be in a relationship with God, and I've come to the view that morals, as I define them, are not enough, and that ethics is grounded deeper than cultural norms. Cultural norms can inculcate bad practices. Ethics itself is a result of religion and deeper feelings and of where we stop trading off. I often say facetiously that I teach Christian ethics in business school and business ethics in the church.

How do you live out your faith at work? First, be worldly. Be a worker, be an investment banker or a real estate broker or a litigator or whatever you are, and if you can't do that successfully, you're in the wrong job. Don't be afraid to take personal risk. Be open. Tolerate questioning. Create a context. Don't burden your work too much with church or outward signs of religion. I believe in Dietrich Bonhoeffer's "hidden religion." Don't wear your heart on your sleeve. Be authentic. Understand that there are covenants in any kind of an organization, both implicit and explicit. Managing change, breaking covenants, setting up new ones is the hardest job a manager has to do.

Be very careful about whom you promote. We spent hours at Morgan Stanley on whom we rewarded and promoted. We never did it perfectly and were always changing the system. Reward character and leadership and not just production. Manage greed. You have to have rewards and punishments as well.

Leave room for personal philanthropy. I've always said if you spend 110 percent of your time working, you're in the wrong job. You are competing against people who spend 80 percent and are successful. If you cannot be well balanced and still compete, you're in trouble.

Build trust, even intimacy. I used to spend hours with my people setting goals, setting standards. Display a certain amount of calmness. Be tolerant of ambiguity and paradox.

In this age of globalization we need a faith-based ethic. We need to understand that the globalization of money and capital markets is really based on a Judeo-Christian culture, because it's a British-U.S. system promulgated throughout the world. And it runs head-on into other faiths and other systems.

We have to understand more about where ethics comes from and where these feelings come from. Culture is shaped by religion, by our deepest feelings about who we are and who we want to become. I see a lot of theology in Peters and Waterman and in Peter Drucker, and a lot of good management in something like the Rule of Saint Benedict—obviously a boundary person.

We're all people of faith searching for ways to be good. In globalization we can come closer together, but we still don't know one another. We can start up a new business fast, but growing wise in the way of life takes a long time. It's never complete, never right, and never perfect. An ethic is deeper than morality or custom. It comes out of our deepest desire to make meaning out of our lives and hence resides in the areas of spirituality and religion. The deepest and most meaningful relationships develop out of this level of interaction. To have integrity is to bring deep meaning to bear in all aspects of one's life. And to deal effectively in a global arena, one must have some notion of the deep meaning imbedded in various cultures.

Kirk Hanson

Milton [Friedman] has set the tone for the debate over business ethics and corporate responsibility for the past 30 years with an article in 1970 that said the social responsibility of business is to increase profits. And so I want to talk a little about what I see as the nature of this debate and where we go from here.

What have the last 30 years been like? We've had three different approaches to the role of ethics in business. One is that ethics has really had no role in business and, while Milton's name has been associated with that, I'm not sure he believes all that has been attributed to him. This position holds that the role of business is to be profitable and to be constrained only by the law. Second is the view of Jim Burke and Norman Lear, whom I worked for for five years and who believe that ethics is good business. If you are ethical, you will be a successful business person. I sometimes got a little uncomfortable with how absolute they were in stating it. The third position is that whatever your belief is, ethics is absolute and has to come before self-interest in business decisions. What do we make of these? I fall into the camp that believes ethics is good business about 90 percent of the time, and that the other 10 percent you do have a very genuine conflict, and there has to be some commitment to ethics as an absolute.

Today the debate over business ethics is being transformed by globalism. American companies realized in the mid-1980s that they were global companies and had to operate in multivalue, multiethic environments. Taking business ethics global, I have come to believe in at least the following four propositions:

- Doing ethics globally is possible. It is not all related to a particular culture. It is not that the world is adopting the U.S. view on ethics. Rather, it is possible to identify some globally accepted ethical norms.
- The ethical behavior of companies does affect people throughout the world and does enhance the bottom line. Ethical behavior affects not just people and stakeholders but also the interests and long-term profitability of the firm.

- You must be aware of and respect the differences in values in various societies. American companies operating in Europe today would not succeed without a sensitivity to Europe's interest in all the stakeholders of the firm. Monsanto clearly did not understand many Europeans' sensitivity about genetically modified foods. Shell did not understand the environmental sensitivity in the rest of continental Europe when Shell U.K. was disposing of the Brent Spar oil platform in the North Sea. So while there are global ethical norms, you also have to have a profound respect for different values.

- Ethics and values, therefore, must be managed in the global corporation. It's a matter of survival and self-interest. You must manage your ethics, your ethical norms, and values of your enterprise like all other behaviors in your organization.

So where are we today? We still have these different approaches to business ethics as we move into this millennium: 1) that ethics has no role in business; 2) that good ethics is good business; and 3) that ethical behavior is an absolute even if it costs you money. We certainly have enough examples that ignoring ethics can cost you money— Columbia Health Care, Coca-Cola, DoubleClick, and others that have not understood some ethical issues facing business in a global society. A global ethic is emerging. Companies must consider transparency, continual self-examination, communication of values, recognizing the obligation to stakeholders, engaging in dialogue with all those stakeholders, continually asking themselves if their actions are ethical. The future role of business ethics in a global society is still uncharted at this point, but it's clear that it is a topic we will be discussing extensively as the millennium develops.

David Brady

For me, ethics is the application of moral principles to everyday life and business problems. There are numerous ethical systems—religious systems, semireligious systems such as Confucianism, and the major secular systems: utilitarianism, Kantian rights, distributive justice. What a true ethical system does is allow you to determine a course of action consistent with the set of moral principles you're reasoning from.

I've always been a fan of Milton's article and views on corporate responsibility. It is ethical, based on a specified axiom (utilitarianism), and is consistent with economic science. What I like most is that it clearly delineates the role of government—government enforces contracts and sets the rules governing fair business behavior. It says that managers are agents, that the principals are the shareholders, and that the rule governing behavior is that the managers *should* maximize shareholder value. As such, it clearly prescribes the course of action so that when a manager has a dilemma, he/she can determine the appropriate course of action.

This reasoning applies in cases where measuring dollar loss can be complicated. For example, in a case like Johnson & Johnson and the Tylenol tampering, the company can calculate the costs of its actions and put it into a framework, and the cost of maximizing profit or gaining credibility can be estimated and the rule applied.

A more popular view of corporate responsibility is that of the Business Roundtable in the United States and its idea of stakeholders. Roughly, the idea is customers, shareholders, suppliers, the government, etc., are all stakeholders in the company and as such are all elements that management has a responsibility to. Managers love stakeholder theory, because they can support any action on the basis of what stakeholders say they want. You balance it off and say, "I couldn't possibly do 'x,' because this group wants one thing and the other group wants the opposite." In addition, the statements regarding the nature of responsibility are purposely vague, and such generalizations allow managers to do what they wish and call it responsibility.

Now while I like what Milton's done, it does seem that globalization presents a bit of a problem. Operating globally, you have local units that are self-sufficient. The center is weak. Some firms focus on scale and uniformity; others use the supply chain model to tap resources and capabilities anywhere. Nike is a classic example. It wanted the least costly producer, so it went to Japan, then Korea, China, Vietnam, etc. Nike also was a global brand—the number one producer of athletic footwear and major producer of athletic gear around the world. To do that, it had to go local, like supporting soccer in Brazil. This approach decentralizes management.

Now, what problems does that create? In the United States and also in Europe, Milton's system works reasonably well. These governments set the rules of what constitutes fraud and liability. But if you're a Nike manager and you're in Vietnam, you don't want to leave the human rights of your workers up to the local government, because, frankly, that's a government that has not been very concerned with human rights in general. This gives managers in some countries different responsibilities. For example, every British Petroleum manager in China is responsible on a biweekly basis for driving out to all the road sites and rural power companies to check and make sure that they're not being built by prison labor.

Milton Friedman

Kirk said 90 percent of the time being ethical is consistent with being profitable. I agree with about 90 percent of what everybody has said. Both David and Kirk have referred to an article of mine from 30 years ago, and that's how I got into this ethical business, which is not my business—I'm an economist. But about 30 years ago I wrote an article for the *New York Times Magazine* on the social responsibility of business ["The Social Responsibility of Business Is to Increase Its Profits," September 13, 1970].

No article I've ever written has yielded me so much money. Not a year goes by that I don't get about $1,000 in fees to reprint it. And the reason is very simple: Business ethics has been a growing subject in business schools. Every business school needs a set of readings on business ethics. Each needs views from left to right, and very few economists were willing to be as extreme as I was. So I had almost a monopoly on the extreme side of the market. I went back and reread this article. I was not surprised that I still agree with it. And I want to read to you both the beginning and the end. Let me emphasize that it deals with the social responsibility of business, not ethics. Those are two very different things. Here's the first paragraph:

> When I hear businessmen speak eloquently about the "social responsibilities of business in a free enterprise system," I am reminded of the wonderful line about the Frenchman who discovered at the age of 70 that he had been speaking prose all his life. The businessmen believe that they are defending free enterprise when they declaim that business is not concerned "merely" with profit but also with promoting desirable "social" ends; that business has a "social conscience"; and takes seriously its responsibilities for providing employment, eliminating discrimination, avoiding pollution, and whatever else may be the catchwords of the contemporary crop of reformers. In fact, they are—or would be if they or anyone else took them seriously that sentence is no longer true—people do take them seriously)—preaching pure and unadulterated socialism. Businessmen who talk this way are unwitting puppets of the intellectual forces that have been undermining the basis of a free society these past decades.

The last paragraph says:

> That is why, in my book *Capitalism and Freedom*, I have called [the notion of social responsibility] "a fundamentally subversive doctrine" in a free society it is an important point related to the globalization problem), and have said that in such a society, "there is one and only one social responsibility of business—to use its resources and engage in activities designed to increase its profits so long as it stays within the rules of the game, which is to say, engages in open and free competition without deception or fraud."

That's the beginning and the end. And of course most of the difficulty is because no one has read the in-between part. That's a discussion of the social responsibility of business. It's not a discussion of what's ethical or not ethical. In my opinion, it's hard to know what is meant by business ethics. Only people, not businesses, have ethics. Ethics is me, the individual, as a person. I'm ethical or unethical. If I'm employed in a business that I think is unethical, I have a clear choice. I can get out of that business and find something else to do. It doesn't seem to me it's ethical for me to do unethical things because the business can let me do it. One common example: Is it ethical to work in a cigarette-producing company? Everybody knows smoking cigarettes is hazardous to your health. So is riding in an automobile. So is skiing. So is swimming.

Is it unethical for me to be an employee in a factory producing cigarettes? No! But is it unethical for me as a manager to make false statements in public? Yes! If people want to smoke cigarettes, if someone decides the pleasure of smoking is worth the risk to his health, that's no different than if he decides the pleasure he gets out of skiing is worth the chance he'll go through a tree.

That's why it seems most of these difficult problems are not difficult in ethical terms. They're difficult in practical terms, difficult in knowing what the costs and returns are. A corporation has an obligation to its owners and stockholders to make as much profit as it can while not violating its owners' ethical concerns or practicing deception or fraud. What that requires will be very difficult to figure out in a place like China. But there I wouldn't say British Petroleum is behaving ethically. I'd say it's behaving responsibly in accordance with its statement. It doesn't want to engage in deception. It doesn't want to tell its stockholders: "Your money comes from prison labor."

The Discussion

Friedman. Insider trading is a made-up crime, but given it's the law, then people ought to obey that law. I want to qualify that. Nobody really believes that it's an ethical precept that you obey every law. If you obey a law that requires you to do something that is unethical or amoral, I think everybody in the room would agree it's a proper human behavior to break that law as long as you're willing to accept the responsibility for that. That was the justification for conscientious objection during the war.

Hanson. I want to push you. It seems what we talk about when we say business ethics really is a single ethic, and it applies to other areas of our lives. And when we talk about ethics in organizations, we're talking first about what the individual manager or employee ought to do. Critics of the tobacco companies try to say it is simply unethical to produce cigarettes, therefore the individuals who work for this company ought to resign.

Friedman. You made a statement there that you don't mean—"It's unethical to produce cigarettes."

Hanson. I believe it is unethical for me to produce cigarettes.

Friedman. Maybe, but it's not unethical to produce cigarettes if it's clear what the facts are and the risks are. If it's unethical to produce cigarettes, then it's certainly unethical to produce skis, automobiles, bullets, guns.

Hanson. I very much differ with you on the ethical obligation. I would argue that my ethical obligation is to not do things that directly harm others. I'm not going to make your ethical decision for you. But I am saying that the people making cigarettes for you ought not to make them.

Brady. I served on the Stanford Committee for Socially Responsible Investing. The question of whether Stanford should invest in R.J. Reynolds came up. The majority had Kirk's position—that we should sell the shares—and they came up with a moral principle that would allow us to sell those shares. They said: You cannot have shares in any company where the sole intention of the company is to harm people. I said, that's fine, and I'm sure Mr. Packard will be delighted to know you're going to disinvest in Hewlett-Packard because HP makes missile-guidance defense systems. That clearly is a product whose sole purpose is to bomb people. They immediately backed up. The point is, it's very hard to define what that set of products is.

Hanson. Because it's hard, don't stop trying to do it.

Brady. Because you succeed in getting legislation passed doesn't make it moral. In South Africa, it was legislated that Blacks did not have rights, and in the United States of America for an extremely long period there was legislation that discriminated against women, Blacks, and Hispanics. That is the distinction between politics and ethics. In politics, by building majorities for positions you favor, you can force your view on other people. But the ethical judgment of whether legislation is moral or not is a separate judgment.

McCoy. Kirk mentioned 90 percent of ethics and profits can be congruent. I'm not sure that's true. I'd say ethical norms are what you are willing to lose for. If you have to win all the time to be ethical, that's not being ethical.

Hanson. I would say that most business ethicists in the United States spend their time trying to convince people that being ethical actually will help you win in the long term. Fulfilling Milton's dictum, we talk about the 90 percent of the time ethics is good for business—do the ethical thing if it is serving the shareholder and the bottom line in the long term. I believe the public is very sensitive to the impact of larger and larger global enterprises on people and the environment. And that's what ethics is about, the impact of my behavior or my organization's behavior on people. My ethical commitment includes both a free society and a set of ethical norms that may include human rights, the protection of human life, etc. My set of values includes your free society.

Friedman. You can't include the free society there. Those of us who believe in the free society believe an organization in which individuals and enterprises are seeking to promote their own self-interest is the best way to achieve those rights. It's not that those rights are something in addition to a free society. It's what a free society is for. By this damn nonsense of social responsibility, what you're doing is pandering in a way to the instincts that say profit is bad, business is bad, everything has to be done through the government and for someone else. It's a philosophy you don't want to accept.

Source: *Stanford Business*, November 2000.

36 Free-Market Environmentalism

Those wishing to learn more about the free-market environmental movement are urged to contact the Property and Environment Research Center at www.perc.org.

With President George W. Bush's selection [in 2001] of Christine Todd Whitman as Environmental Protection Agency administrator and Gale A. Norton as secretary of the interior, there was considerable interest in their libertarian, market-based policies, sometimes referred to as *free-market environmentalism*. Free-market environmentalism has been described as a philosophy that is grounded in property rights, voluntary exchange, common law liability protection, and the rule of law—all of which seek to integrate environmental resources into the market system.

Definitions

Free-market environmentalism conflicts with traditional environmentalism in its visions regarding human nature, knowledge, and processes. With respect to *human nature*, man is viewed as self-interested. This self-interest may be enlightened to the extent that people are capable of setting aside their own well-being; but good intentions will not produce good results. Instead of intentions, good resource stewardship depends on how well social institutions harness self-interest through individual incentives.

Knowledge and information cannot be general and global, but must be time- and place-specific. These visions of knowledge and human nature make free-market environmentalism a study of *process* rather than a prescription for solutions. If we can rise above self-interest and if knowledge can be concentrated and specific, then the possibility for solutions through political control is feasible.

Many environmental problems are caused by the *"tragedy of the commons."* If access to a valuable resource is unrestricted, people entering the commons to capture its value will ultimately destroy it. Even if each individual recognizes that open access leads to resource destruction, there is no incentive for him/her to refrain from overgrazing the common pasture or overharvesting the fish. If he/she does not take it, someone else will, and therein lies the tragedy. There is no community in which to regulate individual self-interest. The individual, who is unconstrained and wastes a community resource—through overgrazing, pollution, or the like—is called a *free rider*. He/she does not pay for the value or cost of what he/she takes away from the community.

Transaction costs become important. It is costly to restrict entry. The costs of organizing and bargaining can be high. *Information costs* are the costs or values attributed to what is taken from the community. What is the cost of my backyard barbecue polluting your air? How much of such pollution should be allowable? What are the costs and benefits of drilling for petrochemicals in the Arctic National Wildlife Refuge? Such costs are difficult and expensive to obtain in the absence of established markets for wildlife habitat, or hiking, or snowmobiling. In order to solve environmental problems, we must find ways of discovering and articulating this type of information. Once such values and costs are determined, rational choices can be made and rights can be marketed or traded.

Free-market environmentalism identifies systematic differences in the way information about subjective values is communicated in markets and politics. In the marketplace, prices convert subjective values into objective measures. In the political process, voting is a signal that communicates the subjective values, especially of special-interest groups. Special-interest groups lower the cost of information to their members, allowing legislation to pass that costs each taxpayer a few pennies, but provides significant benefits to the special group.

Community Management Systems

Community management systems have evolved over hundreds of years to manage issues such as the tragedy of the commons. They seem to contain six basic factors:

- Boundaries must be clearly defined so that individuals know what they can use and others know when they are trespassing.
- Rules are required to determine how the value of the resource is parceled out.

- Rules must be specific as to time- and place-specific resource constraints, or there will be pressure to change them.
- There must be effective monitoring of the rules, and a system of rewards and sanctions imposed.
- Dispute-resolution mechanisms at the local level are necessary.
- The rules must not be subject to change by higher levels of government.

An example may be given of the destruction of the Nepalese forests. The national government chose to ignore previously successful community arrangements, and all the forests were placed under central control of the government. The act led to a chain of destruction that resulted in the removal of almost half of the trees in Nepal's forests. Nepalese villagers began free-riding, systematically overexploiting their forest resources on a large scale. They had lost control of their forests.

Examples of free-market environmentalism occur in areas such as grazing rights, hunting, multiple use of government lands, recreational land uses, water rights, pollution, fisheries, and the like. The argument is made that entrepreneurial pragmatists in the environmental movement have come up with incentive systems, such as trading unused rights to pollution or rewarding ranchers for protecting endangered species, that have led to more positive outcomes than either the government command and control systems or the legal process.

Market-based property rights evolved on the frontier, which was once open to all. Cooperative systems evolved for the ownership of land, livestock, and water. As the perceived value of assets changes over time, so do the incentives. With the use of global positioning systems, DNA testing, and radio and acoustical tagging of species, it is possible to imagine such solutions as tradable rights in whale harvests.

Public funding and bureaucratic controls have not solved such problems as lost salmon runs in the Pacific Northwest or the upkeep of our national parklands. The Endangered Species Act creates perverse incentives for landowners to take preemptive actions to eliminate wildlife habitat, rather than to preserve it.

Oil and gas leasing on public lands pits environmentalists, development companies, and state and local interests against one another in the political process, where the stakes are high and the winner often takes all. This fosters acrimony rather than cooperation among disparate users of natural resources. Free-market environmentalism emphasizes well-defined and enforced property rights. Where environmental groups own energy resources in sensitive wildlife reserves, they become willing to make trades because they see costs in not deploying a valuable asset. By forcing price and opportunity cost discovery, free-market environmentalism can assist in the determination of rational choices where all might benefit.

Conclusion

Critics of free-market environmentalism include those who state that environmentalism is a moral issue and should not be decided by cost/benefit analysis. Others claim that rights to magnificent landscapes and wild animals are more important than the rights conferred to property owners. They state that environmentalists would be willing to pay more for such rights if only they, or the government, had the resources. The case is made that the distribution of wealth favors private landowners over environmental preferences.

I would agree with critics who state that environmentalism is a moral issue. Pure air and water and gorgeous sunsets have aesthetic values and cannot be evaluated solely in dollars and cents, but must be valued out of our deepest sense of who we are and who we want to be. These deep intuitive yearnings, which stem out of our foundational beliefs, cannot always be bargained away. Living out an ethic, even an environmental ethic, is not about always winning. It is about what we are willing to sacrifice for. Always equating ethics with winning diminishes the depth of ethical commitment.

Moreover, the command and control systems imposed by various government levels give some assurance that the public's will might be done. Systems based upon virtue, free bargaining, and perfect information are commendable and should be used wherever possible. Given human nature, however, a system of rewards and punishments should also remain available.

It is my view that free-market environmentalism offers a creative and positive way out of the morass of overregulation and endless litigation. Rather than painting everyone as either for us or against us, as the Sierra Club and others are prone to do, this concept forces us to think hard about costs and benefits—to balance the rights and duties of all parties and to come up with a more balanced and effective solution.

Understanding free-market environmentalism is important for any property owner who wants to gain a better understanding of the environmental movement, or wants to protect his or her property rights, as well as for those who would like to better understand the public dialogue we can expect with Whitman and Norton, among others, over the term of the current administration.

Source: *Real Estate Issues* (CRE Perspective column), fall 2001.